Disciplining Girls

Disciplining Girls

*Understanding the Origins of the Classic
Orphan Girl Story*

JOE SUTLIFF SANDERS

The Johns Hopkins University Press
Baltimore

© 2011 Joe Sutliff Sanders
All rights reserved. Published 2011
Printed in the United States of America on acid-free paper
2 4 6 8 9 7 5 3 1

The Johns Hopkins University Press
2715 North Charles Street
Baltimore, Maryland 21218-4363
www.press.jhu.edu

Library of Congress Cataloging-in-Publication Data
Sanders, Joe Sutliff.
Disciplining girls : understanding the origins of the classic
orphan girl story / Joe Sutliff Sanders.
p. cm.
Includes bibliographical references and index.
ISBN-13: 978-1-4214-0318-2 (hardcover : alk. paper)
ISBN-10: 1-4214-0318-8 (hardcover : alk. paper)
1. Girls in literature. 2. Children's stories, American—History
and criticism. 3. Children's stories, Canadian—History and
criticism. 4. Orphans in literature. 5. Child rearing in literature.
6. Sentimentality in literature. 7. American fiction—19th century—
History and criticism. 8. American fiction—20th century—History
and criticism. 9. Canadian fiction—19th century—History and
criticism. 10. Canadian fiction—20th century—History and
criticism. I. Title. II. Title: Origins of the classic orphan girl
story. III. Title: Orphan girl story.
PS374.G55S26 2011
813'.409352352—dc22   2011009969

A catalog record for this book is available from the British Library.

*Special discounts are available for bulk purchases of this book. For more
information, please contact Special Sales at 410-516-6936 or
specialsales@press.jhu.edu.*

The Johns Hopkins University Press uses environmentally friendly book
materials, including recycled text paper that is composed of at least 30
percent post-consumer waste, whenever possible.

For Melendra

Contents

Acknowledgments

In the pages that follow, I attempt to write with intellectual detachment about sentimentality. For a few paragraphs, however, I have no choice but to speak with genuine sentimentality about the people who infused this intellectual exercise with such joy.

I have been fortunate to have had excellent mentoring since leaving graduate school. At Kansas State University, Anne K. Phillips, Dan Hoyt, Phil Nel, Karin Westman, and Naomi Wood have been foremost among a department full of colleagues eager to support me and this project. A University Small Research Grant at K-State paid for the indexing of the book. At California State University in San Bernardino, Juan Delgado and Rong Chen pulled every string they ethically could to help me in my few, happy years there. James R. Kincaid (of the University of Southern California) thought nothing of lending his advice, attention, and name to my wide-eyed ideas. Brian and Jennifer Attebery (of Idaho State University) have been mentors since long before they realized I was learning from their loving, charitable examples. June S. Cummins and Jerry Griswold (of San Diego State University) gave so generously of their time, advice, and collegiality that I sometimes wonder whether they regret giving me their home telephone numbers. C. W. Sullivan (of East Carolina University) explained how a scholar should behave and frequently bought the beer.

As this book finally wound to a conclusion, it received tireless help from Michelle Ann Abate, Jerry Griswold, Marah Gubar, Luz Elena Ramirez, and C. W. Sullivan.

The list of people who have commented on the arguments in this book is too long to include here, but there are a few people whose contributions were so specific that I can still see their impact on the book. Bess Fox, Kristi Branham, and Mary Hall read the early, rambling close readings that fed the eventual arguments of *Disciplining Girls*, and their patience enabled those arguments to develop. Dale M. Bauer, David Miller, Steve Weisenberger, and Ernie Yanarella generously served on a dissertation committee that consistently asked the right questions. Jessica Lewis Luck and Chad Luck gave encouragement and revision ideas for what became the final chapter. Lucy Pearson explained how to reconceive my reading of individualism in *Pollyanna*. Karen Sands-O'Connor provided rigorous friendly conversation that helped restore confidence in my points about individualism and privacy. Joseph Thomas pointed to the larger theoretical context that my arguments about abuse occupy. Sherryl Vint explained that the Persons Case was actually more germane to my argument than Canadian suffrage. Patricia Murphy drew my attention to specific Victorians who articulated a kind of mother who paralleled the republican mother in useful ways. Matt McAdam, at the Johns Hopkins University Press, has been that most comforting sort of editor: one who is enthusiastic about a manuscript yet makes both the highs and lows of the process of publication something one can survive.

I am deeply grateful to Claudia Nelson for her thorough and generous reading of this manuscript. Her advice helped develop a broader backdrop for the argument throughout the book, and her ingenuous reactions provided the sense of audience I needed at the most delicate points of revision.

I am also grateful to two anonymous readers who served at the *Children's Literature Association Quarterly*, where an earlier version of chapter 10 was first published. Richard Flynn, then-editor of the *Quarterly*, guided the revision process of "Spinning Sympathy" with grace.

The Huntington Library provided a beautiful environment and access to *Tattered Tom*, which is—criminally—out of print. The Martha Blakeney Hodges Special Collection and University Archives at the Walter Clinton Jackson Library at the University of North Carolina at Greensboro provided extraordinary help as I explored the outer reaches of my argument. I am particularly indebted to Rosann Bazirjian, William K. Finley, Carolyn Shankle, Hermann Trojanowski, Sean Mulligan, and Beth Ann Koelsch, who led me by the trembling hand through UNCG's legendary archives of girls' books in series.

I am constantly aware of my singular luck that Virginia L. Blum agreed to be my dissertation director. She knew things she had no professional obligation to know and read drafts whose number and frequency were a burden of which she never complained. If there are words to explain the depth of my thankfulness for her thick-headed belief in my work, I don't know them. She is a model of the person I would like to be, a smart person who thinks hard about the many things in this world that give her joy.

My dear parents, sisters, and brother have had the good grace to do nothing more critical than smile as I have pursued this project. They have also given more gifts to support that pursuit than is reasonable by any standard. One example deserves pointed mention: my beloved sister-in-law, Alicia Sutliff-Benusis, donated a summer of part-time child care to let me write a chapter. I love each of you and promise to ask more about what you're doing the next time we talk.

When we were dating, Melendra Sutliff gave me a book she had loved as a girl. This was part of an exchange we had been practicing throughout our court-ship, a trade that helped us learn each other better. Although I won't mention the books I gave her from my own youth—frankly, I'm shocked she married me in spite of what those books said about me—it would be negligent not to state here at the outset that *Disciplining Girls* exists because Melendra gave me a copy of *Emily of New Moon*, and I was so moved by the complexity and artistry of Lucy Maud Montgomery's novel that I had to write this book to discover how *Emily* came to be. Since then, Melendra earned the money so I could go to graduate school, took care of the children so I could be the kind of professor I wanted to be, and rejoiced over the successes of this book as though they were her own.

For the record, they are.

Disciplining Girls

Gender, Sentiment, Individualism, Discipline

Disciplining someone effectively is a subtle process. On the one hand, successful discipline requires documentable results: the disciplined person stops one behavior (drinking, lying, stealing, speaking) or starts another (exercising, listening, sharing, studying). These outcomes of discipline are observable. Yet on the other, the power that underwrites discipline is at its fullest when it cannot be seen. If the evidence of discipline is tangible, the *techniques by which* a person or institution exercises discipline often struggle to hide themselves, to appear as so good, so natural, that they become invisible to analysis and therefore critique. It is in this strange mixture of what is seen and what is kept secret that discipline becomes most effective.

Literary historians have been interested in discipline for a very long time, and with good reason: literature excels in the games of smoke and mirrors that both invoke power and conceal it. Richard H. Brodhead has made this point about popular novels by U.S. women writers in the mid-nineteenth century, and the first waves of scholarship on the sentimental novels that were the nation's first bestsellers celebrated the power sentimentalism imagined for women. Writers such as Myra C. Glenn have documented the heated debates through which sentimental culture changed popular disciplinary ideology, shifting it from an emphasis on punishing the body to an emphasis on the efficacy of love—what has come to be called affective discipline or moral suasion—to prompt a less abusive and more lasting form of control. More recently, scholars such as Laura Wexler and Lora Romero have complicated readings of sentimentalism by pointing out that the modes of discipline championed by sentimental novels had profoundly negative effects on Americans outside the structures that privileged white women. But a few key points remain in common even between the increasingly nuanced analyses of affective discipline. First, these readings agree that even if it sometimes failed to deliver on its promises, even if its rules excluded many players, affective discipline offered power. Second, scholarship repeatedly asserts that literature was a primary site of the nineteenth-century debate over discipline. And third, these analyses agree that it is the job of literary scholarship to unmask the strategies of discipline these novels contrive to present as natural. These few points of consensus remain even as critical disagreement over midcentury affective discipline continues.

But something strange happens when literary historians address the end of the sentimental period, late in the nineteenth century. According to prevalent understandings of the period, the fierce debates that characterized the question of discipline in nineteenth-century America fizzled out once the sentimental novel began to slip from bestseller lists. Although discipline was, everyone agrees, a provocative topic worked over and revised endlessly in the middle of the century, by the late 1880s, American readers and writers had evidently lost interest. The great arguments that had fueled a cultural shift from corporal punishment to affective discipline had finished their work, and there was nothing more to be said.

It can hardly be surprising that this conclusion is false. Literary debates over discipline did not disappear. They did not even drift into some marginal literature that few people read. Instead, they remained right where they had been: in very popular books penned by women. What's more, they continued in female-authored books that featured orphan girls, just as had many of the most popular sentimental novels. The debate over discipline did not disappear, but it did switch audiences: it became the domain of children's literature.

Disciplining Girls is a book about the *next* fifty years of affective discipline in the United States. It explains how the continuing debates about affective discipline were recorded and advanced in a specific kind of girls' novel that flourished after and borrowed liberally from the midcentury sentimental woman's novel. As with other theoretically informed readings of sentimentalism's literary history, it is eager to untangle the repercussions, consequences, and rules of moral suasion. To that end, it grounds its observations in the mid-nineteenth-century novels that laid out the formula for girls' novels. It also extends and complicates the celebrations and condemnations of sentimental novels that have dominated discussion of those works, marking the costs of the power offered as well as the illusory nature of much of that power. But this book is fundamentally a work of literary history about children's literature. It argues that the first wave of very popular fiction marketed for girls borrowed ideas about power from earlier women's fiction but that this wave also tried to distance itself from that fiction. The result was a revised version of sentimental fiction that offered to girls a constantly changing vision of affective discipline's power. These revisions would have to take into account shifts in turn-of-the-century representations of bodies, individual identity, and the mothers who had once been at the center of affective discipline.

DISCIPLINE AND GIRLS

Concerns with discipline penetrated virtually every aspect of U.S. culture during the nineteenth century. People whose skin color, nation of origin, or class complicated their place in nineteenth-century society were very concerned with it because it determined how they were treated by police, armies, and even owners. Women were concerned with it because it represented a rare opportunity for some modicum of power. Men were concerned with discipline because it influenced their careers, especially if they were soldiers or politicians. And children were concerned with it . . . well, children were perhaps more concerned with discipline than anyone else. This is because, obviously, "discipline" is a favorite term for what parents do to children. But in the years after the peak popularity of sentimental novels, children were not only objects of discipline; they were also, of all things, its agents. In this way, children and discipline affected every other demographic in the culture. Children, and especially little girls, were prominent figures in the negotiations of gender and control.

Two examples help illustrate how gender, control, and discipline intertwine in this literature and the culture of which it was a part. In E.D.E.N. Southworth's bestselling novel *The Hidden Hand*, an orphan girl named Capitola has been taken in by one of the local patriarchs, a man nicknamed "Old Hurricane" for the fury that descends on him when someone defies his orders. But rage as he might, Hurricane has little control over Capitola. He turns for help to a local clergyman, saying,

> She won't obey me, except when she likes! she has never been taught obedience or been accustomed to subordination, and [she] don't understand either! She rides and walks out alone in spite of all I can do or say! If she were a boy, I'd thrash her! But what can I do with a *girl*? (174)

Hurricane's question echoes in the recollections of a real-life girl. On December 5, 1890, a young L. M. Montgomery recorded a similar conflict in her diary. Writing of her friends in the town to which she had recently relocated in order to live with her widower father and his new wife, Montgomery reflects,

> To-day we were all a little hilarious and poor Mr. Mustard lost his patience, kept a lot of us in after four, and gave us a sum in compound interest, a yard long, to work. The rest of them did it, or tried to, but I was just bound I *wouldn't*. If he had kept me there until midnight I wouldn't have made a figure. But he couldn't exactly rawhide a girl, so he had to let me go with the rest. (Montgomery, *Journals* 35)

Between these two stories, one fictional and the other biographical, a problem becomes clear, a problem that would plague mainstream culture at the turn of the century. When Montgomery, a girl from rural Canada, grew up, she became one of the most famous novelists throughout the English-speaking world, and the popularity of the novels she wrote in a tradition inherited from sentimental novelists such as Southworth has yet to abate.[1] Central to the words of both the fictional girl and the girl who would create memorable fiction about girls is an anxiety about power, about how the gender of the dispenser and recipient of discipline interferes with discipline.

That anxiety takes two forms, and they are evident in two questions that are implicit in Old Hurricane's lament. The first is obvious: What can be done with girls? But if the question is obvious, it is not simple. This question meant many things to a nineteenth-century reader. How can girls be disciplined? How does their gender inflect their experience? How does it limit or expand their role in culture? What can be required of them, both as physical objects and as symbolic constructions? Discipline, gender, duty, and representation were crucial questions in the nineteenth century, and fictional orphan girls proved exceptionally well-suited to bearing each question in turn as their authors formulated their answers. In a comparatively short-lived genre of novels featuring orphan girls who infiltrated the hearts of their reluctant guardians, these authors used their endearing protagonists as canvases on which to paint the dangers and potential of gender-defined discipline and privilege.

The second question in Old Hurricane's complaint is less obvious. Clearly, he wants to know how to rule his adoptive *daughter*, particularly as opposed to a hypothetical son, but he also wants to know how to *rule* her. Implicit in his question about girls, then, is this question: what can be done with fathers, with the patriarchs whose duty it is to rule? When Hurricane asks for advice on how to manage his daughter, he has run into the limits of masculine privilege. He has yelled, he has bullied, he has threatened to withdraw economic support, he has flaunted his every right as a straight, white man, but it has gotten him nowhere. As histories of the family show, American families began the nineteenth century with authority securely situated in the father, and indeed the state had made a habit at this point of trading privilege with the father in order to preserve its own power.[2] But over the course of the nineteenth century, during the very decades that Southworth's novel was repeatedly serialized and reprinted, the state began to break up that power, distributing some of it to children, some to wives no longer under the legal erasure of coverture, and, as Michael Grossberg has documented, more than a little to itself. Therefore, when these novels turned to speak of power, the inevitable question was just this: what can be done with fathers? What does the rule of law mean? What are the limits, if any, of masculine privilege? What guidelines should it observe, and who shall dictate them?

Because the turn-of-the-century girls' novels I am exploring were the junk novels of popular culture, they presented an ideal venue for the kinds of political musings I am describing.[3] They were born into the world in guises that kept them from being too closely scrutinized and to this day have spent most of their print lives well below the scholarly radar. Because the formula of the genre dictated that these would be tales of good girls who on the whole did what they were told and grew up to become good women, their narratives could ask questions and probe institutions in ways that might have raised eyebrows elsewhere. If a girl disobeyed her father, was punished, and grew up to become a model citizen, it might be easy to forget that she had once asked troubling questions. These novels were a safe space in which their female authors could consider gendered privilege—how it should be defined, reshaped, and directed—and ways it could be used to deal with the cultural anxieties they loaded onto their imagined girls.

As I explore these questions of discipline and privilege, I simultaneously construct a history of U.S. culture at the turn of the century (two of the novels I examine were not written by Americans, but they were widely consumed by American culture and therefore presumably fit comfortably with the hopes and fears of the American reading public). The history these novels tell clarifies how they built upon one another, which will in turn clarify both the novels themselves and the history of the argument over discipline, one that continues today.

PRIMARY TEXTS

This study takes for its center a very specific group of now-canonical novels, the last several of which were explicitly for children. The most obvious characteristic of the genre is the span of decades in which the genre became popular. At the beginning of this period is the genre's foundational text, Susan Warner's 1850 novel *Wide, Wide World*, a text that has been essential to contemporary discussions of midcentury discipline. The first novel clearly intended for girl readers to follow in the footsteps of Warner's novels was Louisa May Alcott's *Eight Cousins*, published in 1875. This novel overlaps with the waning days of sentimentalism's popularity, but it serves well as the clear beginning for the version of the orphan girl formula novel published for children. After *Eight Cousins*, very few writers of adult fiction continued to use the formula, but many children's writers followed Alcott's lead and were frequently rewarded with high sales figures. Remarkably, this very popular form came to an abrupt halt in the American literary marketplace shortly after the passage of the Nineteenth Amendment. The historical density of the genre's publication ends with Montgomery's *Emily* books, the first of which is the 1923 *Emily of New Moon*. The period with which my book is broadly concerned, therefore, extends from 1850 to 1923, though the first of the children's novels in the genre was published in 1875 and the last was published in 1923, making a nearly exact half century of the genre in the market of girls' fiction. Such a short period of time allows me to work with a closely related set of children's texts, and the blurring at the beginning of the genre invites comparisons with the sentimental novels that articulated the genre formula so clearly.

The plot and other elements of the sentimental orphan girl genre are likewise easy to characterize. In these novels, an orphan girl enters a home far from modern urban life, a home that is reluctant to accept her, and by the end of the novel she has worked her way into the hearts of the people who live there, transforming the children and adults until they love and even resemble her. I have rather arbitrarily decided not to include novels that feature this formula but feature a boy protagonist. But really, there seem to be very few of those. *Little Lord Fauntleroy*, by the author of two of the novels clearly within the orphan girl genre, is a significant exception. In fact, nearly every question I ask in these pages can likewise be applied to *Fauntleroy*, and since its protagonist works in service of the same goals as his novelistic siblings, this novel seems to be more an exception that proves the rule than a disruption of the genre's boundaries.[4] Horatio Alger's 1871 *Tattered Tom*, Kate Douglas Wiggin's 1898 *Timothy's Quest*, and Eleanor H. Porter's 1916 *Just David* are three novels at the borders of the classic genre, and for the sake of preserving my focus on novels that are both clearly in the sentimental tradition and central to the history of children's literature in the United States, I do not treat them here. Alger's novel splits its morality between Tom/Jane's mother and her kind (male) benefactor, which reflects, despite the novel's decidedly urban setting, many of the points I make about Alcott's *Eight Cousins*. Wiggin's novel, also a story that has a modern (and occasionally urban) setting, uses two orphans rather than one and speaks more of the adults than the children, but it features an orphan who disciplines by accident, as does the protagonist of Wiggin's later *Rebecca of Sunnybrook Farm.*[5] Porter's *Just David*, published after her phenomenally successful *Pollyanna*, is so derivative of the earlier book that points of comparison are numerous. Indeed, *Just David* often reads as a hasty rewriting of *Pollyanna*, with many characters dropped, left undeveloped, or simply shoehorned in when following the model of *Pollyanna* requires them. I also refer to Joanna Spyri's 1880 novel *Heidi* only in passing, although it has assumed a canonical status: Spyri's novel was written so far removed from the Anglophone tradition of sentimentalism that I am hesitant to include it in this history. Nonetheless, much of what *Heidi* contributes to the history of the genre is also covered in my discussion of turn-of-the-century kindergarten theory. Finally, I have chosen to address sequels to these novels only tangentially, both because those books are rarely canonical and because it is usually in the initial work of a genre series that an author seems to feel the most pressure to adhere to a formula, and the faithfulness of these texts to the central formula is what provides the means of seeing how iterations of the genre treated the subject of discipline.

Therefore, the list of books *Disciplining Girls* considers as central to its project are these nine, the first two of which are more properly sentimental novels that set the terms of the conversation for the subsequent seven postsentimental novels, all of which are books for children:

— Susan Warner, *The Wide, Wide World* (1850)
— E.D.E.N. Southworth, *The Hidden Hand* (1859)
— Louisa May Alcott, *Eight Cousins* (1875)
— Kate Douglas Wiggin, *Rebecca of Sunnybrook Farm* (1903)[6]
— Frances Hodgson Burnett, *A Little Princess* (1905)
— L. M. Montgomery, *Anne of Green Gables* (1908)[7]
— Frances Hodgson Burnett, *The Secret Garden* (1911)
— Eleanor H. Porter, *Pollyanna* (1913)
— L. M. Montgomery, *Emily of New Moon* (1923)

SECONDARY CONTEXTS

One of *Disciplining Girls'* most deliberate assertions is that the insights of literary historians about mid-nineteenth century women's writing have much to tell us about texts published in the wake of sentimentalism. Most studies of the domestic and sentimental traditions date the waning of those traditions around 1875.[8] Tracing the inheritance of children's novels published at the turn into the twentieth century back to midcentury traditions allows readings of the later period to make use of powerful existing insights about the earlier period. Specifically, insights into sentimentalism permit readings of later girls' fiction to take for granted a political dimension widely noted in the earlier modes. Nancy Armstrong, for example, in writing about the British sentimental tradition, describes how the novel deemphasized real property and public political power as markers of social worth. It then emphasized separate spheres, along the way making desirable a kind of woman characterized by nontactile capital, namely goodness, charity, sacrifice, modesty, and other intangible personal traits. Valuing women according to their private attributes allowed a logic in which women, who were defined according to their exclusion from the public political sphere, could never be political because they were women, who were, everyone knew, facets of the private sphere. The circularity of that logic meant that what women said was a priori apolitical—even when it was explicitly political. By "represent[ing] political conflict in terms of sexual differences that upheld a peculiarly middle-class notion of love," domestic fiction passed itself off as complicit with masculine power (41). As domestic novels painted the home space as "the complement and antidote" to the man's world of exchanged ideas and other commodities (48), the writers assured themselves and the dominant power structure that no matter how political their statements might sound, they could not be political because they were phrased in the feminine tradition. As a result, sentimental writers found a protected venue in which they could discuss political points—such as power and discipline—without fear of opprobrium for having made political speech.

In this space of nonpolitical political dialogue, important cultural work could be done. Cathy N. Davidson has described how even the seduction novel— which appears to be about women without power at perpetual risk of domination by masculine agency—provided the early American woman with an opportunity to "view her life as largely the consequence of her own choices and not merely as the product of the power of . . . the father's authority, the suitor's (honorable or dishonorable) guile, the husband's control" (123). And Lori Merish claims that sentimental novels presented a story of subject formation not through the conventional masculine narrative of rebellion and transcendence but through a combination of individual desire and acquiescence to the dominant power structure.

I continue this line of inquiry, viewing these novels as candy-coated narratives that understand gender in ways that are complexly subversive as well as complicit. Like Armstrong, Davidson, and Merish, I see sentimental fiction as a place for working out what it means to be a woman in America in the emerging industrial age. But I also trace the changing nature of this discourse, as the scope of the politics encoded in these tales turns from sweeping to personal. As orphan girl novels entered the twentieth century, they made use of but often played down the interpersonal energies so vital to the sentimental narrative. For example, death and mourning take on new significance in turn-of-the-century girls' novels. The loss of beloved, angelic children up to and including *Uncle Tom's Cabin's* Eva St. Clare is all but absent in the new girls' novels, whose main characters are clearly not adults who learn to change their ways in the wake of a child's death.[9] In fact, it is a significant aspect of this genre and one of the ways that this genre separates itself from sentimentalism that in them the children *don't die*. But death is not absent in these novels. Rather, it is built into the genre formula: the protagonists are, after all, orphans, so they are defined by death, but this time by the death of adults. Moreover, whatever lingering personality and physical traits they may have inherited from their ancestors (and these novels frequently make a point of saying that the girls share features with dead relatives), the children inevitably move on following the death of their parents. At the beginning of this literary history, the lives of the protagonists are still shaped by the deaths of their parents, but as the genre moves closer to today, it increasingly emphasizes the girls' individuality. These are not children who waste away when the beloved parent is gone but girls who survive both their parents and their parents' deaths.

SENTIMENT AND GENDER

The subject of this book is the literary interplay of power and gender over the issue of discipline, and at one point readings of power and gender in literature were fairly straightforward. Recent scholarship, however, has complicated conventions about the divisions between public and private, masculine and feminine, that existed in postbellum culture. Therefore, before I offer my own readings of power and gender, I want to enter a debate that has grown increasingly nuanced. And although I contradict some of the most pyrotechnic claims being made, I hope to extend the larger points of some of the most exciting scholarship on the subject. Specifically, I want to show that disciplinary strategies of the nineteenth and early twentieth century were read in terms highly inflected by gender to their contemporary practitioners and objects, and I want to show that in a genre of novels about orphan girls, female authors demonstrated that a decidedly feminine version of power was not only valid; it was capable of transforming and directing masculine power.

At the center of the recent debate over gender and nineteenth-century American culture is *Sentimental Men*, edited by Mary Chapman and Glenn Hendler, an anthology of articles dissolving the borders between the separate spheres. There are two arguments that this group of scholars makes, though those arguments are sometimes difficult to separate. The volume as a whole questions the idea that there were separate spheres of masculine and feminine, public and private in the nineteenth century, documenting various sites of interpenetration between them, and suggests that an insistence on such a separation has hindered rather than helped savvy historical readings. This is a useful contribution to the study of the period's literature to say the least. Specifically, it denies us the comfort of looking only for what we expect about gender in only the places we expect to find it. The most important contribution the volume and the works that have surrounded it make, therefore, is this insight that in practice the worlds of domesticity, sentimentality, economy, and public debate all overlapped with each other, no matter how much members of this time period claimed otherwise.

I depart from this claim when it goes on to suggest that the real overlap in energies we once thought discrete means that the barriers between those venues either did not exist or did not matter. In places, such statements are innocuous enough, as in Chapman and Hendler's introduction, where they avow that "the contributors to *Sentimental Men* question any uncomplicated gendering of sentiment as feminine, demonstrating that the ideology of separate spheres was suffused by contested discourses" (8). In his 2001 *Public Sentiments*, a monograph that builds on the ideas of *Sentimental Men*, Hendler argues that "sentimentality in the nineteenth century was never as feminine nor as private an affective structure as we assume it was" (43). Both statements are clearly laudable in that they call for the kind of reassessment of assumptions that is the sign of healthy scholarship, but in his essay "Bloated Bodies" in *Sentimental Men*, Hendler uses this reassessment to imply that readings of sentimentality as feminine cannot be right. Writing on antebellum sentimentality, for example, he argues that "sentimentality needs to be analyzed as more than a feminine literary genre or mode, and as more than a rhetoric that women deployed in political and protopolitical efforts." This pays off for Hendler in the figure of the sentimental reformed (male) drunkard, whose "widespread popularity and emotional power are evidence that nineteenth-century sentimentality has been too quickly categorized as a form of feminization and a force of privatization" (127). However, as much as I may agree with the suggestions that sentimentality is not a purely feminine phenomenon, the sentimentally redeemed man is *precisely* evidence of feminization. Hendler is, to put it plainly, right that sentimentality can (and, his *Public*

Sentiments compellingly argues, must) be to some extent public, but he is wrong that sentimentality to a nineteenth-century American could have been read as utterly free of femininity.

Sentimental Men's defeminization of sentiment rests on a reading of sentiment informed only by the sex of the bodies performing the sentimental acts. If a man performed a sentimental act, this argument goes, the act was read by nineteenth- and early twentieth-century culture as masculine no matter what other social forces may have contextualized the act. Thus Hendler can read the sentiment of Horatio Alger's novels and conclude that those librarians who agitated against the banning of his books did not see that sentiment as feminine. For these readers, Hendler surmises, what guarantees "that male sympathy is not feminizing is, simply if tautologically put, that it is a relation between males" (*Public* 107). Therefore, no matter how feminine such sympathy might be in other texts, sympathy cannot be feminine if it is exchanged between male writers and readers. The transformative power of the reader/writer's sex is complete, according to this theory, so that "sympathetic absorption in narrative," which "was by the 1840s seen as a—perhaps *the*—quintessentially feminine characteristic" ("Bloated Bodies" 130), ceased to be feminine the moment that a male group of reforming alcoholics such as the Washingtonians used such a method of absorption in their own meetings. Hendler himself plays up the violations of stereotype in written descriptions of the meetings, observing that the meetings "sound like collective scenes of sentimental reading, with the pale, solitary, emotionally responsive woman reader replaced by a mass of tipsy but tearful red-nosed auditors" ("Bloated Bodies" 130). It is the male body present in this otherwise feminine narrative that prevents that narrative from being feminine.

Scott A. Sandage, another contributor to *Sentimental Men*, makes a similar argument in his study of letters written to J. D. Rockefeller asking for financial aid. His study is an astute tour of another site in the public sphere, the world of business, making use of a supposedly private tool, namely that of the sentimental personal letter, for its own ends. As does Hendler, he sees the relation between male petitioner and male capitalist as one defined not by the socially inflected tone of their exchange but by the sex of their bodies. One letter, by Fitch Raymond, made especially heavy use of sentimental tropes to induce the millionaire's sympathy, but to Sandage those tropes became masculine because they were exchanged by men:

> Raymond's language ("to faint & perish") would hardly seem like manly talk,
> if sentiment were an exclusively feminine domain. But it was not; Raymond

appealed to an implicit understanding among entrepreneurs that unexpected and often irretrievable ruin threatened even the best of them daily, and therefore bound them together in male communities of sentimental obligation. Sentiment was as appropriate in the market as it was in the parlor. (184–85)

Because they were men, their symbolics could not and should not appear—to themselves or us, the argument goes—as feminine.

But the argument that men cannot perform feminine acts or, more importantly, acts that are read as feminine does not hold, even in the essays making those arguments. Even in early twenty-first-century culture, stereotypically feminine acts are not stripped of feminine inflection simply because their performers are masculine. If that were the case, words such as "sissy" would have long since dropped out of the language.[10] Rather, feminine acts performed by men are feminine acts now and were so at the turn of the twentieth century. Although Sandage maintains that sentiment was not always feminine and thus could be as appropriate between men as it was between women, the men who wrote these letters apparently felt otherwise. This is why, as Sandage himself points out, the men writing their sympathetic petitions *repeatedly* apologized for doing so. They apologized for writing the letters, they apologized for taking up the time of such a busy executive, and they tried throughout their letters to distance themselves from the sentimental strategies of their letters. Clearly they did *not* feel that sentiment was appropriate in this capitalist venue, because one does not apologize for doing something one deems appropriate. The *Sentimental Men* theory of defeminized sentiment is a useful reminder that we should not overemphasize the femininity of sentiment, but there is likewise no need to strip sentiment of its feminine inflections, as Hendler does in his essay on the Washingtonians. He defines their homosocial activity as nonfeminine because it is restricted to physically male participants, and as a result he misses the gendered inflection of the Washingtonian's ideology as they phrased it themselves: "We don't slight the drunkard; we love him, we nurse him, as a mother does her infant learning to walk" (qtd. in "Bloated Bodies" 137). The Washingtonians themselves called their activities feminine. Although we can argue that it may not have been *as* feminine (private, domestic, anticapitalist) as they claimed, how can we argue that they did not think it was feminine in the face of evidence that they themselves labeled it as such?[11]

The fact that we can find instances of sentiment, suasion, disciplinary intimacy, and other traditionally feminine strategies outside putatively feminine spheres is not evidence that this power was not feminine. Rather, it is evidence that this power worked. To readers looking back a hundred years, the factitious quality of the separate spheres is so obvious that it is difficult to remember that no matter how arbitrary those boundaries may have been, no matter how frequently they were violated from either side, the boundaries were real to the people who maintained them and allowed themselves to be ruled by them. Certainly it is true that the boundaries were artificial, and the mounting evidence of men who used "feminine" discipline and women who used "masculine" power is an important reminder of that fact. But should we really be so surprised that white, straight, middle-class men saw an efficacious power that belonged—however tenuously—to one of their disenfranchised Others and then went and colonized that power for themselves? Is this a new chapter in the history of Western power? It is not even really a new chapter in the story of men and sentiment, since until roughly this point in history men could use sentiment without threatening their manly personae, as the decades of successful male sentimental writers had demonstrated.[12] Men used feminine power for their own ends in spite of the fact that they and their culture read it as feminine; they did so because this power worked. However tempting it may be for us now to erase the political significance of the clearly arbitrary lines between masculine and feminine spheres in postbellum culture, doing so places out of reach a historically informed reading of that period's artifacts. Sentimentality, sympathy, suasion, and disciplinary intimacy were feminine modes of power by the lights of U.S. citizens between the Civil War and the granting of suffrage, regardless of who used them.

An insistence on the presence of gender, particularly femininity, allows provocative readings of the political stakes of sentimental fiction and its heirs. The women's suffrage movement is an especially interesting case for studying the boundaries of the not-so-separate spheres because it involved women leaving the home and using both public and economic spaces—stereotypically masculine venues—to advance the cause of female empowerment. Therefore, the movement is by definition one of the sites of overlap between public and private. And yet the lines between feminine and masculine remained largely intact. "It is evident," as Charles Strickland has said in his study of Louisa May Alcott, "that sentimentalists had little or no sympathy with the slogans of nineteenth-century feminism. The cause of women's rights received no votes among most sentimental novelists, who held up passivity as an ideal and who regarded any imitation of masculine traits as a surrender of the woman's claim to superior moral virtue" (26).[13] The objection Strickland sees the sentimentalists as making is not precisely that women were abandoning the private sphere but that they were abandoning the feminine sphere. In fact, in order to make their objections to suffrage known, they had to make those opinions public, to elide the boundaries between public and private. But they spoke publicly in defense of a division based on gender. Gillian Brown has argued that many public women, for instance Catharine Beecher, saw political activism as "a fall from domestic purity, and hence from domestic power and its superior political influence through self-subordination and moral exemplification" (26). Beecher believed strongly in gaining more recognition for women's efforts but not at the expense of femininity. She mocked the quest for suffrage, proclaiming first that men had physical power and women the power of love and then that women could get what they needed by relying on the love they had engendered in men, not by forcing men to give them the vote (Beecher and Stowe 468). Insisting on the femininity of sentiment—and of, as in Beecher's example, the affective discipline it championed—reveals important ironies that highlight the capacity for public power in ideology that had its roots in domestic traditions. The challenge for sentimentalism and the girls' fiction that followed it was to wield that power in ways that engaged more complexly with femininity.

There is one more conventional understanding of sentiment that I want to challenge, and here I agree with and expand on the propositions of recent scholarship. In *Public Sentiments*, Hendler demonstrates that although sentiment is usually cast as a private phenomenon, it also and indeed necessarily takes place in public spaces; further, the intersubjective nature of sentiment (especially in its form as sympathy) requires a public dimension. Nineteenth-century writers of every sex and race knew this and used sentiment in their public conversations— novels, tracts, speeches, and so forth—to achieve social change. This argument is useful for understanding the public implications and requirements of a sentimentalism that I maintain must be read as feminine, even when that sentiment was publicly posed as the opposite of obviously political endeavors such as suffrage. Likewise, consider Karen Sánchez-Eppler's essay in *Sentimental Men*, in which she reads nineteenth-century Sunday school tracts and points to the mostly female group of missionaries whose sale they supported. Sánchez-Eppler finds that sentiment could be used in these cases to justify and even fund the efforts of women beyond domestic borders, making women and the sentiment they wielded not only public but imperialist. The "domestic empire" she postulates "seems oxymoronic not only because it would conflate—as these stories do—home and world, inward sentiment and expansionist adventure, but also because in geopolitical terms it would erase the distinction between the national and the international" (403). Such findings demonstrate "the inadequacies of depicting American empire-building as a reaction against, and a manly alternative to, the bourgeois, feminine home culture of sentimentality and domesticity" (400). The alternative she posits is that pursuits read by the U.S. citizenry as public and masculine could be performed by women and discussed in recognizably feminine terminology, particularly in cases where the texts in question invoked sentiment.

The important insights of current scholarship on gender boundaries in the nineteenth century, then, are that, first, the public and private overlapped, and, second, although feminine modes of operation were still considered feminine, they could be used effectively and even to public acclaim both inside the home and well beyond it. Together, these are crucial points for the project of tracing the history of debates over affective discipline in literature about orphan girls. They help explain why a culture otherwise dismissive of women and femininity could witness and even applaud the growth of disciplinary power in the hands of female writers. These points also help explain how easily girls could fit into the project of sentimental-style discipline, with all its public and political ramifications. Further, in what is one of the most compelling mysteries of the narrative of disciplinary changes, these points frame the question of why a critical venue for this discourse of affective discipline moved from sentimental novels featuring influential mothers to novels that draw little girls to the center of the disciplinary arrangement, girls who not only take the place of mothers but who are often also given the mission of fixing them.

The narrative of my book is driven by these intersecting forces: the public implications of private affection and the heavy weight of gender in discipline powered by love. It is a literary history that shows how new novels for girls repeatedly revised a generic formula advanced by older bestsellers to tell a story in which fictional girls enjoyed fictional strength.

DISCIPLINE'S OWN INDIVIDUALISM

At the center of this book is the literary history of affective discipline, and a theme of great importance to that history is the subject of individualism. Questions of affective discipline are necessarily questions of individuality, of the boundaries between one person and another. Corporal punishment *depends* upon bodily boundaries, announces them with the explosions of pain along one's skin that are intended to correct the person inside. But affective discipline is a technology through which the disciplining subject says to the disciplined object, "Learn to shape your interiority like mine; organize your thoughts after my model and let your actions radiate from that similarity; desire what I desire." Such a blurring of the distinction between the people in a relationship characterized by loving discipline was held up by reformers of the mid-nineteenth century as one of its improvements over physical punishment. For Lyman Cobb, for example, who theorized at length on the nature of good discipline, "The system of flogging forms almost *a complete barrier* to [moral] instruction. It is wholly unnatural; it *closes up* all the avenues of the good feelings which ought to exist" (38). Affective discipline, in contrast, maintains and expands the "avenues" between subject and object; it repeatedly elides borders to allow love to transfer ideology from one person to another.

Therefore, as I narrate the literary history of affective discipline out of the sentimental era and into a period wherein women increasingly represented themselves as individuals rather than as part of a group, I pay frequent attention to the viability of individuality during the same segment of literary history. "Individualism" was a term of considerable importance to the mid-nineteenth-century writers who theorized affective discipline; it was frequently understood as a term that symbolized a distasteful modernity that threatened loving bonds. Horace Bushnell's influential *Christian Nurture*, for example, repeatedly inveighs against "the tendency of all our modern speculations . . . to an extreme individualism" for exactly that reason (20). Bushnell opposes modern individualism on the grounds that it ignores or, worse, frustrates the transmission of "character" and "virtue" from parent to child (21), a transmission he characterizes as documented and endorsed by scripture (23, 28–29). In a characteristic burst of animosity toward a model of human interaction that denies what Cobb might call the affective avenues of discipline, Bushnell declares that

> we possess only a mixed individuality all our life long. A pure, separate, individual man, living *wholly* within and from himself, is a mere fiction. No such person ever existed or ever can. I need not say that this view of an organic connection of character subsisting between parent and child lays a basis for notions of Christian education far different from those which now prevail, under the cover of a merely fictitious and mischievous individualism. (22)

But Bushnell's opinion was more suited to the era of sentimentalism than to that of twentieth-century girls' fiction, even such fiction as the classic orphan girl novels, which were otherwise adamantly nostalgic for premodern sensibilities. As the orphan girl formula continued to expand the powers of the same moral suasion that Bushnell championed even as it evinced growing unease with moral suasion, novels relying on that formula similarly struggled to imagine a disciplinary relationship with individuals with *firm* boundaries. Iterations of the formula throughout the middle of the century generally played down the importance of individuality; iterations of the formula in the new market for girls' fiction did not.

Unfortunately, the very act of invoking a definition of individualism for a project that deals extensively with women writers, especially women writers who were so keenly aware of the sentimental roots of the affective power at stake in their fiction, is complicated at best. Patrice DiQuinzio has summed up the central complication well in her work on the history of motherhood. Motherhood is itself, she demonstrates, a term with important implications of its own for the literary history of affective discipline. DiQuinzio points to an ongoing tension between individual and group identity that has riddled arguments over the rights of women. She writes that

> feminism in the United States has to rely on individualism to claim women's equal human subjectivity, because the intelligibility and political effectiveness of this claim are a function of its being expressed in terms consistent with the dominant ideology. If feminism cannot show that women are subjects as individualism defines subjectivity, then it cannot argue for women's equal political agency and entitlement. (xiv)

Therefore, feminism and the history of motherhood and women's rights have been tied inextricably to an argument for individualism, to an argument that women be regarded as liberal subjects possessing a full complement of rights. However, as DiQuinzio also points out,

> feminism also resists and challenges individualism—because of its relationship to essential motherhood, because it inadequately conceptualizes important aspects of women's situations and experiences, and ultimately because it inadequately conceptualizes subjectivity itself. (xiv)

Thus, the arguments for giving women full rights *also* frequently rest on the idea that women are *not* individuals. Rather, they are echoes of a type: any one woman is, like all other women, maternal by inclination; she is a demure moral paragon, and therefore she deserves rights because she and the womanhood she represents will guide the nation well.[14] Although these arguments are less powerful today, they held significant weight during exactly the decades of the orphan girl novel's transition from sentimental woman's fiction to turn-of-the-century girls' fiction. Thus, it is not at all surprising that the tension DiQuinzio locates within the turn-of-the-century feminist movement also surfaces in the transitioning orphan girl formula.

That tension is central to the argument about individualism that runs through these books, from *The Wide, Wide World* to *Emily of New Moon*. Just as DiQuinzio has articulated this tension for studies of women's culture, Kent Baxter has demonstrated that turn-of-the-century discourse about adolescence also rested on concepts of individuals whose individuality was defined by their failure to fit into a type. Baxter points to early twentieth-century theorists such as G. Stanley Hall and Margaret Mead, who talked about the tension between the individual and types defined by genetics or culture, a tension that defined a period of adolescence from which an individual could emerge. The sentimental and postsentimental orphan girl story both anticipates and participates in this structure of defining individualism. Thus, the novels frequently ask questions about their protagonists that foreground the nationality of the girl—as might Mead's theories. They also frequently examine the overlap between the girl and her family, often in terms of the genetic similarities on which Hall focuses. Again and again, the orphan girl novel defines or refuses to define its girls as individuals based on their difference from or similarity to other people, often entire categories of people. Convinced of the power of a mode of discipline that dissolves boundaries, early orphan girl novels tend toward sentimental dissolution of the protagonist in other identities. Unhappy with the sentimental model's cost to recognizable subjectivity, orphan girl novels published closer to the passage of women's suffrage define the boundaries around their protagonists more sharply.

The fact that individualism is such a fraught topic in books by women, particularly women writing during the waves of feminist activism DiQuinzio highlights, is only compounded by recent scholarship pointing to the inequalities that individualism often obscures—and sometimes encourages. As many scholars—Chris Newfield perhaps most emphatically and Cyrus R. K. Patell most recently—have pointed out, mainstream America loves to tell its history as one characterized by the awakening of individualism. Such a characterization is a holdover from earlier modes of literary and cultural scholarship in which the transcendent white male author boldly rebelled against convention, popularity, or women. As such, studies on this subject have a tendency to ignore the oppressive potential of individualism, which itself has a tendency to naturalize heterosexuality, whiteness, maleness, and membership in the middle class. Patell has considered individualism in two of the most celebrated contemporary American authors, Toni Morrison and Thomas Pynchon, and argued that their work demonstrates how honest debate about democracy and justice in the United States has been stymied by an automatic opposition to any ideology that yields privilege to a group at the expense of an individual. The result, Patell argues, is an emphasis on individual rights that has most often operated as a justification for oppression of groups who do not fit the demographics of the transcendent, protected-at-all-costs individual in question. But individualism is touted as an avenue of upward mobility immune to the very forms of prejudice that have been woven into its definition. What this means is that "for the victims of sexism, racism, and other forms of group-oriented discrimination, the promises of individualism are simultaneously the source and the frustration of hope" (22).

In the current scholarly landscape, therefore, it is difficult to talk about individualism without irony. This is noticeably true when writing about fiction that descends from the domestic tradition, which figured as the status quo against which the male canon rebelled and, by rebelling, defined individualism. Writing about Fanny Fern's *Ruth Hall*, one of the most widely read domestic novels of the nineteenth century, Gale Temple makes a point that resonates with Patell's comments about Pynchon's and Morrison's fiction, written more than a century after *Ruth Hall*. Fern's best seller, Temple claims, frames its "critique of patriarchy into a potentially reactionary direction" (155), but in the end it encourages an understanding of individuality that calls for dissolution into the homogeneity of white privilege. The domestic heroine therefore, Temple argues, only became an individual by renouncing any difference between herself and the tastes of bourgeois culture, that is to say, by giving up her individuality. If this is true, then individuality itself is at best a limited possibility in woman's fiction. Can the story be much different in the girls' fiction for which it set the pattern?

The contradiction Temple exposes is not necessarily an impediment to studies of individualism. By understanding that the promises of individualism are always already broken, especially for those demographics the patriarchy does not favor, a genre history that tells of victories awarded and then forgotten in the progress of the emergent individual makes more sense. An awareness of the intimate relationship between individualism and its disavowed other, domesticity, also allows for a more nuanced reading of individuality in women's fiction following the Civil War. For instance, the history of individualism in the nineteenth century may have been written in previous decades as one of men transcending domesticity, but work by scholars such as Gillian Brown demonstrates that "nineteenth-century American individualism takes on its peculiarly 'individualistic' properties as domesticity inflects it with values of interiority, privacy, and psychology" (*Domestic Individualism* 1). By putting the domestic space at the heart of individualism rather than in its exhaust, Brown is able to consider the contributions of the culture of domesticity to the culture of individualism. Thus the home space, rather than being the foresworn country, "contains the ideal condition for self-possession: a sympathetic and secure proprietorship" (45). This opens up a new question for studies of the orphan girl formula, because the stability of the home—which allows security, which allows possession, which allows individualism—is denied to the protagonists of orphan girl novels by their very premise: orphans are by definition without a home. Through careful use of discipline, these girls are able to win homes of their own—always metaphorically but often also literally—and that ownership is a metonym for the other forms of possession that define the individual at the center of these novels. Ownership therefore becomes a marker of the possibility for individualism in domestic narratives across the history of the orphan girl formula.

Brown works out of C. B. MacPherson's insights on possessive individualism, who notes that one of the most important commodities to be owned in the liberal democratic tradition is the legal right. From Locke through Jefferson to Emerson, MacPherson argues, the notion of alienable rights is a given. The alienable nature of rights means that they can be traded, forfeited, and in all other ways treated as a commodity by the possessing citizen. But when scholars of the liberal tradition talk about rights, they almost exclusively mean *adult* rights. The distinction between adult and child rights in white culture became more important in the nineteenth century with the cultural formation of a new kind of child, and the major figures in domestic ideology were deeply involved in defining for adults what was to be the relationship between adults and children.[15]

Catharine Beecher's domestic manifesto the *American Woman's Home* was just one of many texts that addressed the topic of that new relationship, a relationship defined by discipline. In a lengthy section on the subject, she makes clear that parents' discipline is underwritten by a monopoly on rights. "The medium course," she opines, "is for the parent to take the attitude of a superior in age, knowledge, and relation, who has a perfect *right* to control every action of the child, and that, too, without giving any reason for the requisitions" (279). Beecher does grant that the careful parent will "kindly" state the reasons for her pronouncements but only when the entitled parent is so inclined: "Never, however, on the demand of it from the child, as a right, but as an act of kindness from the parent" (280). For Beecher, the only rights pertinent to the child-parent relationship, indeed, the only rights pertinent to the discipline of children, are those owned by the parent. Those rights are to be guarded jealously and unremittingly by the parent, who must guard against losing them to children, no matter how beloved those children may be.

More important than the content of Beecher's theorem, though, is the shrillness with which she delivers it. Beecher did not announce the distribution of rights with the expectation that her pronouncement would be universally accepted; her italicization and repetition are evidence that she understood she was making a case that she anticipated would meet with opposition. Florence Montgomery's British domestic novel *Misunderstood*, published in the same year (1869) as Beecher's treatise, contributed to that opposition. Gillian Avery has drawn attention to a subtle shift in parent-child relations evident in Montgomery's novel that inverts the positions Beecher belabors. In the novel, young Humphrey dies following a disagreement with his father. This in itself is nothing shocking—mid-century domestic fiction is lousy with dead children—but the symbolic weight of this death certainly is. "In books of an earlier epoch," Avery argues, Humphrey's "death would be used by the author to show what the results of disobedience are. Florence Montgomery, however, uses the death of Humphrey to punish the father who has not taken enough trouble to understand the child" ("Children's" 35).[16] Whereas Beecher's child was required to acquiesce to a parent who might explain if she felt so inclined, Montgomery's parent was consigned to a life of punishment by the specter of a child whom he failed.

The argument over children's rights was no more clearly settled in Beecher's homeland. Cobb and Bushnell, for example, may have agreed on the subject of the power of moral suasion to blur the boundaries between children and the disciplinarians they loved, but they disagreed pointedly on whether children had rights that must be respected in the disciplinary relationship. In his 1847 condemnation of corporal punishment, Cobb repeatedly argues that "parents and teachers should always remember that *children* and *pupils* have RIGHTS," that "the RIGHTS OF CHILDREN" are to be "properly REGARDED by parents and teachers," and that "when the RIGHTS of children are thus appreciated and respected by parents and teachers, they will feel the *responsibility* which rests on THEM" (195). He goes on to enumerate children's right to patient oversight, food, clothing, amusement, and instruction, as well as their right "to *be heard in their own defence*," and, in a memorable phrase, "*to breathe the air of heaven*" (196). But in *Christian Nurture*—also first published in 1847—Bushnell argued, with the same interest in moral education, for the opposite point. Parents, he said with approval,

> appoint [the child's] school, choose his books, regulate his company, decide what form of religion, and what religious opinions he shall be taught, by taking him to a church of their own selection. In all this they infringe upon no right of the child, they only fulfill an office which belongs to them. Their will and character are designed to be the matrix of the child's will and character. (20)

For these authors and the deeply conflicted culture of which they were representatives, a child's possession of individual rights was bound up with the theories and goals of affective discipline. As long as it remained so, the question of whether a child could possess an individual identity would remain cloudy at best.

As time passed and the maternalist sensibilities of writers such as Beecher faded, the culture awarded children more rights that more clearly illuminated an interior subjectivity. Most obvious of these was what Nancy M. Theriot has called the "right to be well-born." This right included the right to be born into families who wanted the children, "but in each case the mother (or at least the parents) was responsible to provide for the right" (128). In a bizarre twist, then, children had to be allowed ownership of a new set of rights, and that ownership could best be guaranteed through obligation of adults, usually the mother, whom Beecher had recently insisted must be invested with full rights. And the new ownership of rights moved deeper into children in ways that were both subtler and more pervasive. This entitlement is most poignant, particularly for studies of literary history, in trends characterizing education and reading habits at the end of the century. These trends emphasized children's private experiences of literature. Christine Pawley's analysis of these habits in an Iowa town during this period reveals how children began studying in accordance with "a newer emphasis on silent, private reading," replacing the traditional practice of learning "to read out loud in class from textbooks that emphasized declamatory skills" (59). These teaching strategies combined with newly available textbooks geared toward specific trades to make the production of private individuals the new mode of public education. As a result of these changes, Pawley concludes, "children were encouraged to see reading as a source of individual enjoyment and fulfillment" (59), providing for turn-of-the-century children's fiction an important conflation of privacy—as in the private, interior act of reading—and individualism. The privacy and individual pleasure of reading helped protect a subjectivity in which the possession of rights could be invested.

Sentimental and postsentimental orphan girl novels, driven by a story about girls adopted into families who are less than thrilled to accept them, begin with the premise that the protagonist is in an inferior position of power and dispossessed of rights or other forms of property. Although these novels follow in the sentimental tradition, which calls for a form of discipline in which the lines between parent and child are softened by love, even the earliest stories narrate the tale of a girl who has the *potential* to be an individual, the potential to be characterized by a discrete, even private interiority. Because these novels span the decades from the conclusion of the sentimental novel's popularity to the early years of women's suffrage, they carry with them the weight of sympathy—which asks individuals to be like each other—as well as democratic representation—which asks citizens to exercise individual voices. The decision to appeal to or disavow individuality, marked by an ability to own property (including the alienable commodity of rights) and an investment in interior desires and prerogatives, had major consequences for the power inherent in a disciplinary model that eschewed boundaries between people who loved one another.

The sentimental orphan girl formula, therefore, has the potential to imagine and celebrate individuality, but it is grounded in stories of "essential motherhood" and "inadequately conceptualize[d] subjectivity," as DiQuinzio has put it, the very sorts of self-erasure that obscure individuality. As Sara Lindey has pointed out, even sentimental writers who called for children's rights did so in ways that, first, were little more than "polite courtesies" (141) and, second, were really more intent on protecting the child's father (145) or the adult who would one day emerge from the shell of the discarded child (141). In the first few decades of sentimentalism and even up through the first sentimental novel written primarily for an audience of girls instead of mothers, novels steeped in this tradition most frequently imagined girls as ciphers for adults, not selves endowed with rights. Written during a period of deep ambivalence over the distribution of rights between adults and children, the sentimental novels that established the orphan formula and communicated that formula to turn-of-the-century fiction for girls often created a semblance of individuality for imaginary girls, all the while quietly insisting that girls performed best as part of a type. The orphan girl novels of the new century, though, would find ways to disentangle themselves from the history of self-effacement that characterized so much sentimental fiction while continuing to imagine the successful exercise of a form of discipline that blurred the boundaries between individuals.

The story of affective discipline in literature is one of misdirection. Mid-nineteenth century sentimental novels about orphan girls promised women (and girls) a peaceful home and influence over men if those women would agree to fill a tightly prescribed role. Novels in this tradition presented the limitations of that role as part and parcel of the power women could wield. By presenting this role as natural, sentimental novels directed attention away from both the roots of that power and its consequences. It should not be surprising that, when fiction for girls replaced sentimental fiction as the nation's bestsellers, the new fiction continued to cloak both the techniques of discipline it endorsed and its debt to the once-popular figures from whom it derived them. *Disciplining Girls* makes explicit the legacy—and burden—of affective discipline that connects the woman's fiction of one era with the girls' fiction of the next.

CHAPTER ONE

The Wide, Wide World and the Rules of Sentimental Engagement

The history of affective discipline in the classic orphan girl novel begins long before there was a clear market for children's literature whose goal was to delight rather than instruct young readers. Susan Warner's *The Wide, Wide World*, published in 1850, crystallized many of the central tenets of discipline in the popular sentimental style, not coincidentally going on to become the first best seller in American literary history. A key strategy for women writers who would attempt to duplicate the financial success of Warner's first novel would be to emulate its ideology. Therefore, just as *The Wide, Wide World* established the formal conventions of the classic orphan girl novel, it also furnished guidelines for the conception and execution of the affective discipline that invigorated its plot. Pivotal elements of those guidelines included the conviction that corporal punishment was inferior to moral suasion. Warner's novel also made central a gendered bifurcation of the production and consumption of discipline, notably as expressed in the central role of mothers and the power this centrality implied over fathers. Further, the technology of discipline by interiority endorsed by *The Wide, Wide World* takes for granted a blurring of identities between disciplining subjects and objects, instituting a pattern of compromised individuality that the genre would revisit and revise many times in the decades to come.

The model of discipline Warner crystallized for sentimentalism and left to the girls' novels of later decades, however, must be understood first as part of a larger conflict. For mainstream U.S. culture of the first half of the nineteenth century, one debate over discipline raged: whether discipline by the hand or discipline through the heart was more ethical. A century and a half later, a preference for loving discipline over physical coercion seems a foregone conclusion, but for the readers who made *The Wide, Wide World* a best seller, that debate was very much alive. And the conditions under which those readers were willing to recognize the ascendancy of affective discipline—transparent emotion, nebulous individuality, gendered allocation of disciplinary prerogatives—suited sentimentalism very well.

MOTHERS AND THE HEART OF NINETEENTH-CENTURY DISCIPLINE

Warner's arguments about discipline unfolded in a midcentury culture deeply aware of the transition it was experiencing from traditional modes of punishment to sentimental-style discipline. Much of the advice literature of the early nineteenth century made that transition obvious, often describing a decreasing interest in the body as the locus for determining a child's future character. Although Dr. William Buchan made it clear in his 1804 treatise that he believed "every man is what his mother has made him," what every man was indebted to his mother for was not his upright character but "the greatest blessing in life, a healthy and vigorous constitution" (2). That constitution was distinctly malleable during childhood, so mothers were enjoined to allow nature to test, but not break, their sons. Buchan offers the example of Edward Watkinson, a young man whose mother did not appropriately manage his body. When Buchan first visited young Watkinson, "at Midsummer," his mother had wrapped him "in clothing sufficient for the rigours of a Lapland winter, and so closely muffled that one could hardly see the tip of his nose" (215–16). With a body so badly mismanaged, Watkinson was too weak to last his adulthood: he died at the age of twenty-one. The child's vital constitution was also under threat from the host of maladies awaiting him at school. Buchan anticipates the mother's wish to improve her son through schooling, but he warns that "learning, however, [sic] desirable, is too dearly bought at the expense of the constitution" (94). The child's body, here at the beginning of the nineteenth century, is too valuable a prize to risk in the name of anything so incorporeal as its mind.

School was often a central site for the debate over the importance of the child's body and mind, and a comparison of how two texts, written decades apart, treated the subject shows how that debate could move in subtle but telling ways. Buchan, for example, argues against "learning" in favor of the physical "constitution." One of the chief threats to that constitution was physical infection:

As thousands of children die every year[,] the victims of diseases caught at schools, and as the health and constitutions of still greater numbers are irretrievably ruined by the confinement and bad air of such places, parents must not be offended at the seeming harshness of my language in reprobating so absurd, so cruel, and so unnatural a practice [of sending children to school]. (93)

The British author P. H. Chavasse, in his 1871 book on children's education, would not disagree with Buchan. Or rather, he would disagree but not over the question of whether children should go to school. Chavasse encouraged a child's education, as long as it took place in the home:

Home is far preferable to a school education for a child. If at home, he is under your own *immediate* observation, and is not liable to be contaminated by naughty children; for, in every school, there is necessarily a great mixture of the good and of the bad; and a child, unfortunately, is more likely to be led by a bad than by a good child. (162–63)

The similarities between the two passages are so many that the few differences are revealing. Chavasse agrees that children should not go to school; indeed, he even agrees that what children risk at school is "contamination." But an important shift has taken place: rather than argue the threat of physical infection, Chavasse argues the threat of *moral* infection.

The increasing interest in and subsequent conflict over the shift from children's bodies to children's spirits cannot be attributed solely to a difference in the nationality of Buchan and Chavasse: multiple figures crucial to the history of childhood in the United States made plain how relevant the value of a child's spirit was to the management of children. Whereas Buchan warned of the threats of public schooling on the basis of physical infection and Chavasse on the basis of moral infection, public figures with a stake in public education frequently made their arguments by appealing to the moral benefits of public schooling. Elizabeth Peabody, who would later serve as an advisor to the commissioner of education, claims in her 1863 *Kindergarten Guide* that the best cure for children's "vicious circle" of "idiosyncrasy" lies in education in the company of not only a moral educator but also other children. "The best conditions of moral culture," she argues, are to be found "in a company large enough for the exacting disposition of the solitary child to be balanced by the claims made by others on the common stock of enjoyment" (Mann and Peabody 14), in short, in a school. Mary Tyler

Mann, or, as she dubs herself in the book she published with Peabody, Mrs. Horace Mann, even dares to suggest that the school environment can provide moral benefit that outweighs the moral damage done by poorly run homes. Reporting on one such improved student, Mann writes that "through my influence she passed much time away from her ungenial home, with friends in whose society she could be happy and unrestrained" (118). Cobb, too, would have been unsurprised at Mann's testimony, for he had earlier written in glowing terms of the ability of the school to address the spiritual inadequacies of home:

> So, if a child may go to a school where order, right principle, virtuous manners, and the love of knowledge reign, and find a respite there from the shiftlessness, vice, and brutality at home, how great is the privilege! In this view, a good school is almost the only mercy that can be extended to the hapless sons and daughters of vice. Their good—most dismal thought!—is to be delivered from their home; to escape the spirit of hell that encompasses their helpless age, and feel, though it be but a few hours a day, the power of another spirit! (100)

These arguments, in which the management of children was so often the flashpoint for disagreement, documented the mid-nineteenth century's increasing preference for ideology that addressed the spirit rather than the body. Even when these American writers disagreed with Chavasse over the importance of schooling outside the home, they agreed that the true target of discipline must be the spirit.

The shift articulated between Buchan and Chavasse, the shift from the primary importance of managing the body to that of managing the heart, was provoked by ardent debate over discipline in nineteenth-century American culture. From the top down, many Americans were asking the same questions: How do we, as a controlling social body, get our soldiers/prisoners/sailors/children to do what we want? The standard answer to this question had always been simple: use some form of the switch until their wills have been broken and they act as they should. Thus a sailor could be beaten with a cat-o'-nine-tails for stealing an officer's champagne.[1] Thus a child could—or rather *should*—be spanked until it stopped telling lies, or fidgeting, or using rude language. But in the nineteenth century, mirroring the transition from an emphasis on the fragile body of which Buchan spoke to the fragile character imagined by Chavasse, a preference for a new kind of control surfaced: discipline by interiority. Rather than punish the body of the offending subject, the nineteenth-century parent/officer/warden might attempt to change the perpetrator's future behavior through suasion. Such suasion took many forms, including reasoning with, educating, admonishing, and even loving the offender. The question of moral suasion versus corporal punishment was relevant to nearly every area of public life in the nineteenth century, including slavery, temperance, worker efficiency, and most obviously, child rearing. Chavasse spoke for many readers of the middle- and late-nineteenth century when he opined that "corporal punishment is revolting, disgusting, and demoralizing to the boy, and is degrading to the school-master as a man and as a Christian" (298). Chavasse certainly felt that children should obey, but he spoke for a rising and influential movement when he argued that striking children was the wrong way to discipline them.

Although men and women both fought on both sides of the issue, corporal punishment came increasingly to be seen as a masculine strategy. Conversely, moral suasion was considered a feminine province.[2] As Myra C. Glenn has said, "Women's allegedly gentle natures predisposed them to substitute moral suasion for corporal punishment in the classroom as well as at home" (32). In other words, it was not just that women argued in favor of moral suasion because they were women but because they believed, as did the overwhelming majority of nineteenth-century middle-class white culture, in the contemporary social construction of femininity. Women expected themselves and one another to act in ways construed as feminine, and a major attribute of "feminine" in the nineteenth century was this stance on discipline.

Women themselves rarely argued with this stereotype in the nineteenth century; instead they became some of suasion's most vocal supporters as they pointed to its efficacy. In her 1866 *How I Managed My Children from Infancy to Marriage*, Eliza Warren relates many examples of her successful use of affective discipline. In a section entitled "Kindness Better Than Harshness," she repeats the tale of one naughty boy who, when caught, was made to say a prayer with his mother rather than fetch a switch. The prayer is carefully calculated to remind the child that disobedience is bad not because it is physically painful but because it is an offense to love:

> "What must I say, Mamma?"
> "Repeat after me: O Lord, I pray to be forgiven for my disobedience to my parents, for the Savior's sake, who, while on earth took up little children in his arms and blessed them." I rested my lips for a moment on his upturned forehead, and said, softly, "Amen." He sprang on my lap, and put his arms around my neck, saying—

"Mamma, may I go to bed? I don't want to play any more; and you will undress me—please, mamma, do."

I readily acquiesced in this request, for I thought the effect of the conversation and subsequent prayer would not so readily pass away. (46–47)

The combination of an offended, *loving* Savior with a mother who kisses her disobedient child as she says "Amen" is a potent one for the nineteenth-century mother. She is careful to extend this policy to all her children, even seeing to it that they treat one another with the same affection. When one child undertakes a task, Warren reports that she has the others "assist . . . as much as possible, and with loving words and kindness" (41). Warren herself uses loving words as she encourages the children to help her pick up their "litters," saying,

"Mamma, [sic] likes to see the room tidy; let us all help to make it so." Then the little feet pattered about, and the little hands were ready to be useful; then a kiss was given to each, and such a joyful clapping and shout at the end of our labor! (40–41)

The deployments and rewards of disciplinary intimacy are complex in this passage. First, it is significant that Warren instructs the reader in the use of children's love for their mother as an impetus to work. Rather than spank or even threaten them, Warren invokes their assumed desire to see their mother happy by simply reminding them that she "likes to see the room tidy." Second, she is careful to reward the children at the end of their labor with a kiss for each. Finally, she implies a reward for the mother who is reading her book, a "joyful clapping and shout" that can be hers, too, if she will follow Warren's method of discipline. While Warren is successfully disciplining her children, she is also modeling that discipline for the reader. Further, she is *practicing* it on the reader as well, making promises of kisses and joyful shouts to the mother who does what Warren tells her.

Warren's treatise was published in 1866, well into the history of sentimentalism as a literary movement, but its dovetailing of private spaces with feminine power draws heavily on sentimentalism's precursors, particularly instances that traded social obligations of mothers with expressions of political power. Linda K. Kerber has used a figure she calls the "Republican Mother" to explain the place of white mothers in U.S. culture from the revolutionary period up through the Civil War. In this figure, Kerber argues, the uncomfortable relationship between women's public lives and domestic responsibilities would be worked out. "In the early years of the Republic," Kerber explains, "a consensus developed around the idea that a mother, committed to the service of her family and to the state, might serve a political purpose. Those who opposed women in politics had to meet the proposal that women could—and should—play a political role through the raising of a patriotic child" (283). What this meant was that although women were represented in culture as domestic and apolitical, they could still have some kind of political power through the same figure—that of the patriotic mother—that was used to keep them out of the centers of power. In other words, women were able to turn an obligation into power. "From the time of the Revolution until our own day," Kerber holds, "the language of Republican Motherhood remains the most readily accepted—though certainly not the most radical—justification for women's political behavior" (12).

But toward the middle of the nineteenth century, a very odd change took place in the intertwined logic of gender and privilege. Always implicit in the culture of sentiment was control: mothers controlled children, virgins controlled themselves, drunkards failed to control their desires, and so on. And, as Mary P. Ryan points out, fiction played an increasingly central role in this culture. "This literature did not present moral postulates and domestic values as the opinions of community leaders," she explains, but "rather . . . embedded them in the daily lives of the common people" (33). Magazines carrying this particular "amalgamation of fiction, didacticism, and domesticity" boomed in popularity (34). The morality espoused by these magazines was one imagined within the bourgeois domestic sphere, a mid-nineteenth century "empire" ruled over by the same figure Kerber found in Revolutionary culture: the mother. The woman who could dictate the rules of the domestic and communicate them to the rest of the public was not just a woman, certainly not a single woman, and not even simply a woman married in a state-approved ceremony. This woman had to be a *mother*, and she had responsibilities that began but did not end in the domestic space. First, she was required to make her children and even husband behave by wielding the power of comfort and approval, commodities made meaningful by the home space, which would remain, at least in popular discourse, the opposite of the public space. But mothers also had to make the nation behave, and they did this by training future as well as current leaders correctly. It was as a mother that an American woman had this power and responsibility. "To put it simply," writes Ryan, "the patriarchal rankings according to age and sex which were so basic to early American conceptions of social order slowly dissolved and, in the process, social energy was rechanneled into the emotional and domestic bonds between women and children" (17–18).

The most important tool the mother had was precisely that "emotional and domestic bond," no more so than when controlling her children. And since adult men had a public sphere to which they were expected to return day after day as well as a system of government that blithely privileged their opinions over that of mothers, it was in shaping children before they left the home that the mother had the best claim to her empire. The interior conscience, a monitor that could be left in charge of children even when mother was not present, was "peculiarly sensitive to affectionate stimuli" and "constituted a critical mechanism of moral guidance" (Kerber 50–51). Mothers increasingly endorsed and exercised discipline through affection—specifically as opposed to physical coercion—as the century aged, and "child-rearing literature of the 1830s and '40s presented numerous methods of establishing the reign of the parents in the child's conscience" (Kerber 51). But once more, the exploration of discipline was not limited to advice columns. Instead, an "association of conscience, guilt, and adult control is found throughout the moralistic children's literature of the 1830s and '40s" (Kerber 53). Literature, especially novels, proved an effective venue for communicating and modeling the sort of control privileged in the empire of the mother.[3]

THE WIDE, WIDE WORLD, BEATING THE CREAM, AND THE NEGLIGIBLE FATHER

No novel was more important to the narrative of the empire of the mother than *The Wide, Wide World*. It tells the story of young Ellen Montgomery, whose ailing mother and unsympathetic father send her to live with Ellen's aunt, the pointedly named Miss Fortune. While there, Ellen struggles to live, despite her aunt's antagonism, by the model of Christian self-effacement that her mother taught her. Neighbors, notably the gruff Mr. Van Brunt and the refined Humphreys family, take pity on Ellen, occasionally standing up for her to her aunt, frequently helping further the education Ellen's mother wished for her, and ultimately providing her with the family conditions that allow her to fulfill the vision her mother once had for her. Ellen is orphaned not long after her parents send her away, and as such she becomes the prototype for the popular orphan girls of fiction that will follow at the turn of the century, but it is the heavy weight of her dead mother that structures the story, determining the girl's formative tragedies while laying out the sentimental rules of affective discipline.

First among these rules is the gendered nature of discipline. The rejection of physical coercion in *The Wide, Wide World* is not universal but governed by the sex of the person doling out the punishment. One aspect of this rule becomes clear in a scene in which Ellen Montgomery, accosted on the road by an unsavory fellow, is rescued by her future husband, John Humphreys. Humphreys leaps to Ellen's aid and beats the villain in no uncertain terms. In a flash, "and Ellen hardly saw how, it was so quick,—John had dismounted, taken Mr. Saunders by the collar, and hurled him quite over into the gully at the side of the road, where he lay at full length without stirring" (401). The text never questions physical coercion in the hands of the romantic, manly figure of Humphreys. In fact his use of physical coercion, far from being a problem, is the key to overcoming a problem in the narrative. In other words, for all the debate over corporal punishment in the culture where Warner's novel appears, her presentation of physical punishment wielded by a man is largely uncritical.

Warner's novel is equally clear in its insistence that a woman's use of corporal punishment is inappropriate. For instance, when Ellen has perpetrated one of the many small crimes that girls of these novels commit, her aunt responds in a way that her *own* future husband denounces. "Come, come!" Van Brunt warns her, "this is getting to be too much of a good thing. Beat your cream, ma'am, as much as you like, or if you want to try your hand on something else you'll have to take me first, I promise you" (133). The implications of physical coercion in this passage are not so simple as they first appear. Fortune threatens physical violence, the central affective figure of the novel—Ellen—trembles in fear, and a more likeable character tells Fortune she has gone too far. But the passage isn't precisely rejecting the threat of physical violence. In fact, Van Brunt makes such a threat himself when he warns Fortune that she will "have to take me first, I promise you." Further, he doesn't even technically warn her against violence. Instead, he suggests that she redirect her violence to a purely domestic endeavor, namely "beating" her cream, which she can do as much as she likes. Moreover, Fortune and Van Brunt adopt the attitude associated with the opposite gender in the coercion/suasion debates: the woman threatens physical violence, and the man warns her to use a less physical mode of discipline. But in fact there is no threat to the gender divide in this passage. What is important here is not that Fortune threatens physical violence (she doesn't actually use it), but that she is rebuked for doing so. In contrast, no one rebukes John for his use of physical coercion. Further, no one in Warner's novel rebukes a woman for using moral suasion. Warner uses Fortune to convince her readers of the value of the sentimental code of discipline and its gendered structure. In Aunt Fortune's hands, this brand of punishment is not only inappropriate; it is even laughable, because whatever physical dominance she may have over the child, Van Brunt—a man— has a much greater degree of dominance over her. These moments of physical violence in a genre that generally deplores such violence insist that it be read as an inappropriate tool for women to use. In this early example of Fortune and Van Brunt, the genre also begins to argue that physical coercion is inappropriate as a means of disciplining children.

Warner does not leave to the reader the project of imagining what mode of discipline should be used in corporal punishment's place. Not only is corporal punishment less than ideal when a parent needs to discipline Ellen; there is also a much more effective mode of discipline available that the people around—and conspicuously apart from—Ellen use to mold her. This form of discipline begins not with threats, and certainly not with beatings, but with love. "In *The Wide, Wide World*," as Richard H. Brodhead argues, "to love one's mother is to wish to do things her way, but to love her and lose her is to have this wish heightened into full-fledged moral imperative" (82). This discipline is inculcated and enforced by means of the love the affectionate parent has fanned in the child's heart. Warner's novel repeatedly endorses this kind of discipline as the best kind for ruling children, and it is even endorsed by people who don't know Ellen. Shortly after Ellen has first lost her mother (to Europe, not yet death), a kindly stranger tells her to ignore the taunts of other people in the face of her duty to her mother, saying, "Never mind being laughed at, my child. If your mother says a thing is right, that's enough for you—let them laugh!" (79). This is the origin of the empire of the mother as Ryan describes it, an empire grounded in the noncorporal discipline of the child who will eventually go out into the wide, wide world. The positions of disciplinarian and disciplined object are clear in the sentimental tradition: the child will learn to love the mother, whose ability to punish the child's body may be lost but whose authority to tell the child what to do is upheld even by strangers. The effective way to discipline Ellen, this foundational sentimental novel argues, is the affective way, and mothers should use it to the exclusion of physical discipline.

Affective discipline is so effective, in fact, that it even works when Ellen is far from the people she loves, which is to say the people advancing Ellen's mother's goals for her. Although they cannot be present to monitor her progress, affective discipline keeps Ellen in line. Key to discipline, as Michel Foucault has demonstrated in his analysis of the panopticon, is the concept of surveillance, a power defined not precisely by the presence of an observing disciplinarian but rather by the felt gaze, by disciplined individuals made to understand that they are being watched even when they aren't.[4] Nancy Armstrong has already documented the importance of surveillance to the domestic tradition, connecting it to precisely this sort of effort to shape young women (19). In *The Wide, Wide World*, Ellen is a good young lady in part because she is such a willing recipient of disembodied surveillance. This is demonstrated when Ellen, now approaching her majority, is forced to live in Scotland with relatives whose mildly liberal spirituality is an affront to the conservative evangelicalism of Ellen's mother. John Humphreys, concerned about Ellen, takes the long voyage to Scotland to make sure she is remaining true to the precepts his family has tried to encourage in her. When John visits her at the Lindsays' home, he asks her to begin writing to him, even though the Lindsays are not likely to approve. John assures Ellen that he will arrange things, and Ellen immediately agrees to do as he wishes:

> "Very well," said Ellen joyously,—"then it will do. Oh, it would make me so happy! And you will write to me?"
> "Certainly!"
> "And I will tell you every thing about myself; and you will tell me how I ought to do in all sorts of things? that will be next best to being with you. And then you will keep me right."
> "I won't promise you that, Ellie," said John smiling;—"you must learn to keep yourself right."
> "I know you will, though, however you may smile. What next?"
> "Read no novels."
> "I never do, John. I knew you did not like it, and I have taken good care to keep out of the way of them." (563–64)

The conscience sharpened in Ellen through her affection for John, the representative of the family most closely aligned with the wishes of Ellen's mother, has guaranteed that she will act as she should.

In this key scene, Warner is both endorsing and extending the role to which affective discipline had previously accorded surveillance. Writing only a few years before Warner published her novel, Horace Bushnell had repeatedly emphasized the importance of "a very close and careful watch" over children in a nurturing disciplinary relationship (287–88), but Lyman Cobb had promised that "a child or pupil, who obeys his parent or teacher from LOVE *purely*, can be relied on, when *absent*, as well as when *present*" (104). Horace Mann, in his role as secretary of the Massachusetts Board of Education, argued on behalf of affective discipline instead of physical coercion in part because of the extraordinary power of the latter to govern pupils in the absence of immediately obvious authority, reflecting that if the scholars seem almost unconscious of the teacher's presence; if they are unobservant in what part of the room he stands, or in which direction he may be looking; if he can step out at the door to speak to a visitor, or into a recitation-room to inspect a class, and remain absent for five or ten minutes without there being any buzz or whirring in the schoolroom,—then one may feel the delightful assurance that such a school is under the sway of a serene and majestic authority,—the authority of the great law of duty and love. (31)

It is clearly "the authority of the great law of duty and love" that governs Ellen in John's absence, and in this sense Warner articulates the discipline at the heart of the orphan girl narrative in plain keeping with its common expression in mid-century culture. Although John did not tell her before her departure that she should stay away from novels, Ellen's affection for John is so strong and so nicely keyed to her conscience that she is able to obey his rules before he has even articulated them, as Mann might anticipate. But there is a bizarre extension of that disciplinary tradition at work as Ellen and John discuss novels. The extraordinary surveillance of this scene, enabled by affection, is not only something the controller desires, as it would have been in the case of Foucault's warden. It is also craved by the disciplined object. In this scene, Ellen rejects her own agency when she brushes aside John's (condescending) explanation and smile, essentially manipulating him *back* into the role of surveillant ruler. What will make Ellen "so happy" is the knowledge that another apparatus of surveillance— regular letter-writing—will be introduced. She manipulates him, in short, into better manipulating her.

John's ambivalent status in the novel—a man applauded for using physical coercion but who also acts as an affectionate proxy for the wishes of Ellen's mother, a nexus for affective discipline who is so easily manipulated by the object of his discipline—is indicative of another rule of sentimental discipline, namely the disingenuous role of men. Other scholars have pointed out the importance of Ellen's mother to the story and specifically to the discipline the novel espouses, but most studies miss the novel's use of the father.[5] This is hardly surprising, since the novel itself often seems to forget him. Although her mother's death is a momentous, traumatic event, Ellen's father dies in a scene that makes it unclear whether he really *has* died. The ship he was to have taken to America sinks, but "it remained a doubt whether Captain Montgomery had actually gone in her." The long period Ellen goes through without any definite news is hardly pleasant, but she doesn't seem to suffer much, and "Ellen rather felt that she was an orphan than that she had lost her father. She had never learned to love him[;]

he had never given her much cause." Rather than grieve for her possibly dead father, Ellen feels relief that he will not reappear and take her away from her new friends, the Humphreys, who *have* given her cause to love them and who, unlike her father, have been accomplices to her mother's designs (381). Because her father never returns to her in this novel or a sequel, it is safe to assume that he is dead, but the passage is almost flippant about the father's death; in another midcentury novel, this is exactly the kind of passage that would set up his "surprise" return in a later chapter. But the fact that Ellen's father does apparently die, and in such a forgettable scene, is indication that the father himself is something less than crucial to the novel's agenda. The novel opens with a father who is irrelevant to the experience of mothers and daughters, and it frequently pushes him to its margins.

Or more accurately, it pushes his *body* to the margins. Although Ellen's father dies offstage and in a scene that has the feel of something written just for the sake of continuity, he is continually reincarnated throughout the novel. His authority remains, even when his body has been discarded. John and the other male Humphreys inherit his authority over Ellen, telling her to mind her mother (79) and read only what will keep her pure. The sentiment that channels Ellen's behavior into acceptable venues also channels her allegiance. Thus, she can think of John's father as her own father—an easy switch made all the easier because Ellen felt no real love for her biological father in the first place. Later, in Scotland, Mr. Lindsay's kindness combines with her own accidental affection for him to grant him the term "father," a term he is insistent that she use. This is ironic, because Ellen had little affectionate connection with her biological father. But affection keeps alive something unattached to the body of the father, a sense of fatherness that does not necessarily have a biological representative. In *The Wide, Wide World*, the father's body is all but inconsequential. The father's authority remains, but it is located where affection places it.

In snipping off the authority of the father from his body, leaving it free to be placed where sentiment directs, *The Wide, Wide World* makes several claims about gender and power, claims that will echo down through the orphan girl plot over the decades. First, the novel warns men—Warner may have made her name in woman's fiction, but she spent a great deal of her life educating men—that daughters will only mourn fathers who use love and, further, only those who *use love as a mother would*. Second, the novel confirms that daughters will only obey fathers whom they love and only in proportion to their love. Finally, it argues that fathers/husbands/brothers must learn to love as a woman would. The net result is that paternal authority is subordinate to maternal authority, masculinity is subordinate to femininity. This is a tradition that both craves paternal authority—remember Ellen's longing for John's instruction—and reforms that authority according to sentimental feminine dictates.

But for all the attention the novel gives discipline and power, the agency imagined by the novel is never in the hands of Ellen for very long. *The Wide, Wide World* is not so conservative a novel as it at first appears, since it both transmutes the body of the father and locates authority where a more feminine mode of discipline says it should.[6] Further, the orphan girl is the character who justifies passing over one form of discipline in favor of another and whose affections define the legitimate rulers. Nonetheless, the power the novel doles out passes through her, never resting under her control. This is very much in keeping with the way the child is typically represented in sentimental fiction, including in the temperance novels Karen Sánchez-Eppler has studied in detail. Temperance narratives written from the beginning of the century through to the passage of the Eighteenth Amendment in 1919 often constructed, Sánchez-Eppler shows, an affectionate child whose love was the motivation and reward of the redeemed drunkard. In this way, temperance authors served their own needs as well as the needs of the fictionalized drunkard father by routing affectionate, reformative power through the figure of the child. But that power never served the child who was used as its lens; rather, "the child's love works to enforce a bourgeois patriarchal order that leaves the child as vulnerable as ever" (3). The same is true of Ellen. The only need met by the men her affection manipulates or labels "father" is the need that she remain under discipline's power, that she become as conservative and submissive as her mother. There is power in affective discipline, the sentimental orphan girl story avows, but that power swirls around the girl rather than remaining for long within her.

THE WIDE, WIDE WORLD: AFFECTIVE REPRESENTATION AND LOCKEAN EDUCATION

In the vision of moral suasion that Warner's novel provides to the orphan girl genre for which it sets the pattern, the structures of discipline do not significantly empower the orphan girl at their center. Indeed, it is sometimes difficult to perceive just where Ellen begins and the other members of the disciplinary cast end. Such permeable boundaries are, however, a necessity for affective discipline that strictly follows the sentimental model. As the prototype of the orphan girl at the heart of disciplinary intimacy, Ellen routinely undergoes erasure as a discrete subject in order to take on the roles of the people she loves. This is a trend that will never fully disappear from the genre, and it always represents the opposite of individualism, a disregard of the girl's boundaries as the traits within the subject are rewritten by the adults around her.

In these instances, Ellen is not represented as an individual, but an occupant of a role. To Aunt Fortune, for example, Ellen stands in for her mother, whom Fortune regards as frivolous. To Fortune, Mrs. Montgomery represents middle-class luxury, affectation without pragmatic use.[7] She particularly scorns Mrs. Montgomery's preference for books to manual labor. One such snide comment provokes an uncharacteristic flash of temper from Ellen. "Mamma isn't a book-worm!" she tells her aunt ("indignantly"). "I don't know what you mean; and she never thinks herself above being useful; it's very strange you should say so when you don't know any thing about her" (140). But Fortune hardly needs, she feels, to know anything about Ellen's mother: she is a type, and Fortune considers her research on the subject done. When Ellen enters her home, then, Fortune does not see Ellen as a yet-to-be-defined individual with yet-to-be-announced tastes; instead, she assumes that Ellen is like her mother. She then embarks on a project of exposing Ellen to the hardships of life as a woman, emphasizing labor and pro-duction at the expense of studying, even preventing Ellen from attending lessons that would enable her to move in the circles of a lady. Fortune is cruel to Ellen throughout, but her cruelty is not always directed at Ellen per se. Frequently she attacks Ellen's mother through the little girl, who is able to represent that mother quite well. Although Ellen refutes her aunt's understanding of her mother, she never argues that Fortune should judge Ellen on her personal merits. Ellen, it seems, agrees that one should see the mother through the child.

Warner's novel itself never contests Ellen's opinion, instead confirming and even extending it. Thus, the novel's likable characters join the despotic aunt in affirming that Ellen represents not herself but her mother. "I remember," Ellen says to her friend Alice Humphreys, "mamma once told me when I was going somewhere, that people would think strangely of *her* if I didn't behave well." Alice responds as though surprised at the suggestion that daughters could rep-resent anything other than their mothers: "Certainly. Why, Ellen, I formed an opinion of her very soon after I saw you" (240). The opinion Alice forms of Mrs. Montgomery is positive, and the affection she develops for Ellen leads her to ask Ellen to serve as her own cipher. Alice is ill and dying slowly, so she has plenty of time to build an affective relationship with Ellen, teach her the fundamentals of what a Christian lady (of which Alice is a model) needs to know, and then draft Ellen into her own service. "I will tell you, Ellie," she says. "You must come here and take my place" (432).

The affection built between Alice and Ellen, as with the mother-daughter bond, allows for a completely successful transfer of "place." Ellen enters the household, takes on Alice's jobs, and most importantly assumes Alice's own affective position in the family. Her success is marked not just by a transfer of residence but also the inheritance of Alice's affective titles: for the remainder of the novel, the members of the Humphreys family call Ellen "sister" and "daughter." Ellen accepts these names and, because she forms affective bonds with them too, calls the patriarch of the family "father," and she refers to John Humphreys, her future husband, as "brother." When Alice passes away, John takes over the instruction of Ellen. The love she has for him is a powerful enabler of instruction, and Ellen takes to her lessons well, as when she is called away to Scotland to await her majority with blood relatives. There, while busy not reading novels, she carries with her John's likeness. Her relatives regard that likeness as too prudish, but try as they might, they cannot erase it from her persona. "There's not a bit of moping about her," says one of her Scottish relatives. "I think John Humphreys has infected her; he has something of the same look himself" (475). At the end of the novel, Ellen moves into a room decorated for Ellen by John, happy to fill another position that is defined by someone she loves. Ellen's story, therefore, is not only the coming-of-age story of an orphan girl and a rise from disenfranchisement to respectability; it is also the story of the happy, affectionate dissolution of that individual's identity into a series of roles. Here at the beginning of the genre's history, the formation of a distinct individual is not so important as the story of the changeling, whose adoption into the community procures for the girl a new face in service of the strongest affective authority at hand. The power inherent in affective discipline works to let other, beloved characters shine through Ellen's transparent subjectivity.

The Wide, Wide World is also a story of educating that changeling so that, while she is abroad, she can carry the community's ideology into foreign spaces and successfully defend it against assault. After Ellen is absorbed into the Humphreys family and educated about evangelical Christian morals in their mold, she is capable of resisting the more liberal theology of her Scottish relatives. When they demand that she read her Bible less often, participate in (to Ellen's mind) less decorous pastimes, drink wine—in short, that she obey them and act as they act—Ellen is able to resist because she has so successfully been educated by her affective, rather than blood, family. She is even uncharacteristically rude in her resistance, as when the Lindsays assail her nationality. When Sophia Lindsay gloats that Ellen will no longer be American but "a Scotchwoman," Ellen replies that she "had a great deal rather be an American" (494). In this way, Ellen does defend her boundaries from incursion by that which is not like her, but not until the book has established that the "her" under attack is the one defined by her affective disciplinarians.

What Ellen has experienced is a model of education that Gillian Brown has demonstrated was well ingrained in the American democratic experience long before Warner set the formula for the classic orphan girl novel. This educational model will trickle down through the history of the genre and limit the extent to which its protagonists can achieve individuality. The Lockean model of education filled a desperate need in the early republic for both consent and individual representation. One of the foundational ideas in the formation of the American democracy, Brown demonstrates, was the consent of the governed, a consent conceptualized according to John Locke's political theories. This consent is characterized by an individual who agrees to something tacitly or otherwise, but in any case in accordance with a belief that his consent will bring about personal gain. A strong, informed individual who is fully endowed with rights is the only individual who can act out the ideal Lockean consent.[8] In the early United States, children's education frequently made a point of trying to build just such an individual. But—and here is the crux of the problem—an individual fully endowed with the right to consent and the education necessary to understand the ramifications of consent might well choose *not* to consent. Although the early nation made genuine attempts to rear individuals who could represent themselves without coercion by the community, the survival of the community depended on finding some way to make sure that the individual would choose— of his own free will—to do what the community wanted him to do. Therefore, as Brown puts it, "self-determination as Locke formulated it entails making the self an object of management while designating the individual as the rightful manager of himself" (*Consent of the Governed* 44).

This paradox had implications for many aspects of early American culture, but it had direct consequences in relation to the education of children. Puritan education systems thus had to endow (male, white) children with all the tools necessary to individual economic and political pursuits that they hoped would drive Lockean democracy, but citizens could only be trusted with enfranchisement after they had been taught to use their privilege in ways that would support the status quo. "They accordingly," Brown asserts, "adopted the Lockean method of beginning to direct children's interest at a very early age. In his own pedagogical plan, Locke regularly stacks the deck presented to the child. He frankly sets out to bring the child into accord with the parents' wishes and values" (*Consent of the Governed* 44). This was done by giving the child complete freedom to explore issues and decide for himself what he thinks about those issues . . . but by simultaneously only allowing the child to be exposed to challenging ideologies and experiences once he has already learned to react to them in the ways his parents encourage. By granting the child complete freedom to explore and grow in a tiny, protected, and carefully selected arena of intellectual development, then allowing the child to graduate to sequentially wider, but just as carefully selected arenas, parents could direct the individual's growth and see to it that he was not faced with a decision about any given social issue until he was already confirmed in the opinion his parents themselves held. The explanation that Locke gives for this manipulation is that it ensures the child only encounters things for which he is prepared. Once the child has grown strong enough to cope with challenges— political ideology, religious heterogeneity, gender codes—the parent allows him to encounter something that will challenge but not defeat him, and this pattern continues until the child is a strong, capable individual. The goal is a child who learns how to think about the kinds of things the parent wants him to think about in the terms the parent wants him to inherit. He is therefore free to make whatever choice he wants, as democracy insists, but ideally he will be unable to make any choice other than that which the educating community requires.

Seen in the context of a culture built on Lockean education, even the most individualistic moments of Warner's novel appear more concerned with community than individualism. When Ellen stands up for her chosen nationality, religion, or drinking habits, she is certainly making a decision in keeping with her own ideology. Because she spends so much time defending her personal opinions against the majority opinion while she is with the Lindsays, she appears at times to be an adamantly individualistic young woman. But a wider view of the novel does not support this reading. Ellen does not encounter the Lindsays until she is ready to encounter them, and her time with them is marked by a series of tests. During that time, she demonstrates that she is acting not out of some personally forged morality but in accordance with the ideology the Humphreys family taught her. This is already evident in Ellen's discussion with John about his concern over the dangers of novels. When she assures him that "I knew you did not like [them], and I have taken good care to keep out of the way of them" (564), she is both marking his affective surveillance and reassuring her readers that a well-disciplined girl will only encounter temptation when she is ready to react to it—of her supposedly individual volition—as her disciplining master prefers. Ellen does not exactly avoid the temptations of Scotland because those temptations conflict with her personal code but rather because they conflict with a code that she composes out of her educator's ideology. The temptations around

Ellen create the false sense of an individual by introducing conflict between the Lindsays' ideology and the ideology into which she has been carefully, willingly, shepherded.

Warner's novel has received extensive attention as the essential sentimental novel, a fundamental example of "woman's fiction." As such, its conception of moral suasion continues to stand out as instrumental in understanding senti- mental-style discipline. But *The Wide, Wide World* also established a formula for orphan girl stories that would long outlast the popularity of sentimental fic- tion. The vision of discipline Warner presented would be invoked in iterations of the orphan girl novel for nearly seventy-five years. But it would not have to wait nearly so long to experience its first revision. That would come before the era of woman's fiction had even come to a close.

CHAPTER TWO

The Hidden Hand and Momentary Individualism

If *The Wide, Wide World* has become the example par excellence of sentimentalism, E.D.E.N. Southworth's *The Hidden Hand* is a much more difficult orphan girl novel to classify. It was first published in serial form in 1859, thus appearing within the same decade as *The Wide, Wide World*. But it was also republished in serial form twice more over the subsequent decades before finally being published in novel form in 1888. It is therefore a story that thrived during as well as immediately after the years of sentimentalism's highest popularity, suggesting that it fit a midcentury sentimental as well as a postsentimental sensibility.

Today, scholarship tends to treat the novel as both sentimental and something quite different from sentimental. For example, Amy E. Hudock speaks of *The Hidden Hand* as part of a sentimental tradition also populated by *Uncle Tom's Cabin*, but she regularly places the word "sentimental" in quotation marks to distance herself from its use. Paul Christian Jones takes for granted that Southworth's novel is sentimental and examines how it further works within a sentimental *abolitionist* tradition, a tack similar to that of H. Jordan Landry, who begins her argument about the novel by referring to the scholarship on sentimentalism and then showing how it is *also* a seduction novel. But Joanne Dobson, whose work on Southworth still dominates conversation on all of the author's work, calls *The Hidden Hand* "a comic subversion of the paradigm, a madcap romp through the conventions" and then argues that Southworth "uses conventional sentimental narrative . . . as the vehicle through which to subvert feminine ideals" ("The Hidden Hand" 227). In this foundational essay on the novel, Dobson calls the book "a peculiarly inverted sentimental novel" that contrasts with Warner's novel

(232) and examines what she calls the book's "sentimental counterplot" (234). This counterplot features "a true sentimental heroine" whom Southworth considers both "a paradigmatic and admirable figure" (235), resulting in a message that is both "subversive" and "hedged" (236). Dobson therefore insists on a point that is easy to forget: *The Hidden Hand* is clearly both a sentimental novel and a postsentimental novel. It both endorses and reconfigures sentimental-style discipline, with implications that are at times powerfully subversive, at others profoundly conservative.

Southworth's novel features two orphan girls who star in parallel narratives. The first, Capitola Le Noir, is adopted by a man known as Old Hurricane, the wealthy rival of Capitola's birth family. Capitola, rescued by a kindly nurse from her uncle's murderous intentions, grows into a lovely, spunky young woman who turns the head of the dastardly Craven Le Noir even as she threatens to expose her uncle's connections with the region's most notorious bandit, Black Donald. Her uncle, Colonel Le Noir, also plays the villain in the novel's parallel orphan thread, that of Clara Day. Clara befriends the long-suffering Marah Rocke and her son Traverse, and when Colonel Le Noir schemes to marry Clara off to Craven in order to lay claim to her inheritance, Marah's meek patience becomes the model for Clara as the girl awaits rescue.

The popularity of *The Hidden Hand* throughout the sentimental period is perhaps due in part to how successfully it grappled with the issues of discipline that drove *The Wide, Wide World*. But whereas Warner's novel was willing to make room for physical coercion as a tool for men, Southworth's novel rejects that mode entirely. It rewards only male characters who will forego the use of masculine privilege. The narrator even avoids tales of masculine prowess when possible, at one point skipping a great battle scene with a shrug: "We prefer to look after our little domestic heroine" (348). The tension between masculine and feminine privilege is one of the novel's most important themes, and it is a theme frequently addressed in terms of discipline.

The only characters who seem capable of using violence are those such as the cartoonishly villainous Colonel Le Noir, who warns Clara, "You are in my power, and *I intend to coerce you to my will!*" (303). Elsewhere, Traverse Rocke longs to pronounce, fight, and rage against Le Noir's successful legal suit to carry Clara away. Traverse desperately wants to "rage [and] do violence," precisely the sort of manly activity *The Wide, Wide World* would allow, but in Southworth's novel such acts are useless (254). In the case of Colonel Le Noir, Southworth links coercive power at a personal, domestic level to bad men, and in the case of his suit, she links his successful coercion to a judge who is "a corrupt politician, whose decisions were swayed by party interests" (254). She later condemns the military actions of the Mexican-American War in similar terms, as Traverse questions a patriotism that requires him to invade another country, this time under the command of Colonel Le Noir (345). At the personal, national, and international level, Southworth rejects physical coercion as ineffective at best, villainous at worst.

The same is not true of all power: the heroes of Southworth's novel, in contrast with Colonel Le Noir, always avoid physical coercion, and even when the other options they devise are not sufficient to whatever challenge is at hand, they are always presented as *preferable* to masculine power. Thus Traverse, after failing in court, praises Clara's response. "Oh, my angel-girl! my angel-girl!" he says to her, "your patient heroism puts me to the blush, for my heart is crushed in my bosom and my firmness quite gone!" (255). In a conversation with Herbert, Traverse's mother recounts her own awful story of dispossession, a story in which her husband misused his masculine prerogative to punish her. Herbert is astounded:

> "Oh, Marah! and you but seventeen years of age! without a father or a brother or a friend in the world to take your part! without even means to employ an advocate!" exclaimed Herbert, covering his face with his hands and sinking back.
>
> "Nor would I have used any of these agencies, had I possessed them! If my wifehood and motherhood, my affection and my helplessness, were not advocates strong enough to win my cause, I could not have borne to employ others." (98)

Marah has carried heavy burdens—malnutrition not the least of them—as a result of this decision, but she still does not regret it. Her contentment is the result of her deep belief in the value of her feminine positions, her wifehood and motherhood. Even the final "advocate" she lists, "helplessness," is not identical with victimhood, because it is a tool of the kind of affective discipline that women in Southworth's novel have as their only real weapon against masculine law.

Although Southworth is advancing an argument about discipline that condemns a masculine form of coercion that Warner was willing to tolerate, the anticorporal discipline she endorses is not always dainty; indeed, it isn't even necessarily kind. Marah Rocke's subplot, the one to which Dobson refers when she speaks of the novel's "sentimental counterplot" ("The Hidden Hand" 234), articulates a model of discipline that would have been very much at home in *The Wide, Wide World*, but the title character's story envisions a mode of noncorporal punishment that Ellen Montgomery would never have endorsed. When Craven

Le Noir spreads rumors that Capitola has dallied with him, she takes matters into her own hands and challenges him to a duel—what at first appears to be a physical means of correcting the young man. He laughs her off, but she draws on him and fires. On his supposed deathbed, Craven makes a clean confession of his lies, at which point Capitola reveals that her revolver charges were filled with no more than gunpowder and dried peas. Hurricane's response is mixed: he is proud of Capitola for her total victory, but, as he says,

> "while you *were* taking your own part, why the foul fiend didn't you pepper
> him with something sharper than dried peas?"
> "I think he is quite as severely punished in suffering from extreme terror
> and intense mortification and public ridicule," said Cap. (376)

Just as Marah Rocke prefers a feminine advocacy, Capitola prefers a mode of discipline that relies on noncorporal punishment: "terror and intense mortification and public ridicule." Southworth directly opposes physical punishment—of which gunning down a cad is surely an example—with a kind of discipline that makes use of relationships rather than broken bodies. It is important to remember, as Warner's novel argues, that affective discipline is generally driven by love, but in her novel on the borders of sentimentalism, Southworth broadens the scope of anticorporal discipline, embracing other sorts of correction through interiority. Love, meekness, and affection all work well, but Southworth also lays claim to an anticorporal discipline that makes use of humiliation.

The outlines of a debate over power and gender that will continue through the rest of the history of the orphan girl story begin to take shape in Warner's and Southworth's novels. Here at the beginning of that history, the central terms of moral suasion are already clear. Coercion and other physical modes of discipline are only appropriate for men, if they are appropriate at all, and noncorporal modes of discipline are always more effective. In the purest sentimental mode, they can control Ellen when she is away from John, and in a comedic revision of sentimentalism, they can humiliate a rake into erasing a stain against Capitola's name. Masculine power and privilege are not only less preferable than the power available through affect; they are also inherently limited, whereas feminine power is not. Finally, although men remain in power at the end of these stories, the father has already begun to destabilize. The fundamental structures of power have not been altered, but the father's power is limited over the orphan girl, and it is her choice that decides where his authority is located. This sentimental management of spirits and bodies would provide a convincing—but not immalleable—pattern for the girls' novels in the decades after sentimentalism.

HEROIC CONFORMISTS AND TEMPORARY SUBVERSION

I began this chapter by pointing to the oddly sentimental/postsentimental nature of Southworth's novel. For the purposes of affective discipline, that ambiguous nature means a broadening of feminine powers at the expense of masculine. It is this expansion of powers—"hedged," as Dobson has said, by traditionally sentimental narratives such as Marah Rocke's secondary plot—that makes Southworth's novel so alluring to scholars exploring subversive texts. "In *The Hidden Hand*," Dobson states, "there is no doubt about the deliberateness of the author's comic subversion of both the conventional narrative and of the feminine conventions that produced it. For this reason it makes an especially interesting contrast to *The Wide, Wide World*" ("The Hidden Hand" 232).

But on the subject of individualism, *The Hidden Hand* does not provide a contrast with Warner's novel. *The Wide, Wide World* rehearses conflict that can create an illusion of individualism, but, as the novel reveals, the project of sentimentalism is the erasure of individuals, not their production. The same is true of *The Hidden Hand*, and it is true both in the "madcap" narrative of Capitola and the sentimental narrative of Clara. Both Capitola and Clara outlast dangerous situations by standing up in the face of oppression, a strong indication at least of individual fortitude, and Dobson goes so far as to imagine Capitola marching with "women's rights activists" (236). But whatever their momentary subversions, these are narratives about the restoration of a temporarily derailed patriarchy and the character types that support it, not about the firm construction of genuine, empowered individuals.

Southworth's novel, like Warner's, produces the illusion of a triumphant individual by surrounding her with adversity, a tempting narrative line for many sentimental novels. Gale Temple has traced this story through, for example, Fanny Fern's *Ruth Hall*. Although Temple grants that the conflict between protagonist and threatening environment does forge a kind of individualism, she argues that the individualism espoused in Fern's novel is one centered in a familiar and comforting reflection of the status quo. This reflection is accomplished via a beleaguered protagonist who holds beliefs that most of her readers share but who speaks and struggles as though her beliefs were being marginalized by a sphere with which she is in vicious competition. This individual is a "fraught individual" because she and her individuality are always by definition under attack from an opposite and supposedly majority opinion. In this way, Temple demonstrates, the novel is "positioning Ruth (and the reader who identifies with her) as a misunderstood and unfairly muted source of positive cultural change" (132). This kind of individualism "is underpinned by a view of society as corrupt, as a continual source of new forms of stagnation and hypocrisy against which one's own dynamic and ever-evolving authenticity can be defined" (150). Temple traces this pattern in other writings by Fern, including her nonfiction. In one essay, Fern imagines "the individual as an oasis of goodness and reform in the midst of a social desert fraught with hypocrisy, inhumanity, and corruption" (150), and in another she "sustains a binary between readers as reform-oriented, fraught individuals, and the broader culture as a cruel, monolithic, and heartless mass" (148). The irony, though, is that Fern is proposing an individual under assault by a tyrannical majority opinion that does not exist. Rather, the supposedly marginalized protagonist (and author and reader) represents the majority opinion, suddenly imagining itself in danger. For example, Ruth Hall must defend her consumerist tastes against her anticonsumer mother-in-law, who is cunning and cruel. In this scenario, the sentimental protagonist wearily but triumphantly champions the cause of feminine consumption even though her mother-in-law, neighbors, and the culture itself seem to oppose her. But critics of sentiment from Hawthorne and Melville to Ann Douglas have observed that nineteenth-century culture was hardly opposed to consumption, that it was, rather, *predicated* on consumption.[1] In this way, the fraught individual is not an individualist at all but a friend of the majority, and Ruth Hall's welcome reabsorption into consumer culture at the end of the novel marks not so much the triumph of the individual as the reassertion of a momentarily displaced status quo.

Various pseudoindividuals populate Southworth's novel and experience a similar reabsorption into communal identity. These characters, in the same mode as Ruth Hall, take dramatic positions that seem to emphasize their individuality, but those positions are carefully constructed from the hallmarks of a type. Marah Rocke, for instance, lives a solitary existence with all the world seemingly arrayed against her after her husband leaves her with their child. But all the melodrama of her solitude owes to her chosen role as long-suffering, faithful wife to her misled husband, hardly the kind of position with which Southworth's bourgeois readers would have disagreed; all the same, Rocke and Southworth both represent her situation as one of isolation, and she has no "advocates" to comfort her (98). Similarly, in the novel's main seduction plot, Clara Day is removed from her family's home, turned into an orphan, and relocated to the home of the evil Le Noir, who intends to marry her to his wretched son. The courts, with a little stretching on Southworth's part, take Le Noir's side, and Clara is left with no defenders as she struggles in solitude to do what any good girl should do: wait until marriage for sex, and wait until love for marriage. Traverse Rocke, too, valiantly stands up for what his audience already believes in—observation of the chain of command, respect for superiors, romantic self-effacement, honorable conduct as a soldier—against a court martial and unit that seem intent on punishing those characteristics.[2] Again, Southworth has to stretch the verisimilitude of her story to create this opposition, because, as one of the characters points out, Traverse could have appealed at any time to another authority to receive relief.[3] But he does not use that right—just as Marah does not search for another advocate and Clara does not resist the court's authority—because the novel requires a manufactured opposition between supposed majority and oppressed—false—individual. The melodramatic conflict is prolonged and in many cases created by these heroic individuals who courageously cling to roles that validate rather than challenge mainstream sentimental ideology.

But the most misleading individualism in Southworth's novel is that of Capitola Le Noir herself. Capitola's early scenes as a spunky cross-dresser living in the cracks of urban society are excellent examples, as her willingness to transgress gender boundaries seems to define her as an individual who eschews rules of behavior determined by her class and sex. It is for this illusory individualism that Capitola has frequently drawn praise, as when Dobson argues that

> Capitola's freedom of spirit is directly associated with her upbringing outside the boundaries of middle-class society and of gender expectations, an implicit recognition of the stultifying effects upon women of conventional socialization. As a white child raised by a black laundress in the slums of New York City, as a girl who spends her early adolescence disguised as a boy, Cap has achieved a unique sense of herself and her possibilities. (introduction xxix–x)

That "unique sense of self" for Dobson is the result of Capitola's childhood "outside the boundaries of middle-class society and of gender expectations," a subversion of the types implicit in "conventional socialization." Capitola is unique, according to this reading, because she is distinct from the groups in which midcentury girls and women were pressed to dissolve themselves.

But the point of the early scenes that Dobson points to as crucial for the formation of Capitola the individual is not to privilege an individual pushing off from group identity. Rather, these scenes represent an opportunity for Southworth to argue in favor of the *reassertion* of gender codes. Consider Old Hurricane's winning argument that "whether a girl in *boy's* clothes or *men's* clothes, or *soldier's* clothes, or *sailor's* clothes, or, *any* clothes, or NO clothes, sir!" one must "treat her with the delicacy due to *woman*hood, sir!" (39). Hurricane's outburst marks him—for the court and for the reader—as a trustworthy custodian for the until-recently rugged individualist, a custodian who will determine the girl's treatment according to her sex, not her temporary individuation from type. And although Capitola has only posed as an individual outside "the boundaries of middle-class society and of gender expectations" for a short time, already Hurricane is able to deliver a speech full of nostalgia for the protection of "womanhood," for the safe return of Capitola to within those boundaries. As for the "possibilities" Capitola's supposed individualism indicates, Hurricane's necessary defense of Capitola, a defense grounded in her status as a woman as distinctly opposed to her outlier identity as a cross-dressing threat to the status quo, effectively brings the orphan girl back under the protection of bourgeois structures. Many female readers of the mid- to late nineteenth century would have picked up on this important shift of agency, for the relationship between Capitola's brief period of subversive empowerment and Hurricane's gentlemanly legal argument mirrored a similar tension that, as J. Stanley Lemons has pointed out, plagued the women's rights movement from sentimentalism through suffrage. One of the most important points of disagreement between these early activists, Lemons suggests, was over how much agency should be given to women and how much protection should be counted on from the government. Laws that would grant rights, activists repeatedly discovered, implied a loss of protection, particularly in industry, and many women protested against the expansion of their rights because they feared that loss. Read in this context, Hurricane's manly protection of the essentially feminine Capitola represents the most conservative reaction to an independent woman endowed with agency: that agency must be removed, and the girl must be given the patriarchy's protection through the intervention of the law. Capitola's early history is thus not a record of expanding possibilities but of a careful herding of the unique girl back into the protective types recognized by the status quo.

Importantly, Capitola herself does not resent being reassigned to a long-term type after her stint as short-term individual. When Hurricane reestablishes Capitola in her proper class and dress, rather than fighting the shift, she gladly gives up her unique identity, "deeply blushing at the recollection of her male attire" (51). Therefore, despite all the dangers to gender codes Capitola faced on the streets, "she has come out of them safe," as Hurricane later says (174), and the novel repeatedly narrates instances in which gender codes themselves have also emerged safe, despite the protagonist's temporary subversions. Although Capitola does occasionally step out of her conventional role as the book goes on, as when she duels—or, more accurately, pretends to duel—with a man, she continues to take the part of feminine goodness, choosing humiliation over bullets in her faux duel, urging mercy in Black Donald's trial, looking with "compassion" on a fallen enemy (398), and even chiding her adoptive father for failing to observe the manly codes of honorable combat (397). Capitola both acts with regularity to affirm the feminine codes she supposedly inverts as a cross-dresser, therefore filling rather than complicating the role she will eventually occupy as wife, and enters the novel because Hurricane sees in her not an individual but the reflection of her father. Capitola's status as sole heir of Le Noir's fortune is what prompts Hurricane to seek her out, not any set of characteristics that Capitola's life on the streets or unique desires have formed into a unique individual. The novel's resolution depends on Hurricane's plans, which are ultimately successful, to use the daughter's reflection of her father to invalidate Colonel Le Noir's wealth. For all her spunky individualism, Capitola is, like the fraught individuals who make up the supporting cast, most important to the novel for how she fills a series of roles.

And whatever momentary individualism Capitola and the other characters might manage, the happy ending is structured such that individuals are again, as with Ellen in *The Wide, Wide World*, dissolved into social roles. This is because the resolution of the novel's conflict is enabled by the healing of fissures in the social structure that date back to before the opening of the novel. Marah and Traverse, for example, were cast from their rightful place in the leisured elite by Hurricane's unjust abandonment, but by the end of the novel they have joyfully been restored to that position. The industry and poverty that isolate them through much of their lives are gladly discarded as they return to their roles in the upper class. Even Black Donald, a thorn in the side of society for most of his life, is safely recruited out of unlawfulness and into productive society. And Capitola herself does not figure at the end of the novel as a force for future disruption and individuality but rather conventionality. Like the other wives, Capitola ends the novel not by railing against the status quo but by fitting herself neatly into a stereotype, chiding her husband when he misbehaves. And although adopting such a typical role may be out of character in light of whatever individualism she may have achieved earlier in the story, it is completely in keeping with the spirit of the happy ending, in which the wealthy are restored to their wealth, the truly evil are punished, the penitent are reformed, monogamous couples are reunited and even mass produced in the double wedding, and the briefly subversive individuals come to occupy conventional roles neatly.

The Hidden Hand's status as a novel that is both sentimental and postsentimental positions the narrative to follow key points in the technology of sentimental-style discipline through to their logical ends. Its disingenuous narrative of individualism is grounded in an understanding of gendered power that is at least as bifurcated as the vision of such power in *The Wide, Wide World*. It is difficult to read Southworth's novel as subversive against the backdrop of the history of affective discipline, but it is no strain to see how this popular orphan girl novel tilted the conversation in favor of a mode of power that it considered feminine. The novel repeatedly moves masculine domains of power—law, force, military hierarchy—to the margins of discipline. More important, more central, more *effective*, Southworth argues, is feminine discipline.

CHAPTER THREE

Eight Cousins and
What Girls Are Made For

If women in sentimental-era novels *could* manipulate men, if Ellen Montgomery could place her father's authority where she wished or nudge her future husband back into the role she preferred, the logical conclusion was that they sometimes *ought* to manipulate men. Similarly, when Craven Le Noir blackened the name of Capitola, she and her adoptive father might have disagreed about the best way to force him to recant, but there wasn't really an argument over whether she *should*. On the one hand, this disciplinary ability offered women some meaningful power. But on the other, it also came with a serious obligation. If women could discipline men, and if they therefore ought to discipline men, then surely they were also responsible for those men. The vices and other moral failings of men, those things about men that could be improved through discipline, were consequently the burden of the women who wielded discipline.

As the orphan girl formula migrated into the novels for girls that began appearing in the late nineteenth century, the exact powers and responsibilities of affective discipline came under revision. The slight changes in the rules of discipline sometimes grew logically out of the patterns established in sentimentalism. For instance, where the sentimental model hinted that girls could modify men and the authority attached to them, the new orphan girl novel expanded that responsibility to highlight specific moral failings in men and how girls could fix them. Girls' novels of the twentieth century would eventually begin to consider how discipline ought to target women, but such was not the case as sentimentalism drew to a close and the first girls' novels in the model of *The Wide, Wide World* took their places on nineteenth-century bookshelves. During the transition from midcentury sentimentalism to turn-of-the-century girls' fiction, the classic orphan girl novel continued the sentimental work of disciplining men, even as it laid the groundwork for a postsentimental revision of girls' subjectivity.

Louisa May Alcott is best known for her crucial contribution to the history of girls' literature, *Little Women,* a quasi-autobiographical novel published in two parts in 1868 and 1869. But much less attention has been paid to her 1875 novel *Eight Cousins.* Although *Little Women* was much more widely read, *Eight Cousins* also plays an important part in the history of girls' novels: it is the book through which the orphan girl formula is transmitted from sentimentalism to literature written and marketed for girls. In it, Alcott tells of recently orphaned Rose Campbell. After the loss of her beloved father, Rose finds herself in the residence of her wealthy aunts, surrounded by boy cousins and one kind uncle, all of whom very quickly come to adore her. By the end of the novel, she has concluded that "I *must* take care of the boys, for they come to me in all sorts of troubles and ask advice, and I like it *so* much" (245). Rose, as befits her status here at the turn from sentimentalism to the new market for girls, is both disciplined and disciplining, learning from her uncle how to manage herself but serving the boys' mothers by managing them. And, for all their good hearts, they are badly in need of management.

The vice of men and boys was hardly a new subject for women writers of the nineteenth century. Indeed, temperance played a critical role in the history of women's public political agitation, women often justifying their incursion into the public sphere on the grounds that temperance was primarily a domestic issue, which is to say an issue over which bourgeois women had particular responsibility. One of the chief hopes of temperance workers was that moral suasion would work to redeem the drinker, and the affective child and loving home space, promising as they did affectionate rewards to the reformed drunkard, served as the primary tools of that discipline.[1] Therefore, the orphan girl formula and the disciplinary ideology that characterized it were well suited for stories about men's vice. But moral suasion was not the only tool nineteenth-century women considered in their fight against male vice, and as these books championing affective discipline made their case, they had to make it against both physical and legal coercion. Karen Sánchez-Eppler points to "the 'Maine Law' of 1851, which forbade the manufacture or sale of intoxicating liquor," as an instance in which the temperance movement eschewed suasion in favor of legislative strong-arming (72). Rather than trying to save the souls or win the hearts of the men who drank, this strategy relied simply on forbidding men to drink on pain of imprisonment or fine. But for sentimental writers, legal coercion was too direct, perhaps too masculine a power. And Alcott, a writer whose work for girls straddles late sentimentalism and the early girls' market she helped shape, would agree with sentimentalism. As Charles Strickland has said, to Alcott, men had "a fatal weakness for tippling," and they could best be saved from that weakness "by the influence of good women" (142). Prohibition is more explicitly a concern of the novel's sequel, *Rose in Bloom*, but the fundamental battle between male vice and female influence is already established in *Eight Cousins*. In her fiction about girls and the dissipated boys they tame, Alcott makes the argument that legal proscription against male vice is not necessary: discipline through love can manage it very effectively.

Rose's maturation is a tale of a little girl struggling with the responsibility that comes of her ability to influence weak men or, more often, boys. As one of her aunts tells her, "You have more influence over the boys than you know. Use it for their good, and I shall thank you all my life" (173). The frame for Rose's deployment of influence, of affective discipline, is therefore one cut from the sentimental tradition. Because Rose is enjoined to use her influence by one of the boy's mothers, she is still acting as an affectionate agent of mothers, just as the stranger Ellen met on the boat encouraged Ellen to embrace the beliefs of her dearly departed mother. Therefore, in a scene that focuses on a male vice the novel finds especially abhorrent, it makes a point of connecting her discipline to the loving mothers on whose behalf she works. Here, the sin is smoking, something one of the boys argues that "every man" does. But Rose protests that it is an awful habit, one that "your mother doesn't like" (172), and she convinces them to give it up. The scene begins by pointing to the boys' affection for Rose (172) and ends with her striking a bargain with the toughest of the boys, one who forces Rose to give up her own new earrings in exchange for his promise to quit smoking. "She felt it was right to do it," the narrator confides, "yet found it very hard." Unwilling to let this opportunity to correct her cousins slip by, she agrees, much to the boys' surprise, and they seal the deal with "a hearty grip," the boys "half pleased and half ashamed" (176). The mixture of affection and humiliation is a blend of the disciplinary techniques championed by *The Wide, Wide World* and *The Hidden Hand*, of the confirmed affection that ruled Ellen and the public disgrace that avenged Capitola's tarnished reputation. It is also a clear instance of the balance of obligation—Rose does find it very hard—and power that comes with the endorsement of affective discipline that the new girls' novels carried over from the sentimental version of the orphan girl story.

But who benefits from this power? Certainly Rose is treated as a hero: the "elders" of the extended family into which Rose has been accepted congratulate her so warmly that they "made her feel as if she had done a service to her country, as she had," the narrator reports. But the narrator is very specific that the benefit is to the nation, not precisely the girl, "for every boy who grows up free from bad habits bids fair to make a good citizen" (176–77). Here, Rose takes on the responsibilities of the republican mother Kerber notes as well as those of the emperor mother Ryan describes. By using her moral influence, Rose creates a better citizen and nation. But she doesn't significantly change the distribution of power. Instead, the earrings-for-cigars trade that Rose makes with the boys will, Uncle Alec assures her, serve some broader power, for "when girls give up their little vanities, and boys their small vices, and try to strengthen each other in well-doing, matters are going as they ought." In this way, then, although Rose touches the power of suasion as it funnels through her, she is doing little to change the patriarchal order in which she lives. All the correction a girl can give will only ensure that boys become the good politicians the country needs in order to thrive. Thus, when Rose finds out that one of her cousins has fallen into a bad crowd, she realizes that "if I'm there and try to make it pleasant, he will stay at home and keep out of mischief" (246). Here it is as though legislative coercion had never been conceived: laws are not necessary because boys will be good if they are taught to desire what is at home rather than in dark alleys. This is one of the main lessons Rose learns, and near the end of the novel she has learned it so well that she, "quite beaming with satisfaction as she spoke," can tell her uncle that "I have discovered what girls are made for. . . . To take care of boys" (245). The novel endorses Rose as a fitting distributor of discipline and boys as an ideal recipient, but that arrangement keeps Rose in a position that has value and gives her joy because in it she serves others.

The power of suasion as imagined in Alcott's novel does not fundamentally change the institutions of privilege around their protagonists, but there is an increasing sense as the genre passes out of the late years of sentimentalism that these girls are able to direct power where they choose. For instance, Rose likes the servant girl Phebe from the moment they meet, and although Phebe remains a sort of servant to her throughout the novel, Phebe's life does improve as a direct result of Rose's affection and in accordance with Rose's wishes. The two of them study together, and Phebe excels in some subjects with which Rose struggles. Phebe even leaves the ancient home where she once seemed destined to spend the rest of her life as a servant, accompanying Rose to school and further improving her social mobility. Phebe follows Rose's instruction because, as she says "with a laugh and sob, 'I think you are the dearest girl in the world, and I'll let you do anything you like with me'" (58).[2] Rose not only manages to influence her cousins to give up smoking; she also has the same effect on Alec himself (172), who elsewhere in the novel figures as *her* disciplinarian. The outcome is that Rose modifies both Alec and Phebe in accordance with her personal desires. This is a small victory, to be sure, and one that can easily be overlooked. But it is a victory that marks an important trend: the orphan girl can influence the people around her to behave the way she wants, sometimes without even justifying that influence in the name of a mother.

The novel, therefore, reiterates a sentimental idea of discipline with one decep- tively small change; the same is true of its handling of individualism. Louisa May Alcott was perhaps the single most important figure in the formation of the new domestic novel for girls in the late nineteenth century, but she has routinely been treated as a sentimental writer, and *Eight Cousins* does little to threaten that status. In her foundational book on midcentury women writers, Nina Baym notes without comment that "Alcott, for her part, presided over the waning days of woman's fiction, when it permuted into children's literature" (*Woman's* 23), and nowhere does Alcott look more like a dean of woman's fiction than in *Eight Cousins'* treatment of the individualism of its protagonist. *Eight Cousins* is just as disingenuous in its portrait of girls as individuals who depart from a type as are *The Wide, Wide World* and *The Hidden Hand.* But buried deep within this portrait is a hint of how girls in future orphan girl novels, ones not quite so firmly tied to sentimentalism, could begin to articulate their protagonists as individuals.

Rose Campbell's individual identity is mixed from the very beginning of her story. She arrives at the home of her aunts as a discrete package, a package all the more worrisome because she is unlike the boy children who swarm across the family home. The novel further confirms Rose's unique identity in the way she is passed from one adult to another, from dead father to teacher to aunts to uncle, as though she were a distinct commodity, unattached by emotion to any other person or group. This individuality, this difference from those around her, is the premise of the book, but Alcott quickly introduces a way in which Rose's individual identity is overwritten. Just as Ellen Montgomery represented her dead mother to her aunt, Rose frequently reminds her new guardians of her father. When Uncle Jem, for example, first meets her, he greets her with a formal handshake. As one individual to another, this is an appropriate greeting; after all, these two individuals have no ties other than the formal ties of blood, no history of affection that would prompt anything more. "But, somehow," the narrator in- terrupts, "when he shook her hand, it looked so small in his big one and her face reminded him so strongly of his dead brother that he was not satisfied with so cold a welcome" (208). Rose is the ideal blank child to take on her father's visage, and as such she inherits the affection of his brother. But "inherit" is too weak a term: Rose calls forth the affection her uncle had for his brother not because it has been handed down to her but because Rose is a cipher for her father.

To Uncle Jem, Rose's obscured identity means she is the automatic recipient of affection and little more, but to the most important uncle in the story, it means she can enable a variety of complex tasks defined by the affection between brothers. Dr. Alec Campbell arrives in Rose's life with the task of rearing her squarely on his shoulders, and again, this premise is founded on the idea that his relationship is with her as an individual. His educational methods require a great deal of personal involvement, and unlike most of the girls in this genre, Rose does not receive her education as part of a mass group of students in a public school. Instead, Alec pays careful personal attention to her diet, exercise, and socialization as well as to more conventional subjects such as math and language. She is his private project, and the other adults make an explicit agreement to stay out of his way as he attends to her development. And yet the relationship he forges with Rose is always interrupted by the specter of her father. As they are discussing how he plans to educate her, Alec says to Rose that

> it is my fault that I am a stranger to you, when I want to be your best friend. That is one of my mistakes, and I never repented it more deeply than I do now. Your father and I had a trouble once, and I thought I never could forgive him. So I kept away for years. Thank God, we made it all up the last time I saw him, and he told me then that if he was forced to leave her, he should bequeath his little girl to me as a token of his love. I can't fill his place, but I shall try to be a father to her. And if she learns to love me half so well as she did the good one she has lost, I shall be a proud and happy man. Will she believe this and try? (34)

The relationship between teacher and student is therefore dominated by the lost father. As with Uncle Jem, Alec looks at Rose and sees her father. To him, she represents another chance to rectify the damage Alec wrought in his relationship with his brother as a result of their "trouble," and the enormous amount of energy he dedicates to her education is from the beginning given to healing that relationship.

Rose, however, is not the only one who disappears into her father's identity here: so does Alec. Their affective relationship, which is the foundation for an extraordinarily effective form of discipline in this novel, attempts to cover Alec with his brother's identity. Although Alec verbally recognizes that he "can't fill"

her father's place, he nullifies that acknowledgment when he declares his intention "to be a father to her." The love she feels for him, the engine that drives
the successful disciplining of Rose, will be measured against her love for her
biological father, and Rose does frequently make comparisons between Alec and
her father, even specifically between their similarly loving and patient methods of educating her (82). Rose and Alec, the individuals who occupy the two
apparently distinctive positions in the teacher-student relationship, are both overwritten by the impression of the dead father.

And although Alec's methods of education are, he declares, new, they are also
dedicated to forging the limited individuality familiar from the Lockean model
of education.[3] Rose is destined to inherit a great deal of money, and although
she will probably someday marry and lose the right to direct her own property in
marriage, there is the possibility that she will come into her majority and choose
not to spend her money as would best benefit the community.[4] The daughter's
use of money had already concerned authors of the sentimental tradition, especially authors of the sentimental best sellers that set the orphan girl formula. In
a scene from *The Wide, Wide World* that has attracted endless critical attention,
Ellen first learns to connect her affection for her mother to successful shopping
and then to exercise affective influence over sympathetic bystanders to ensure
that subsequent shopping is similarly successful. In *The Hidden Hand*, the use
of money, especially inheritance, is a major source of conflict in the narratives
of both Capitola and Clara. For these loaded plot threads to make sense, the
novels must locate legitimate ownership of property in an individual with a legal
identity: Ellen must have the right to her money and purchases, and Capitola and
Clara must lay a legal claim to the enormous financial inheritances their devoted
fathers wished for them. Therefore, the sentimental tradition carries with it an
opportunity for individuality by means of the ownership of real property. But, in
keeping with a pattern found throughout sentimental novels, Alcott's novel struggles to find a way to contain that potential for individuality. Here, the Lockean
model of democratic education again comes into play. If a woman can own property like a man, the novel seems to argue, then like a man she must be educated
to use her individual rights in such a way that they will serve the community.
With the girls' novel's focus on children and education, that imperative becomes
even clearer. To that end, Alec in his role as educator must train Rose to choose
of her own free will to make the decisions that the majority requires her to make.

As Alec teaches Rose about the care of her inheritance, he claims to be endow-
ing the child with agency to act independently. "I shall take care of things till you

are of age," he says while teaching her the methods of accounting, "but I mean that you shall know how your property is managed and do as much of it as you can by and by. Then you won't be dependent on the honesty of other people." Rose is dismissive of his concerns:

> "Gracious me! As if I wouldn't trust you with millions of billions if I had them," cried Rose, scandalized at the mere suggestion.
>
> "Ah, but I might be tempted—guardians are sometimes. So you'd better keep your eye on me, and in order to do that you must learn all about these affairs," answered Dr. Alec, as he made an entry in his own very neat account book. (83)

Their exchange is reminiscent of the conversation between Ellen Montgomery and John Humphreys in *The Wide, Wide World* when John asks Ellen to take responsibility for herself, but Ellen manipulates John back into a position from which he may maintain discipline over her. However, in *Eight Cousins* Alec manages to avoid taking long-term responsibility for Rose by invoking a fear the sentimental tradition had long expressed, that of guardians who misuse the wealth of their charges. In a shift that echoes the gradual relocation of disciplinary authority to the little girl, Rose is asked to take up the action of surveillance— "keep your eye on me"—that Ellen insisted on ceding to John but that, tellingly, Rose accepts. Therefore, *Eight Cousins* observes its close relationship to sentimentalism both through its conviction that guardians "might be tempted" and its assertion that girls have rights connected to the ownership of property, rights that distinguish Rose as an individual.

But the delineation of Rose as an individual is, again in keeping with sentimental traditions, framed in ideology that hedges on that individuality by keeping Rose safely ensconced in a role. The relocation of the responsibilities for her wealth to Rose requires the kind of legal recognition of ownership by an individual that the sentimental tradition has already implied. But the training of the use of wealth does not stop with the safeguarding of personal possessions—far from it. Rose's extraordinary wealth, Alec worries, will present the growing girl with an especially hard task, and not only because people might try to take it. Rose asks,

> "But, really, shall I be rich by and by?"
> "I am afraid you will."
> "Why afraid, Uncle?"
> "Too much money is a bad thing."

"But I can give it away, you know. That is always the pleasantest part of having it, *I* think."

"I'm glad you feel so, for you *can* do much good with your fortune if you know how to use it well." (84)

Ironically, if she is to use her wealth well, an individual must both carefully patrol her property to make sure that even well-meaning uncles do not misspend it *and* give the money away. The training Alec offers—or, rather, on which he insists— begins with the promise of individuality but includes with it instruction on the use of wealth in ways that adhere to a bourgeois code of feminine charity. As Alec teaches Rose about her wealth, the promise of individuality through ownership incurs a series of critical exceptions. First, as in other examples of Lockean individualism, the individual gains access to the powers of subjectivity as she learns how to use them as her community desires. Second, affective discipline—this time, flowing from the loved uncle to the girl—speeds the path of Rose's normalization: her love for Alec makes her want to manage wealth *as he does*, not at all according to any individual dictates. Finally, the borders of the individual implied by the ownership of great wealth come under an ongoing obligation to dissolve themselves, the money passing from Rose to the objects of her charity as she, in Alec's phrasing, distributes wealth "well." Here, the novel makes clear that to use property well means *not* to own it.[5]

Alcott's interest in this subject reflects not only her proximity to the sentimental period but also her awareness of a modern concern, a concern of which her readers certainly would have been aware: girls' spending. Although fiction for women and girls never lost sight of the fact that feminine spending was always regulated by coverture, it repeatedly took to imagining how to control women's limited role in economy.[6] Thus, as Catherine Keohane has demonstrated, saving for charity in the eighteenth century took on various forms so that women who were involved in the spending but not earning of money could be controlled. In eighteenth-century bourgeois culture, Keohane argues, saving and spending well was cited as "the most immediate Female business" (qtd. in Keohane 43). Thus one of the main tasks of the housewife was governing her own desire. Lynne Vallone claims that a concern with feminine saving figured strongly in the nineteenth century as well, showing up repeatedly in literature not just for women but also for girls. In the nineteenth century, she reports, "the instability and liquidity of the American economy, where fortunes were made and lost with alarming frequency, also affected the advice books for girls, which almost unanimously advocated for its readers training in some marketable skill or trade in the unhappy event that some evil befall the girl and her family" (118). A 1927 study of girls' culture found that this pattern persisted into the twentieth century, emphasizing in no uncertain terms that girls and unmarried women could be expected to spend in ways that helped their families at the expense of their personal desires:

> Another prevalent misconception is that the majority of girls and women go to work for pin money. . . .
>
> Studies made by the Women's Bureau show that "contributing all earnings to the family fund is a very general practice among women wage-earners," as 68% of those investigated, in one city, did so. Families are frequently dependent in part on the contributions of their women, and sometimes wholly so. In one of the Women's Bureau studies, as many as one-third of all single women living at home were the sole breadwinners in their families. (Walter 68)

A long history of concern that girls spend their money just so thus attends *Eight Cousins*. The novel's concern that Rose learn to spend her money well operates as an attempt to demonstrate to girls how to use the wealth that was theirs as individuals. Earnings were, as with Rose, best spent not in gratifying individual desires, but in serving others.

But all the ink spilled on the issue of girls' spending also points to a force for individual identity that sentimentalism both recognized and even sometimes praised. Desire, sentimentalism recognized, was at the heart of both good spending and bad. And although woman's fiction of the nineteenth century frequently championed self-denial, the disavowal of desire does not precisely eliminate it. Gillian Brown has located what she calls nineteenth-century fiction's "objective of desire in keeping individual identity intact" (*Domestic* 118). Desire begets taste, and in Brown's reading of the sentimental tradition, it is "the exercise of the tastes by which a person distinguishes himself" (101). Gale Temple locates a specific instance of this kind of individualism in the sentimental novel *Ruth Hall*:[7]

> Ruth's uncommonly distinguished and superior individuality, which the phrenologist can decipher in the very bumps and lines of the skull, is constituted by, even dependent upon, her existence as a judicious, yet freely-spending consumer. Her exquisitely delicate and sensitively arranged self has very specific tastes, needs, and desires that must be met for Ruth to find happiness, which is portrayed as her right as an American. (145)

It is, according to Temple's reading, the desires themselves that define the individual, and the exercise of those desires is the evidence of individuality. Temple's argument works consciously with Brown's articulation of possessive individualism, but María C. Sánchez draws similar conclusions even though her model of individualism in Fern's novel disagrees with Brown's. Sánchez believes that scholars have overemphasized the importance of possessive individualism in *Ruth Hall*. Instead, she argues, we should consider how Fern uses class and taste to set off the individual protagonist from the characters around her. The sheer naturalness of Hall's desires mark her as different from the mass market, but her desires for things produced for that market demonstrate her individuality: "Ruth is a distinctive woman, in part because she knows how to make distinctions" (26). By contrast, the characters against whom Fern pits Hall are homogenized and villainized by a "monstrous lack of discrimination" (35). Desire and its practice were, for the sentimental tradition, evidence of individuality, and even in this tradition that so famously endorsed self-denial, it was frequently a mark of women the novels celebrated.

Alcott's novel embraces the ambiguous role of desire in sentimentalism; *Eight Cousins* embraces the right of the individual to exercise desire even as it narrates the refusal of such exercise. Therefore, although Rose is a conveniently blank screen on which her relatives can project the face of her father, it is also true that Alcott marks Rose with a variety of personal desires. She dislikes oatmeal, cherishes the "splendid boxes of goodies" her relatives send her at school (39), and longs so desperately for earrings that she pierces her ears without Alec's cherished approval, much as her cousins disregard their mothers' disapproval of pulp novels and cigars. The novel therefore recounts multiple instances in which the children express themselves through taste.

The scene of Rose's miniature reform movement, during which she takes out her earrings in exchange for a promise that the boys will give up their own vices, not only serves to illustrate the limited form of power Alcott imagines for her protagonist but also articulates the disingenuous role of desire in the novel. The adults of *Eight Cousins* rarely stand in the way of the children's desires, recognizing the right that individuals have to pursue their tastes. But the function of the reform scene is to explain how a disciplining girl such as Rose can guide individuals to choose to abjure desire. It is the children's right as individuals to have tastes, and indeed the conflict to which the children's various desires lead mark them out as distinct from their parents, but it is the duty of good members of the community not to pursue those desires. The result is a strengthened community, and the adults thank Rose for her initiative. Alec personally applauds her, pointing out that the gendered responsibilities of men are solidified by girls and mothers who teach boys to deny such desires, and he assures Rose that her actions will "help their mother keep these sons fit friends for an innocent creature like yourself" (182–83). And although Alec promises Rose herself a better husband, what he is really promising is better observation of gender regulations: men will be appropriately manly toward their appropriately feminine wives. In this way, even Rose's future reward, her as yet unnamed husband, speaks not to her own needs but to the maintenance of the community status quo. As with ownership of property, ownership of desire is the right of the individual, but, also as with property, desire must be foregone by the individual in favor of the majority's needs. The sentimental impulse in Alcott's novel keeps individuality permanently in balance with responsibilities to the community.

The individual in Alcott's novel gains and loses legitimacy in these negotiations as she acquires the rights to property and desire, but she is carefully educated to use those rights as her community requires. Significantly, as Alcott begins to popularize in books for girls tropes that had already proved popular in novels for women, she keeps the ambiguous nature of sentimental individualism but quietly drops the disingenuous promises of individuality, the false faces of individualism that the orphan girl formula used in *The Wide, Wide World* and *The Hidden Hand*. It can hardly be said that Alcott championed individual desires over communal obligations. But the emphasis she retained from sentimentalism on an individual's right to her own desires would lay the groundwork for a more emphatic individuality in the orphan girl novels to come.

With Alcott's orphan girl novel, the era of sentimental individualism, of girls who play at subjectivity only to take up the positions of loved ones and majority opinions, comes to a close. But this is not to say that turn-of-the-century orphan girl stories would embrace stridently individualist protagonists. On the contrary, the impression of sentimentalism would remain on the orphan girl novel even into the years immediately following passage of the Nineteenth Amendment. But part of that impression was an awareness of how selfhood could be defined by desire. In books written during a period in which consumer culture flourished, the path to identity through taste and ownership provided a means by which women writers could populate a sentimental formula with girls who were recognizably themselves.

CHAPTER FOUR

Rebecca of Sunnybrook Farm and the Threat of Affective Discipline

Although the orphan girl novel came to popularity in the nineteenth century, it was during the opening decades of the twentieth century that orphan girl novels proliferated. Taking a page from *Eight Cousins*, girls' fiction of the new century invested its protagonists with more disciplinary agency, simultaneously pushing for more distinct subjectivity for girls involved in the affectionate relationships that drove sentimental-style discipline. But the resulting orphan girl novels did more than merely flatter girl readers with promises of a new centrality in the melodrama of discipline. Orphan girl novels of the twentieth century laced their promises of moral influence with distinctly unsentimental reevaluations of suasion itself. In the new century, the genre began to give voice to its first notes of disappointment with affective discipline.

At the forefront of the new century's revision of the orphan girl genre stood Kate Douglas Wiggin, a woman already well known for her fiction as well as her highly visible role in promoting the growing kindergarten movement across America. It is in her popular explanations of kindergarten theory that Wiggin lays the groundwork for the revisions to affective discipline that would animate the new wave of orphan girl novels. In *The Relation of the Kindergarten to Social Reform*, Wiggin both takes the efficacy of affective discipline for granted and points to a significant problem at its heart, a problem that has to do with individual identity.

The discomfort Wiggin here voices clearly—and at which she will hint when she writes her own version of the orphan girl novel—grows out of the tension between suasion and legislative coercion. What she focuses on is the dangers

of moral suasion to the emerging child. Although sentimental versions of affective discipline—including those of the children's novels that overlapped with the
closing years of sentimentalism—sold affective discipline in part based on the
permanent bonds it created, Wiggin argues for a disciplinary model that weans
children from their sentimental mothers and teachers. Children will certainly
feel affection for good teachers, Wiggin explains, but children who fail to separate themselves from the sentimental disciplinarian should be regarded by the
kindergarten teacher as students whom the kindergarten has failed. What is so
startling about Wiggin's explanation of her ideas is that her phrasing sounds like
a direct indictment of the ideology of moral suasion, the very model of discipline
that had been tied so closely to feminine modes of instruction in previous decades. She writes that

> the kindergarten attempts a rational, respectful treatment of children, leading
> them to do right for right's sake, abjuring all rewards, save the pleasure of work-
> ing for others and the delight that follows a good action, and all punishments
> save those that follow as natural penalties of broken laws,—the obvious con-
> sequences of the special bit of wrong-doing, whatever it may be. The child's
> will is addressed in such a way as to draw it on, if right; to turn it willingly, if
> wrong. Coercion in the sense of fear, personal magnetism, *nay, even the child's
> love for the teacher, may be used in such a way as to weaken his moral force.*
> With every free, conscious choice of right, a human being's moral power and
> strength of character increase; and the converse of this is equally true. (8–9,
> emphasis added)

Wiggin's warning about the coercive nature of discipline through love is particularly surprising because she elsewhere endorses exactly that model. The point of
Froebel's Gifts, a book she coauthored to explain to potential kindergarten teachers the program's fundamentals, is to show how carefully designed geometric
toys can draw children out of their private world and into a world of relations
with other people. The kindness Wiggin insists kindergarten teachers must use
with their pupils will, she points out, join with this intersubjective relationship
to form an excellent basis for discipline. Therefore, her warning about "personal
magnetism" stands out as a significant departure from the sentimental design of
discipline: Wiggin here voices a rarely spoken qualm about affective discipline.
If it is true that children should be led to difficult tasks and adult morality by
a teacher for whom they feel affection, Wiggin implies, it is also true that the
teacher must disown the power of that bond, instead relying on children's sense

that what is good is what will bring them pleasure. The kindergartener's job is to educate the desires of the student, then let those desires guide the student.

Wiggin's ambivalence over affective discipline sets the tone for the next phase of the orphan girl novel. That ambivalence is characterized and driven by a conviction that has been earned through the previous iterations of the formula: as *The Wide, Wide World, The Hidden Hand*, and *Eight Cousins* all argue, there is power in affective discipline. If there is power in it, and if there are times when that power ought to be used, are there not also times when it ought *not* to be used? Are there times, in fact, when affective discipline works too well? Wiggin's nonfiction certainly indicates that there are. But power is notoriously addictive. It is one thing to argue, as did the sentimental orphan girl story, against the power of physical coercion by offering moral suasion as a more ethical and effective alternative, but it is quite another to foreswear a kind of power that works. In the orphan girl novels at the beginning of the twentieth century, then, women writers had to negotiate not only the genre formula but also the struggle between affective discipline's attractive power and a growing sense that this useful form of discipline was somehow wrong.

Wiggin's writings about kindergarten theory help illuminate the next book in the genre's history, Wiggin's 1903 novel, *Rebecca of Sunnybrook Farm*. In this story, the bright and imaginative Rebecca has to leave her mother's home because the outstanding debts incurred by her father before his death make it necessary to send one of the many siblings off to live elsewhere. Her mother's sisters—the strict Aunt Miranda and the loving Aunt Jane—adopt Rebecca accidentally, thinking they are volunteering to accept Rebecca's more demure sister. But they make the best of Rebecca's presence, seeing to her education no matter the personal inconvenience. Rebecca, for her part, becomes a cherished member of her new community, charming the eligible but indolent Adam Ladd and flourishing in every educational opportunity that comes her way. Despite the constant threat of financial disaster, Rebecca thrives, simultaneously warming the hearts of the people around her.

Surrounded by those glowing hearts, Rebecca is able to command significant power, power with pointed benefit to the girl herself. As with other novels in this genre at the turn of the century, Wiggin's book places the child, not the adult, in the role of disciplinarian. Rebecca is rarely the target of discipline; she is instead its most accomplished practitioner. The most frequent form of discipline directed at her is that of the scolding, such as those she receives from her Aunt Miranda, but they do little to change her; her mistakes are honest ones, and it is really experience that teaches her, not any form of discipline executed by adults. Rather, Rebecca is herself extremely gifted at disciplining other people. When, for example, Rebecca runs away from her adoptive home, stopping first at the Cobbs' house to say goodbye, Jeremiah Cobb correctly sees that Rebecca is making a poor decision, one that will limit her choices for the rest of her life. However, Cobb is not good at talking, and indeed the narrator confides that his "mental machinery was simple." Still, that machinery can move smoothly "when propelled by his affection or sympathy. In the present case these were both employed to his advantage" (86). Because of his affection and sympathy for Rebecca, Cobb is able to give her the advice she needs, even though she herself is unaware that she needs it. In this scene, the driving force of affective discipline—love—remains unchanged from the sentimental pattern. However, as in other iterations of the orphan girl formula at the beginning of the twentieth century, here the girl is at the center of the disciplinary relationship, not her mother. Further, it is Rebecca, not the people she has disciplined, who benefits from this arrangement. Although the narrator indicates that affection and sympathy work in this scene to Cobb's advantage, it is Rebecca whom he is able to help. The only sense in which Cobb's action is "to his advantage" is that it is a service—talking Rebecca out of a bad decision—that will benefit the girl he loves.

There is one other significant change to previous models of affective discipline that emerges in this scene, and it is one that reappears throughout Wiggin's novel. Whereas affective disciplinarians in earlier books frequently designed discipline around love, Rebecca's use of affection and sympathy to motivate the people who love her is rarely intentional. This is clear, for example, in that Rebecca does not get what she wants when she tells Cobb of her plans to run away. Her conversation with him is designed to prompt him to let her go, but the affection she has inspired in him prompts him instead to give her what she needs. This stands in direct contrast with Rose contracting with her adoring cousins to give up their bad habits. Rebecca is good at discipline, but she is especially good at it when she doesn't realize she is using it. Elsewhere, when an older Rebecca approaches an unruly horse whom the Cobbs have trouble getting to take a bit, Rebecca again disciplines without seeming to know she has done so. Mrs. Cobb later relates how Rebecca approached the horse oblivious to his awful temper:

> And I declare if she wan't pattin' Buster's nose and talkin' to him, and when she put her little fingers into his mouth he opened it so fur I thought he'd swaller her, for sure. He jest smacked his lips over the bit as if 'twas a lump o' sugar. "Land, Rebecca," I says, "how'd you persuade him to take the bit?" "I didn't,"

she says, "he seemed to want it; perhaps he's tired of his stall and wants to get out in the fresh air." (245)

Rebecca's claim that she didn't persuade the horse is disingenuous, as Mrs. Cobb's story hints, but it is true that Rebecca didn't *realize* she was persuading him. In this way, Wiggin's protagonist is able to use affective discipline without exactly encouraging the kind of dependency against which Wiggin's nonfiction warns. Moreover—and this, too, echoes the philosophy of the kindergarten— Buster does what Rebecca wants because she has manipulated what *the horse* wants, thus disowning the affectionate bond between the subject and object of discipline. Rather than raise the whip to this horse and force its body to perform as she wishes, and rather than fostering a love for her in its heart, Rebecca identifies what the horse wants and uses that longing to direct it. The result is a sketch of a new form of affective discipline, one that retains the power of moral suasion without endangering the growth of "moral power and strength of character" that are so important to the mission of the kindergarten.

This is a very thin line for Wiggin to walk. On the one hand, she is continuing the tradition of writing narratives that center on increased power for girls, but on the other she is exhibiting a reluctance to endorse fully the form of power that had been synonymous with the orphan girl formula for fifty years before the publication of *Rebecca*. The result is a deeply ambiguous form of moral suasion. Affective discipline in the new century is colored from its beginning by this conviction of the power inherent in such discipline, power that was both attractive and, in Wiggin's opinion, fundamentally dangerous as well.

Rebecca also revises the traditional narrative of affective power by introducing a new tool for discipline that manages both to guarantee power and to allow the disciplining girl some distance from her actions: in addition to motivating men through affection and sympathy, she can also move them through stories. Wiggin devotes most of her text to meditations on other aspects of discipline, but she gives storytelling a place of resonance in the novel's penultimate chapter. In this scene, Adam Ladd, the wealthy bachelor whom Rebecca charms and who becomes the key agent of her financial reversal of fortunes, puts the girl on a train, taking pains to "assure her of his sympathy" (219). After he has seen her off, Ladd—or "Mr. Aladdin," as Rebecca has come to call him for his unexpected generosities—sits waiting for the next train. There, he reads a copy of *Arabian Nights* he intends to give Rebecca soon. While reading his tales of Arabian nights, nights in which a woman spun tale after tale to exercise over her murderous husband the only control she could imagine, a transformation comes over

Ladd: "He turned the pages idly until he came to the story of 'Aladdin and the Wonderful Lamp,' and presently, in spite of his thirty-four years, the old tale held him spellbound as it did in the days when he first read it as a boy" (279). At this point in the narrative, there is little need to charm Ladd, who has already helped Rebecca without her knowledge, so what is the point of charming him here? Perhaps it is to hint at the power that Rebecca will have over him should he, as he seems to intend, one day marry her: Scheherazade, after all, is a wife of a wealthy man, and if she can direct the desire of her husband, perhaps Rebecca can, too. But of course that power is deferred. Wiggin's novel ends shortly after this scene, and its only sequel returns to Rebecca's girlhood rather than exploring her future, perhaps married, life. What this scene does do, then, is introduce another form of affective discipline. This new face of discipline promises to work on affectionate men, directing their power in such a way as to benefit the orphan girl. But it also offers an indirect form of influence. Stories, after all, do not demand. Instead, they model, shape, and nudge. The final tool of affective discipline that Wiggin describes is the one that best satisfies the requirements for discipline she needs. First, it is powerful. Second, it can be disowned.

Rebecca therefore illustrates the struggle writers of the twentieth century engaged in with their sentimental foremothers. The orphan girl formula at the beginning of the twentieth century had not fully separated itself from the sentimental model of the nineteenth century—and why would it have? Novels in the sentimental mode had been earning staggering sales figures for decades, and the disciplinary model at the heart of sentimentalism promised a degree of power, an opportunity to reform men that held as much appeal for bourgeois women in the decades leading up to prohibition as it had in the decades leading up to abolition. But one theorem of sentimental ideology—that girls should be able to own, and, by owning, create legal and social subjectivity that valorized individual identity—posed a real threat to the strategy of intimate discipline that provided the through line for sentimentalism's orphan girl story. Literature for girls in the first decades of the twentieth century, tied formally and ideologically to literature for women from the previous century, wrestled right up to the end of the genre with the rules of affective discipline and how a discrete individual could figure into a disciplinary relationship. In part, the shift in the history of affective discipline from an emphasis on girls receiving discipline from adults to girls dispensing discipline themselves was enabled by these girls who were more dramatically themselves. Those "selves" would be defined by the tastes and desires cultivated in the newly protected interiority of fictional girls.

The beginning of the period in which these literary developments take place was marked by the ambiguous individuality that characterized the sentimental fiction of a previous era. Nowhere does this individuality surface more clearly than in turn-of-the-century discourse about education, specifically the discourse about kindergartens. Developed from Friedrich Froebel's German model, kindergartens embraced the idea that children had desires. In fact, the kindergarten movement struggled to recognize an individual, if predictable, child in its theories. As a result, it offered a way of thinking about children that promised to turn their desire from a problem into an avenue to selfhood—as long as they desired what they were supposed to.

Wiggin, who ran the first free kindergarten in California, wrote copiously on behalf of the movement throughout the last two decades of the century, penning fiction to raise money for the San Francisco Public Kindergarten Society as well as treatises in popular magazines and books touting Froebel's theories. In essay after essay, Wiggin articulated the centrality of children's needs to the concept of kindergartens. In her argument for the public funding of kindergartens, for example, she made the point sharply:

> As to the final adoption of the kindergarten there is one preliminary question which goes straight to the root of the whole matter. At present the state accepts the responsibility of educating children after an arbitrarily fixed age has been reached; in California, six years. Ought it not, rather, if it assumes the responsibility at all, to begin the educate the child when he *needs education?* (*The Relation of the Kindergarten to Public School* 3)

For Wiggin and the other members of the early kindergarten movement in the United States, the child had specific, locatable needs, and it was those that should guide parents and teachers (and taxpayers) as they puzzled over how to relate to children.[1] Wiggin's essays and books on the subject were all but evangelical in tone as they argued with and wooed readers in an attempt to get them to support the kindergarten movement. At the end of *Froebel's Gifts*, the text she coauthored with Nora Archibald Smith, she intimated that any student of pedagogy would convert to Froebel's theories not simply because his theories were true in the abstract but because they accorded with what children in fact believed. Such a convert "has come to look at things in the child way" (201).

It was by paying attention to what the child wanted that kindergarten theorists proposed to develop them as individuals. The goal of the kindergarten teacher was not to develop a child who would cling to the adult's morality or affection but who would individuate from the teacher and become an independent thinker, to foster a child who had agency, direction, and desires that sought fulfillment. The boundaries around the fledgling individual were so important that the authors repeatedly cautioned educators to watch out for the problems that an uninterested or harried teacher could visit on the students—thus the adult was less the model for and more the threat to the emerging individual.[2] Wiggin and Smith argue that this pedagogical method is different from others precisely because of this awareness of the child and his borders.[3] The authors discovered that when they used methods *other* than Froebel's, methods grounded in adult notions of what a child should learn, "sometimes the child's mind obstinately declined to follow the prescribed route; it refused to begin at the proper beginning of a subject and go on logically to the end, as the books decreed, but flew into the middle of it, and darted both ways" (ix–x). The pedagogy of the kindergarten, on the other hand, was not "written in the seclusion of the study," a fact that guaranteed Froebel's methods "have the virtues, too, of work corrected and revised at every step by the 'child in the midst'" (v–vi). If children could not precisely be trusted to spring into the world fully educated to their position and use, they could be counted on to explain what they needed, and the successful teacher would become successful by listening. Rather than imposing her notion of what they needed on them, she would wait for them to express those needs themselves and thereby guide their education.

Children's desires were therefore central to their instruction. The kindergarten teacher used a series of increasingly complicated and abstract physical objects, and these objects were keyed to what children wanted. By engaging children's interest and leading them through this careful schedule of toys, the teacher made use of children's innate desires to lead them progressively to become the kind of well-rounded individuals Froebel hoped for in his theories. These objects, educational toys called "gifts," were "designed to lead to the mastery of material objects" but at the same time they were intended to be "always connected with the child's experience and affection" (27). By studying the tastes of children, Wiggin insisted, Froebel proposed a regimen of work and play that was

> developed with infinite love and forethought to meet the child's wishes and capabilities; every one of them has been so delicately adjusted to meet the demands of the case, and so gently drawn into the natural and legitimate channel of childlike play, that they never fail to meet with an enthusiastic reception from the child, nor to awaken the strangest interest in him. (119)

The third gift, for example, "satisfies the growing desire for independent activity, for the exercise of his own power of analysis and synthesis, of taking apart and putting together" (59). Wiggin and the other early proponents of the kindergar-

ten movement made clear that these gifts did not meet children's desires accidentally but rather were specifically crafted after extensive observation of what
children wanted at what point in their development. The goal of kindergarten
was to produce individuals, Wiggin declared, unlike previous educational models. The methods for building an individual rested entirely on attention to the
child's desires.[4]

But for all Wiggin's protests, the model of education endorsed by the kindergarten movement still clung to key ideas associated with earlier conceptions
of childhood development. For example, Wiggin endorsed the development of
individuals who possessed their own desires and wielded their own authority not
for the sake of children but because such individuals represented "an opportunity
for amalgamation of races, and for laying the foundation of American citizenship" (*The Relation of the Kindergarten to Public School* 16), for the communal
obligation that undergirded education in the Lockean model. Moreover, Froebel's strategy of individuation was almost identical to Locke's in that the child
was to be exposed at first only to simple tests, then gradually more complex tests,
following a course indicated by the child's progress. Put more accurately, though,
this course was determined by the *anticipated* progress of each child. This logic
took for granted that all children were similar enough that their growth could be
charted in the same way. The derision Wiggin and others expressed for methods of childhood development that did not listen to the "child in the midst"
concealed a willingness to homogenize the experiences of individual children
and tick off their progress along a path that was just as prescribed as any other
developmental model. Kindergarten theorists even used the same arguments to
justify the use of this slowly expanding circle of exposure, warning of the threat
any other path of development would pose to "the imperfectly trained pupil,"
who "shrinks in half-terror and helplessness, feeling no hope of becoming master
of these strange new impressions" (Wiggin and Smith 98). Both models imagined a child whose progress would follow a certain route, and both had difficulty
even conceiving of children who would not follow the anticipated progression.
For example, the first six of Froebel's gifts, the "Building Gifts," anticipated a
certain kind of child who wanted to "investigate" and "transform" (54), characteristics that kindergarten theory expected of the child at that stage in his development. Although Wiggin and Smith argued that the child "must have full liberty
to make the various experiments which suggest themselves to him," the "latent
energies" they were "endeavoring to rouse" (36) were the energies appropriate
to the child *if* he followed Froebel's chart; if there were such thing as a child
whose development blazed another trail, kindergarten theorists seemed unaware

of him. In this way, the early American kindergarten movement both insisted on a selfhood constructed on desire and a structure into which children would fit as predictable types.

Kindergarten's popularity was therefore a marker of the continuing conflict within American culture about individuality, particularly in children. But emerging from that conflict was a genuine effort to wean children from adult influence quickly. Key to the distinctions between adult and child, the turn-of-the-century kindergarten movement argued, was an acknowledgment of a child's possession of desires. Those desires would characterize a child with whom adults could interact without rendering obsolete the boundaries between one individual and another. And it is significant that as this construction of a child with interior desires was gaining ground, one of the major figures in popularizing the notion was a writer of sentimental-style orphan girl stories. The same woman who argued that "the child has a right to a place of his own, to things of his own, to surroundings which have some relation to his size, his desires, and his capabilities" (*Children's Rights* 15) would practice her call for children's individual identity in her essays on education, but she would sharpen it in her fiction.

In *Rebecca of Sunnybrook Farm*, Wiggin confronts head-on some of sentimentalism's favorite tools for eliding the difference between individuals and types. As her protagonist navigates a variety of affective relationships, Wiggin emphasizes the desires that characterize Rebecca's individual identity, and the choices that are the expression of that desire become a powerful tool for articulating how Rebecca is unlike those with whom sentimental stories would be inclined to align her. Those desires originate from an interiority that, Wiggin demonstrates, the girl is licensed to define.

In sentimental stories of this formula, the protagonists frequently find their own identities overwritten by those of their deceased ancestors. This is precisely the case for Rebecca, but in a departure from the sentimental pattern, the way Rebecca reflects other people is complicated from the start. When Rebecca first enters her aunts' home, she is read by at least one of her aunts not in terms of her unique identity but as an echo of her disappointing father. Because Rebecca's aunt Miranda has always disapproved of Lorenzo Randall, she frequently singles out aspects of Rebecca's character that she insists show "the Randall" coming out in her. Rebecca has her father's artistic ability (20) and "happy disposition" (272), two inappropriate traits in Miranda's opinion, so to her aunt Rebecca is "an everlasting reminder of her foolish, worthless father" (54). When Miranda watches Rebecca skip home from school, she is even more annoyed to see that Rebecca moves "with her father's dancin'-school steps" (78). And although Rebecca and her mother both still feel affection for her father, Miranda argues that "dead husbands are usually good ones; but the truth needs an airin' now and then, and that child will never amount to a hill o' beans till she gets some of her father trounced out of her" (82).

This is the crucial difference between Wiggin's treatment of the issue and that of Warner, Southworth, and Alcott: Rebecca's father *can be* trounced out of her. Simply because Miranda can expect Rebecca to stop being like her father, the orphan girl is for the first time an individual who can choose (if after a cruel form of education) whom to reflect. This is the central conflict between Rebecca and Miranda. As Rebecca says, "Nothing I can do suits Aunt Miranda; she's just said it will take me my whole life to get the Randall out of me, and I'm not convinced that I want it all out, so there we are!" (211). Rebecca's personality is a necessary battleground for the conflict between Randall and Miranda, and the space cleared, the novel seems to say, is the space in which the individual girl will choose which family to inherit.

But even that is too simple a representation of the struggle that takes place over Rebecca's identity, because there is another father besides Lorenzo Randall whom Rebecca inherits, and by the end of the novel she can also invoke or discard him. When a group of missionaries comes to town, Rebecca's aunts are too ill to keep up the Sawyer tradition of church attendance, so they reluctantly send her in their stead. Before the service is over, Rebecca hears that it is also a family tradition to invite visiting missionaries to stay at the Sawyer home, so she extends an invitation to them. Her aunts, not strong enough to play the part of host, are distraught, but Rebecca manages the entire affair admirably, and one of the visitors mentions to Miranda that Rebecca's actions were reminiscent not of the Randalls but of Miranda's father, Deacon Israel Sawyer. For the first time, Miranda feels something akin to affection for Rebecca:

> The memory of old days had been evoked, and the daily life of a pious and venerated father called to mind; the Sawyer name had been publicly dignified and praised; Rebecca had comported herself as the granddaughter of Deacon Israel Sawyer should, and showed conclusively that she was not "all Randall." (170)

One of the church leaders, Deacon Milliken, points out that Rebecca not only acted similarly to Grandfather Sawyer but that she acted *un*like Lorenzo Randall. "I thought at first," he says, "seein' she favored her father so on the outside that she was the same all through; but she ain't, she's like your father, Israel Sawyer." Milliken then overrides Miranda's protests and says that Rebecca sat "in the same seat he used to when he was leader o' the Sabbath-school" and delivered her invitation with poise that exactly recalled her grandfather—"there was mor'n one spoke of it" (177).

Clearly Wiggin is borrowing from the sentimental orphan girl story the idea that girls in disciplinary relationships can be ciphers. However, because Wiggin presents two incompatible ancestors and then insists that Rebecca is able to negotiate their representation, she suggests that the screen on which they are projected has some power to contort itself. Rebecca can, to put it another way, express her own selfhood through her ability to manage the identities that crowd imperfectly inside her. In the same way that Locke, Jefferson, and Emerson—as Gillian Brown and C. B. MacPherson have argued—saw alienable rights as commodities that could be traded, therefore defining subjectivity, Rebecca's ability to swap her ancestors' likenesses suggests her own subjectivity. Rebecca is likewise able to choose the strengths she needs from either father, taking the dramatic flair of one in a school presentation, the demure hospitality of another at church, even discarding her father's infamous financial incontinence while *retaining* his ability to write compellingly. Here in the latter half of the history of the formula, Rebecca complicates the transfer of identity that was taken for granted in earlier novels through her ability to mitigate the father—indeed, fathers—she has inherited. Rebecca does not unconsciously represent either father, but having been forced to realize that her representation is negotiable as a result of the ongoing conflict with Miranda, she becomes an individual endowed with the privilege of taking on whatever mixture of personalities she prefers for herself. The result is an individual defined by the ability to own, exchange, and modify the fathers she has inherited.

This tool for delineating Rebecca as an individual is one that relies heavily on interiority. Wiggin uses Rebecca's ability to negotiate inherited traits to draw lines between Rebecca and the adults around her that can be momentarily crossed, but the lines are drawn by the character; she makes choices that derive from her unique tastes and inclinations. Further, it is significant that what Rebecca is negotiating is *character*—a sense of familial obligation, a "happy disposition"— rather than physical traits. I have noted how the orphan girl formula divorces the father's spirit from his body so that fictional girls can manipulate it as they wish, and that disembodied sense of the father plays right into a pattern in genre fiction that Cathy Boeckmann has pinpointed between the years of 1891 and 1912. Boeckmann's study, which focuses on the competing philosophies of inheritability and environmental influence, examines how fiction of the period struggled to locate racial identity, which it first accomplished by cataloguing visible signs of race. But when novels (and news) of passing made the unreliability of visual

markers of race painfully clear, the inheritability of *character* became an important tool for tracing racial lineage. *Rebecca* suppresses any knowledge of race
issues, but it demonstrates the same logic: character is the locus of identity, the
marker of difference between one individual and another.[5] Rebecca's individuality is clear because there is something uniquely Rebecca that can decide when
the boundaries of self are crossed and when they are not. But as Boeckmann's
logic would have it, that individuality is situated in character, in her interiority,
not in her visible body.

Rebecca represents an important step in the development of the individual
girl. Because she comes into the novel with her father's identity scribbled over her
own, because she announces from the opening chapters that she intends to gain
property but use it to benefit others, Rebecca is the inheritor of the self-effacing
girls of the sentimental novel. But because she is able to decide whom she will
reflect, there is simultaneously in her character the indication that she is an individual who can discriminate and choose according to her personal taste. This is
not an unqualified endorsement of individualism, but it is a crucial change, and
it is one that Wiggin remarkably introduces within the sentimental sensibilities
of affective discipline.

CHAPTER FIVE

A *Little Princess* and the Accidental Power of Stories

Rebecca of Sunnybrook Farm was the first of the classic orphan girl novels to suggest the affective power of storytelling in the hands of disciplining girls, but Frances Hodgson Burnett's 1905 novel, A *Little Princess*, was more dedicated to exploring the power of storytelling than any other book in the genre. The great popularity of *Rebecca* touched off a revival of the sentimental orphan girl story, one that both longed for the power of affective discipline and looked at such discipline as a tool in bad need of revision. *Rebecca* guarded against the costs of that power to disciplining girls by complicating the self on whom adults attempted to project their identities. And, even more significantly, it strove to imagine a girl who could enjoy the power of discipline without quite exercising that discipline herself. In A *Little Princess*, as in Wiggin's novel, story is an effective tool of discipline, and, also as in Wiggin's novel, discipline that relies on affection is strong but imperfect. In *Rebecca of Sunnybrook Farm*, for the first time, a story in the orphan girl tradition points to the limits of moral suasion, not just its powers and techniques; A *Little Princess* would take up the revisionary spirit of Wiggin's novel even as it magnified *Rebecca*'s sense of the disciplinary potential of storytelling. At the same time, though, it also increased the risk of girls disappearing into the role provided by the stories that surround them.

A *Little Princess* opens on seven-year-old Sara Crewe. With her is Captain Crewe, a successful speculator in India and Sara's "young, handsome, rich, petting father" (6). They bid a tearful farewell to one another at the prestigious London boarding school of Miss Minchin, who fawns over Sara—and Captain Crewe's money. But when Sara's father dies unexpectedly, Miss Minchin shows her charity by turning Sara from the star pupil into a despised maid, heaping indignities—and a great deal of work—on the orphan girl. In her attic room, Sara tells stories to herself and a few friends to keep herself from depression, unwittingly setting off a chain of events that reconnects her to her father's wealth.

A *Little Princess* participates in the ongoing narrative of affective discipline at first by playing conscientiously by sentimental rules. Physical coercion, for instance, remains only in its ineffective uses by the cruel schoolmistress, who starves Sara and confines her to a miserably uncomfortable room. In contrast, the early chapters portray affective discipline as would a nineteenth-century novel about suffering orphan girls. Such discipline is remarkably effective when it is used, for example, on Sara, notably by her father. Sara's father has discovered—as he tells Miss Minchin—that Sara doesn't really need correction. She will, like Rose of *Eight Cousins* or Ellen of *The Wide, Wide World*, do what her presumed disciplinarian—namely, her father—wants without even having been told to do so. This is because Sara loves him so completely. Just before her father leaves, the two share a tender moment that outlines the depths of Sara's affection:

> "Are you learning me by heart, little Sara?" he said, stroking her hair.
> "No," she answered. "I know you by heart. You are inside my heart." And they put their arms round each other and kissed as if they would never let each other go. (19)

The love she feels for her father riddles Sara's being to the extent that how she acts, what she learns, and the ways she thinks are defined in accordance with that love. In one scene, Sara is greatly embarrassed as a result of a misunderstanding over a proficiency she has acquired out of love for her father. After her father departs, Sara attends French lessons with the other students, but the work is so far beneath her abilities that she is unsure of how to respond to it. She attempts to tell Minchin of her problem, but Minchin refuses to try to understand and instead summons the French tutor, Monsieur Dufarge, to instruct Sara. And indeed Sara has never technically studied French:

> Madame had not understood. She had not learned French exactly—not out of books—but her papa and other people had always spoken it to her, and she had read it and written it as she had read and written English. Her papa loved it, and she loved it because he did. (26)

Sara's father loves French so much, the narrative tells us, because his deceased wife was French, but this affective relationship gets only passing mention and quickly disappears from the novel. Here one of Burnett's first breaks with the sentimental tradition is visible: in a sentimental novel, the affective power of the mother would have been paramount, but in this book the relationship between father and child is more important, as it was between orphan girls and their (adoptive) father figures in previous girls' fiction. After Sara explains—in fluent French—to Monsieur Dufarge the misunderstanding that has taken place, the tutor tells Minchin that "there is not much I can teach her. She has not *learned* French, she *is* French" (27). If it is true that Sara knows her father by heart, it is also true that her heart beats with the impulses it has learned from his out of that love.

At the beginning of the novel, this version of affective discipline—the old standard—remains in power, but as the pages go by, it seems less and less convincing. Sara is a typical sentimental heroine at first, and the tension of the novel is generated by the reader's perception that Sara must survive both morally and physically until the day when, if she is lucky, the man who knows the truth about her father's fortune and his untimely death will arrive to restore her to the upper class.[1] As a typical sentimental heroine—at least at the beginning of the novel—Sara wins influence by effacing herself. Thus, as one of her rivals realizes, "Sara was a leader, too, and not because she could make herself disagreeable, but because she never did" (38). But Sara is an effective leader through submission over only the other girls at the school, not the adults. In the weeks following her father's death and her abrupt descent to the working class, Sara realizes that as effective as disciplinary intimacy may be between little girls, it's a very poor mode of power for children over adults:

> During the first month or two, Sara thought that her willingness to do things as well as she could, and her silence under reproof, might soften those who drove her so hard. In her proud little heart she wanted them to see that she was trying to earn her living and not accepting charity. But the time came when she saw that no one was softened at all; and the more willing she was to do as she was told, the more domineering and exacting careless housemaids became, and the more ready a scolding cook was to blame her. (94)

In the same way that Wiggin's word of caution to too effective teachers was remarkable because it expressed concern about a mode of power that had been widely celebrated by the sentimental writers preceding these girls' novels, Burnett's illustration here of the limitations of affective discipline, especially in its old form of self-effacement, is a startling word of dissent in the discourse of affective discipline. Whereas Wiggin worried that sentimental-style discipline was too effective and therefore ought to be revised, Burnett indicates that it ought to be revised because sometimes it fails to work at all.

The answer A *Little Princess* posits to the problem of the limitations of senti-mental disciplinary technologies of the sentimental novel is a form of influence engendered by storytelling. Whereas previous novels made a point of the virtue of feminine strategies of mercy and public sentiment, pointedly in contrast with physical coercion, the disciplinary energy of Burnett's novel relies almost exclu-sively on making the disciplinary objects feel that they are part of a story. Thus, when, before her financial reversal, Sara befriends the young maid Becky, Bur-nett conceives of storytelling as the opposite of physical discomfort. Sara begins a story for Becky in the privacy of her room, then stops the tale, worried that "you haven't time to hear it now . . . but if you will tell me just what time you come to do my rooms, I will try to be here and tell you a bit of it every day until it is fin-ished. It's a lovely long one—and I'm always putting new bits to it." The promise is wonderful to Becky, who has been eavesdropping on Sara's stories as she tells them to the other girls already. If Sara will hold up her end of the bargain, Becky sighs, "I wouldn't mind *how* heavy the coal boxes was—or *what* the cook done to me" (57). The promise of stories is more important than the pain of the physi-cal world. That world represents not only trials but also possible rewards, yet for the audience of Sara's stories, those things matter no more than does the pain. Although Becky, as an undercompensated worker at Minchin's school, does not receive enough food to eat, even the treats, such as meat pies, Sara shares with her each day are not so important as the opportunity to hear Sara's stories:

> However heavy it was, and whatsoever the temper of the cook, and the hard-ness of the work heaped upon her shoulders, she had always the chance of the afternoon to look forward to—the chance that Miss Sara would be able to be in her sitting room. In fact, the mere seeing of Miss Sara would have been enough without meat pies. (65)

The contrast between physical and sentimental is the same as it has been before, but now the desired commodity is the girl's story, the latest face of affectionate discipline.

In *Rebecca*, where the first hint of story's power emerges in this genre, the reading scene is carefully overdetermined: Ladd is a wealthy, marriageable man who is reading a book chosen in accordance with his affectionate history with the girl protagonist, so the metaphors of the scene convey the power of the reading relationship subtly. A *Little Princess* throws such subtlety to the winds. Sara tells stories to her friends, her maid, the neighbor, herself, her dolls, her students, and nearly everyone else who will listen to her. And the narrator makes quite plain what is at stake in storytelling. Even when Sara is still wealthy and well edu-cated—the wealthiest and best-educated student at the school, in fact—it is clear that everything else pales in comparison with her ability to enchant an audience:

> Of course the greatest power Sara possessed and the one which gained her even more followers than her luxuries and the fact that she was "the show pupil," the power that Lavinia and certain other girls were most envious of, and at the same time most fascinated by in spite of themselves, was her power of telling stories and of making everything she talked about seem like a story, whether it was one or not. (46)

Through stories, Sara exercises a great deal of control over most of the characters in the novel, not just willing listeners or reluctant ones such as Lavinia and the other envious girls. She tells stories, for example, that quiet a temperamental child (43–44) and help educate a slow student (173–74). The fact that her stories are usually fictional does not in any way limit their power, and Sara can even use them to control herself, as she does after her fortune is lost, and she is forced to move out of her warm and luxurious room into a tiny, cold room upstairs. All her friends and fellow students expect her to fold under the change, which takes place in less than a single day, and more than one little girl asks how Sara will manage.

> "Sara," she said, "do you think you can bear living here?"
> Sara looked round also.
> "If I pretend it's quite different, I can," she answered; "or if I pretend it is a place in a story." (101)

The stories she concocts to ease the pain of her physical life fight a long battle with the tribulations of her new poverty, and they seem to be her only hope for outlasting her tribulations. She maintains, for example, her sweet and gener-ous disposition despite her worldly problems by imagining herself a mistreated lady: "She was a proud, brave little chatelaine, and dispensed generously the one hospitality she could offer—the dreams she dreamed—the visions she saw—the imaginings which were her joy and comfort" (175).

The resolution of the conflict hinges not on Sara's learning to use stories ap-propriately—she is a natural—but on learning to expand their scope. At the be-ginning of the novel and right up until the climax, Sara thinks of stories as ways to help those in her immediate proximity, including herself. But by telling her stories, she brings about the happy ending in which her fortunes are restored and even increased. The servant of the man who is looking for her has been eavesdropping on her stories, and he reports these fancies back to his master, who is ill and wracked by guilt over the death of his friend and business partner, and together they decide to start making Sara's stories come true. They pay careful attention to her desires and fulfill them down to the last detail, providing a lamp with just this color shade, a meal with just this sort of platter. At this point in the novel, Sara is shocked to discover that stories are not local, private phenomena. She has no idea who has been providing her with such secret treasures, and she can see no way that her benefactor could know of her private wishes. With the intervention of her benefactor, however, she realizes that stories don't just dominate the spirit but dictate real life as well. "And to think I used to pretend and pretend and wish there were fairies!" she exclaims. "The one thing I always wanted was to see a fairy story come true. I am *living* in a fairy story. I feel as if I might be a fairy myself, and able to turn things into anything else" (201). In a moment of clarity, Sara tells Becky that "*everything's* a story. You are a story—I am a story. Miss Minchin is a story" (115). Stories are not just for pacifying children. They are for controlling reality.

And although Sara's biological father is only in her story briefly, still, the novel makes it clear that the role of men is no less under the jurisdiction of affectionate disciplinarians than before. Sara provides from her meager meals crumbs that a rat—a father rat—takes back to his home, and in the process she wins his trust. This fluffy bit of anthropomorphism adds nothing to the plot, and as such its importance to the formula's theme is easy to miss, but Sara is instrumental to this little father's ability to provide for the family. The relationship between father and family in other scenes is enabled by the little girl and her discipline, and there, too, stories are the favored tool of her discipline. In addition to the dramatic effect they have on Sara's world once the kindly neighbor, Tom Carrisford, hears them, these stories also shape Carrisford's reality. His illness is the direct result of his guilt over his friend's death, and Sara's stories at first merely serve to distract from his pain. But as time goes on, her stories so move him that he is prompted to use his great wealth on her behalf. When Minchin starves Sara, Carrisford provides her with food. When Minchin refuses to replace her ragged clothing, he sends her new clothes. He uses his privilege on her behalf in general because of the affection her stories have stirred up, but he also attends to her desires, giving her not just things he wants her to have, but things she has told him—through her stories—that she wants. At the climax of the novel, Sara's fortune is restored through the connection provided by those stories, restored by the affectionately motivated Carrisford.

Carrisford represents an opportunity not just to direct masculine privilege but to manage fatherhood itself. This is in part because the friend whose death tortures Carrisford to the point of illness is none other than Sara's father, and the wealth Carrisford mistakenly withheld from that father is waiting to be handed down to Sara. But when Sara looks at Carrisford, she sees a connection to her father forged by affect. Carrisford gazes on Sara "with the look she remembered in her father's eyes—that look of loving her and wanting to take her in his arms. It made her kneel down by him, just as she used to kneel by her father when they were the dearest friends and lovers in the world" (223). The relationship she lost with her father is recovered in Carrisford, and once more the ties of affective discipline are to thank for restoring the family. The affective discipline that caused Sara to obey her father has been transferred to Carrisford, who loves her first because of her stories. And although Sara was unable to help her biological father when he was ill, Sara's presence, by the end of the novel, heals Carrisford, reinstating him to his original vitality. The girl who reconnects the rat father to his family in her oubliette is likewise responsible for reconnecting her own father with the family.

It is storytelling that has attracted the most attention in scholarship about *A Little Princess*, but frequently the critical interest in storytelling leads to frustration with the novel's vision of individualism. Mary Cadogan and Patricia Craig, for example, have little to say about *A Little Princess*—although they write at length about Burnett's better-known orphan girl novel, *The Secret Garden*—but they do make a point of criticizing the novel's "passion for princesses and angelic children," commenting that such passion "was at odds with [Burnett's] respect for individuality and democracy" (68). Their dismissal of the novel is not typical for the field, however. Elisabeth Rose Gruner, for example, pursues the use of storytelling through the novel in an avowed effort to understand how stories shape their audiences and to what extent such influence can be resisted. Such an agenda is inevitably one framed by issues of discipline, and Gruner's article is concerned with storytelling in terms immediately familiar from the history of affective discipline within which the orphan girl genre is written. Sara's stories, Gruner argues, "teach—both the content material . . . and a less tangible sympathy or identification. Narrative, within the novel and perhaps of the novel itself, allows for sympathetic identification and even for moral growth" (176). Gruner's point about "sympathetic identification," a process through which the affection-

ate author and audience erase the boundaries between themselves, is directly relevant to the kind of individualism possible within sentimental structures. Such
identification plays a significant role in the relationship between fictional Sara
and her fictional playmates and, crucially, between fictional Sara and her real-
world readers (174). Whereas Cadogan and Craig shrug off the book's importance
in part because of its anti-individualist tendencies, Gruner struggles to find value
in the book *because* it bridges the hearts of readers and narrators. Rather than
denounce the book for its invitation to sympathetic identification, Gruner seems
to argue that sympathetic identification is inevitable, and the reader's task is not
so much to resist such identification as it is to choose carefully which texts one
should allow access to one's heart. Gruner points to how Sara revises her own role
models—Cinderella and Marie Antoinette, two of the princesses to whom Cadogan and Craig no doubt object—but does not precisely infer from such revision
that readers should differentiate themselves from Burnett's orphan. Rather, for
Gruner, Sara is "a better role model" for contemporary readers than are previous
princesses (175), and she implies that Sara's "power to reshape her destiny and to
identify imaginatively with others" (178) is something for readers to emulate. In
short, Gruner performs a surprising revision of Harriet Beecher Stowe's famous
desire to create "right feeling" in her readers: taking for granted that sentimental
stories will result in a dissolution of self, she argues that we must make sure that
the stories we read themselves have right feeling first.

Gruner's engagement with the novel, characterized simultaneously by a keen
awareness of the book's sentimental manipulations as well as the consequences of
such manipulations, provides excellent insight into the novel's mission. Gruner
does champion the novel, concluding for example that "Sara's storytelling imagination is her mainstay, her defense against the violence and degradation by a
world controlled by the tyranny of the vulgar and cruel" (171). But for all the
power Gruner sees in such loving stories, she also worries that even Sara's teaching is "of a peculiarly passive kind" (177). Although storytelling and sympathetic
identification can "alleviate misery" and "nurture," she acknowledges that "the
transformative power of the stories functions only in one direction, still maintaining the hierarchies firmly in place" (179).

Gruner's essay is in part a response to an earlier essay by Elizabeth Lennox
Keyser, itself concerned with the implications of Sara's compelling ability to tell
stories. For Keyser, what Gruner would later call "sympathetic identification" is
certainly a source of power, but it has likewise a tendency to erode individual
identity, a tendency that Keyser implies is not just a problem for contemporary
feminists but also for Sara. When one wealthy little boy, for example, sees the

destitute Sara and immediately assumes she fits the identity of one of the pathetic characters in a story he has heard, Keyser protests that, far from liberating the listener, "absorption in stories can lead one to misread reality. Further it shows how Sara's habit of viewing herself and others as fictional characters has begun to trap her in the roles that others would have her play" (236–37). Here, Keyser alludes to another way that the novel reveals the *failures* of sentimental disciplinary strategies, similar to Sara's failure to soften the hearts of her oppressors through "silence under reproof." Although the novel seems to emphasize Sara as storyteller, it also, as Keyser points out, reminds the reader that Sara is the object of stories, and not always to her benefit. As the sentimentally suffering princess, Sara has encouraged the people around her "to project whatever they wished on to her, so that she has been in danger of losing her own identity" (238). The conversation between Gruner and Keyser underscores the sentimental origins of Sara's penchant for disciplinary storytelling as well as an awareness of the threat such discipline poses to the individuality of the disciplining girl, an awareness that the novel itself seems to possess.

Previous readings of A *Little Princess* have been justifiably fascinated by how the novel imagines the use of storytelling, but there is also an element of the technology of affective connections that is nonverbal. The novel's understanding of how stories move people also contains a crucial component powered by sight, and this, too, has complicated implications for Sara's empowerment. Sara, for example, sees Carrisford when he is ill and guilty, and she pities him. As a result, she is already disposed to like him when they meet. Elsewhere, Carrisford's servant watches Sara through the skylight as she tells her stories, and the fantastic changes to her room that Sara makes as she pretends that it is a lovely space instead of a verminous attic affect him as well. Sara also watches a happy, wealthy family through their window, envying their domestic bliss, setting up the happy ending when Sara is not only returned to the upper class domestic hearth but also becomes close friends with this very family. Most importantly, however, Carrisford cannot see Sara until the end of the novel. This, more than Minchin's unkindness or Sara's hunger, is the crucial problem in the novel. It is only when Sara is presented to Carrisford's sight that the mystery is solved and Sara restored to her proper station. Being seen is a key factor in affective discipline, which is why Ellen Montgomery craves spiritual surveillance by John and the other disciplinarians she loves when they cannot watch her physically. This is another way in which the traditionally private discipline of affection is necessarily public: it cannot take place entirely within the disciplinarian or the disciplined subject.[2]

The discipline that works on the fathers, biological and otherwise, of these novels relies heavily on the girls presenting themselves to be seen.

Although A Little Princess inherits a model of discipline powered in part by surveillance, surveillance that will become less important and even offensive in later orphan girl novels, there is a significant change in the genre that finds expression in Burnett's novel. Whereas Ellen, Capitola, and Rose are very conscious of the discipline they were enacting, Rebecca and Sara represent a new disciplining girl, one who frequently disciplines accidentally. This is fundamentally the same pattern we see when Rebecca unconsciously motivates Jeremiah Cobb through sympathy or convinces his horse to desire what Rebecca desires. Sara can use stories and other forms of intentional discipline to keep Lottie from crying or help Ermengarde remember her lessons, but the most spectacular successes she has come about when she doesn't know she is being heard. Although she speaks her desires aloud, she has no idea that Carrisford's servant is listening to her, and if she had known he was listening, she might have changed what she said. Increasingly, when these girls use affective discipline successfully, they do it without meaning to.

It seems likely that this newly accidental discipline comes about because, as in the case of Wiggin, women writers at the turn of the century were growing uncomfortable with the ramifications of emotional manipulation. Wiggin and the orphan girl novelists who wrote so compellingly in this tradition borrowed from sentimentalism knew the disciplinary structures that underlay the formula that guided their plots, and they could hardly have missed the power offered to women and girls through those structures, but in the new century, they began both to endorse affective discipline and distance their heroines from it. Thus, starting with Rebecca and continuing pointedly with Sara, the new orphan girl protagonists best used affective discipline when they used it accidentally. Although it was once the right of a woman, indeed her obligation, emotional manipulation of men in the early years of the twentieth century was no longer a morally uncomplicated exercise, even and especially for the women writing in the sentimental tradition.

Not only does the new discomfort with moral suasion force good discipline to become accidental; Burnett's first orphan girl novel also explicitly outlaws the crueler forms of affective discipline. When Sara's fortune is restored, she leaves Minchin's school without a backward glance. Minchin is upset by this and angry that her "kindness," as she has always called it, goes unrewarded. Her sister, however, has quite a different reading of what has happened. In an extended and powerful speech, Amelia Minchin criticizes her sister for the many evils she has committed, even taking herself to task for overworking, underfeeding, and generally abusing a girl who had done nothing wrong. But, as Amelia points out, Sara would never stoop to retribution:

> "And now you've lost her," she cried wildly; "and some other school will get her and her money; and if she were like any other child she'd tell how she's been treated, and all our pupils would be taken away and we should be ruined. And it serves us right; but it serves you right more than it does me, for you are a hard woman, Maria Minchin, you're a hard, selfish, worldly woman!" (230)

But however much the two of them may deserve public humiliation, Amelia is right: Sara will not use it against them. Amelia's speech is as comical as it is lengthy, filled with gasps, sobs, hysterical laughter, and finally brought to an end by smelling salts. But it reveals an important change in the history of non-physical discipline. Whereas nineteenth-century novels relied on reputation as proof against misuse of power, the most public face of affective discipline is no longer appropriate for these authors. Recall, for example, Capitola's punishment of young Le Noir after he maligned her own reputation. Rather than fill him with lead, as Hurricane thinks she should have done, Capitola relies on "intense mortification and public ridicule." This, for sentimental-era novels, is a correct, feminine alternative to physical coercion. But for early twentieth-century girls' novels, public disgrace is not an appropriate disciplinary technology. Affective discipline in this new age of the orphan girl story requires discipline to be both fortuitous and kind.

In her first orphan girl novel, Frances Hodgson Burnett performs the complicated task of both following the rules of sentimental-style discipline and pointing to the limitations of moral suasion. She simultaneously expands the powers of suasion through the effective storytelling strategies of her protagonist and demonstrates the voracious appetite of such stories, an appetite that can consume the discrete identity of even its skilled teller. In so doing, Burnett models the early twentieth-century understanding that affective discipline is too powerful a tool to ignore but too complicated a tool to be endorsed wholeheartedly.

CHAPTER SIX

Anne of Green Gables and the Return of Affective Discipline

With all the changes *Rebecca of Sunnybrook Farm* and *A Little Princess* make to the formula of affective discipline, it might seem that L. M. Montgomery's first orphan girl novel, 1908's *Anne of Green Gables*, is something of an anachronism. In the previous orphan girl novels of the new century, the genre pulled itself away from public and conscious affective discipline as well as from most of the other hallmarks of affective discipline in the sentimental tradition. It embraced story-telling as a way to enchant and thereby direct objects of discipline, particularly because storytelling allowed girls to discipline the people around them obliquely, sometimes even accidentally. With those changes in mind, Montgomery's first novel feels nostalgic: whereas the other books immediately preceding it dis-tanced themselves from affective discipline in the style of sentimentalism, *Anne of Green Gables* relentlessly recounts the successes of moral suasion. But in doing so, it echoes Wiggin's warning that the disciplinarian may regret her success.

Anne of Green Gables' portrait of sentimental-style discipline is thorough. Anne herself, for example, is frequently a target of discipline through love in ways that Ellen Montgomery was but Rebecca was not. Anne comes to Green Gables full of "queer" ways, including a complete lack of understanding of the Christian faith Marilla Cuthbert, her adoptive mother, wants to instill in her. To go about making Anne into a Christian, Marilla first tries forcing her to recite a prayer, but immediately the adoptive mother realizes that the "simple little prayer, sacred to white-robed childhood lisping at motherly knees, was entirely unsuited to this freckled witch of a girl who knew and cared nothing about God's love since she had never had it translated to her through the medium of human

love" (99). Marilla frequently tries empty morals and harsh (though never corporal) justice on Anne, but none of them works so well as affection. Matthew, her
brother and the only other occupant of Green Gables, is shy and kind, and the
only sort of attention he ever gives the child is loving. As a result, "he was free to
'spoil Anne'—Marilla's phrasing—as much as he liked. But it was not such a bad
arrangement after all; a little 'appreciation' sometimes does quite as much good
as all the conscientious 'bringing up' in the world" (263). Although harshness
never makes Anne act as Marilla wants her to—in one scene, Marilla's lack of
compassion drives Anne to lie, a sin for which Marilla later blames herself—acts
of kindness never fail to stir up obedient affection. As Marilla says, Anne is "one
of the sort you can do anything with if you only get her to love you" (96). Anne's
affection makes her obedient to all the right codes: like Ellen, she promises not
to read anything she should not (317), and like any good middle-class girl, she
declares that she does not envy the exquisite jewelry another woman wears but
prefers her own string of pearls. "I know Matthew gave me as much love with
them," she confides, as ever went to another woman along with more expensive
gifts (356). Anne looks very much like a disciplinary object who would be at
home in a girl's novel decades earlier.

   In a break with novels from the beginning of the tradition, Anne does use the
same kind of affective discipline, with the same successful results, on the adults
around her. The touch of her hand causes "something warm and pleasant" to fill
Marilla's heart ("a throb of the maternity she had missed, perhaps" [126]), and
an impulsive kiss "thrilled her" with a "sudden sensation of startling sweetness"
(144). The sight of Anne's pathetic face moves her to unaccustomed love, and the
knowledge of Anne's desires motivates Matthew to go to the store and buy Anne
exactly the sort of dress she has secretly wanted. Because Marilla refused to make
for Anne any new clothes other than "good, sensible, serviceable dresses, without
any frills and furbelows about them" (127–28), Anne's clothing has always been
less pleasant than that of the other girls, but she has never complained. When
Matthew arranges for a dress with puffy sleeves to be made for Anne, one of
his neighbors thinks, "I'm sure the child must feel the difference between her
clothes and the other girls'. But to think of Matthew taking notice of it! That
man is waking up after being asleep for over sixty years" (270). Here, Matthew's
motivation is clear to the reader, who benefits from Montgomery's floating point
of view by being able to watch Matthew's chain of thoughts as he infers Anne's
taste in clothes and acts on his love for her to buy this particular dress. Therefore,
there is some sense in *Anne of Green Gables* of the change that has taken place in

the story of affective discipline over the decades, the increasing ability of girls to discipline adults. However, and much more importantly for the orphan girl genre in the new century, the fact that *Anne* repeatedly points to the successes of affective discipline, indeed of affective discipline that is cunning (at least on Marilla's part) rather than accidental, makes its take on discipline feel out of touch with the direction of the rest of the genre. Affective discipline, which had begun to falter in *A Little Princess*, has new life in *Anne of Green Gables*.

The novel even resurrects physical correction—a mode of discipline so odious to most of the postsentimental orphan girl novels that they simply ignore it—in order to denounce it once more. For example, Marilla's neighbor and close friend Mrs. Lynde eagerly advises Marilla to use punishment rather than suasion. She recommends to Marilla the use of "a fair-sized birch switch. I should think *that* would be the most effective language for that kind of child" (116). But Lynde is not, at least until she changes her opinion of Anne, a sympathetic character. In fact, her children are conspicuously absent from the novel, perhaps implying that the mother who uses "a fair-sized birch switch" is a mother who should expect to be alone in her old age. Contrast this with the scene Eliza Warren painted in her guidebook for child rearing: whereas Warren's narrative followed up suasion with clapping hands and kisses for all, Montgomery makes Lynde's home notably quiet.

The novel does acknowledge some of the changes that have been made to affective discipline in the genre's recent history, but overall its take on affective discipline reiterates the genre's first ideas: affective discipline is an effective tool by which to control children as well as adults.[1] *Anne* contributes to the genre not by reinventing affective discipline but by arguing that *parents will regret using it*. In other words, *Anne* argues not just that affective discipline works, but that it works too well. Late in the novel, the narrator points out that Marilla herself knows this, although she may not admit it. "Marilla had almost begun to despair of ever fashioning this waif of the world into her model little girl of demure manners and prim deportment," the narrator explains. "Neither would she have believed that she really liked Anne much better as she was" (246). Matthew, too, whispers an objection to affective discipline where only the reader can hear, saying, "Don't give up all your romance, Anne. . . . A little of it is a good thing—not too much, of course—but keep a little of it, Anne, keep a little of it" (302). The march of discipline is unceasing, though, and Anne does grow up. This should make Marilla happy, since she has been busily stamping out Anne's childishness since the moment the girl appeared at her door. But the adoptive mother is surprised to find "a queer, sorrowful sense of loss" (331). Later, after she reads some of Anne's poetry—now polished and skillful, unlike the doggerel she'd earlier produced—Marilla begins to cry. Anne asks for an explanation, and Marilla says,

> I just couldn't help thinking of the little girl you used to be, Anne. And I was wishing you could have stayed a little girl, even with all your queer ways. You're grown up now and you're going away; and you look so tall and stylish and so—so—different altogether in that dress—as if you didn't belong in Avonlea at all—and I just got lonesome thinking it all over. (358)

The insight *Anne of Green Gables* brings to the genre is a surprisingly sorrowful warning of what happens when affective discipline works on little girls.

The truth is, though, that as the genre progresses, the girls need discipline less and less. As Marilla realizes very soon, "Anne was smart and obedient, willing to work and quick to learn; her most serious shortcoming seemed to be a tendency to fall into daydreams in the middle of a task and forget all about it until such time as she was sharply recalled to earth by a reprimand or a catastrophe" (101). Although the girls make humorous mistakes at the beginning of their stories—such as when Anne disastrously attempts to change the color of her hair or bake a cake for her teacher—they are never disobedient or defiant. Increasingly, the novels become tales of changing not the girls but the parents. For Montgomery's novel, this means that Marilla comes to appreciate the girlishness in Anne that love eliminates.

In fact, Marilla's regretful realization of what happens when children are successfully disciplined is perhaps best understood as a narrative not of how Anne receives discipline but of how she—unwittingly, of course—dispenses it. A scene from late in the novel suggests that this is just the case. When Anne returns to Avonlea after a successful career at Queen's College, she discovers, "in her own white room," a "flowering house-rose" that her adoptive mother has set on the window sill (375). The flower is more than a sign of welcome to the returning daughter; it is a marker of one of the novel's most important subplots: the transformation of the adult at the hands of the child. When Anne first came to Green Gables, Marilla—like a latter-day Aunt Fortune—set her face against any signs of frivolity, one of which was flowers in the bedroom, something for which Anne longed. Because Marilla at the end of the novel anticipates Anne's tastes and acts in accordance with them, the "house-rose" is evidence not only that Marilla has changed but that she has been molded by Anne's tastes.

Anne is, in many ways, the most disingenuous of the postsentimental orphan girl novels. Its tale of a girl who is successfully disciplined harkens back to sentimental orphan girl stories, making it a book out of step with the drift away from such narratives at the turn of the century. But even as Montgomery repeats this story, she frames it with poignancy by showing Marilla bemoaning the success of her discipline, therefore both telling the sentimental tale of the successful disciplining of a girl and wistfully wishing that story had never taken place. Similarly, even as it tells the story of how Anne comes into line with Marilla's wishes, the novel meticulously recounts the effect that Anne is having on her adoptive mother. In fact, a careful reading of the book reveals that Montgomery seems much *more* interested in Marilla's transformation than in Anne's. If *Rebecca* is the story of a girl whose individuality is confirmed by her interiority, tastes, and judicious management of character, *Anne* is the story of how its protagonist both—lamentably—gives up many of her most romantic impulses and provides a schematic—a recognizable pattern of characteristics that define Anne as an individual—for changes to be imposed on the mother.

The most obvious of Anne's interior traits that transfers to and redefines Marilla is a broad ability to, as Anne puts it, imagine. Before she has decided to allow Anne to stay at Green Gables on a trial basis, Marilla is frequently disturbed by Anne's imaginative personality: "She had an uncomfortable feeling that while this odd child's body might be there at the table her spirit was far away in some remote airy cloudland, borne aloft on the wings of imagination," the narrator explains. "Who would want such a child about the place?" (79). Shortly thereafter, Anne tries to make up a more "romantic," as she puts it, history of her years before Avonlea, but Marilla will hear none of it. "No," she says, "I don't want any of your imaginings. Just you stick to bald facts" (85). Anne's imagination is a major factor in the disruption she causes in her new home, as she is unable to concentrate on the mundane tasks of farm life, preferring instead the Tennyson-inspired visions of nobility that riddle the novel. Marilla therefore sees it as one of her chief goals to train these flights of fancy out of the girl, but despite herself, she develops something of an imagination herself. For example, she intuits the longing Anne has for a grown-up-style tea party with her best friend and even suggests it for her. Anne is beside herself with joy, clasping her hands and exclaiming, "How perfectly lovely! You are able to imagine things after all or else you'd never have understood how I've longed for that very thing" (178). The "imagination" Anne flags here is the product of Anne's discipline on Marilla; although Anne is herself an object of discipline in the novel, and Marilla thus impresses qualities on her, the child's qualities themselves become qualities that are impressed on the adult.

The battle between Anne's frivolity and Marilla's demure spiritual pragmatism is also one that produces a more mixed victory than might be expected. Anne makes outlandish and frequently inappropriate comments, and although Marilla at first stomps them out, Montgomery is careful to describe a character arc through Marilla's laughter, or initial lack thereof, that shows Marilla becoming more like Anne. When the girl says that another woman looks like "a gimlet," "Marilla smothered a smile under the conviction that Anne must be reproved for such a speech" (95). When Anne makes a similarly rude comment to their neighbor, Marilla "was as angry with herself as with Anne, because, whenever she recalled Mrs. Rachel [Lynde]'s dumbfounded countenance her lips twitched with amusement and she felt a most reprehensible desire to laugh" (118). Anne does apologize for the comment but so floridly that the apology seems more a game to her than penitence, and "Marilla was dismayed at finding herself inclined to laugh over the recollection. She had also an uneasy feeling that she ought to scold Anne for apologizing so well; but then, that was ridiculous!" (125). Elsewhere, Marilla collapses into "such a hearty and unusual peal of laughter that Matthew, crossing the yard outside, halted in amazement," asking himself, "When had he heard Marilla laugh like that before?" (175). Later, when she scolds Anne for another rude comment, she finds herself "striving to overcome that unholy tendency to laughter which she was dismayed to find growing upon her" (189–90). By the end of the novel, Marilla has given in and laughs without explanation or apology (e.g., 384). What she has learned from Anne is not just to laugh but to allow herself to say and do things that are socially inappropriate — precisely the behavior she has been educating out of Anne. Thus she can laugh at rude comments and even scold Mrs. Lynde herself (393), the very woman to whom she earlier forced Anne to apologize for rude behavior.

In Marilla's transformation, the novel imposes the traits that defined Anne onto Marilla herself. This transformation has direct consequences for the figure of the malleable child and hence for the history of individualism in Montgomery's genre. It is during this phase of the history of affective discipline that the fictional girl's duties transition from accepting discipline to dispensing it, and that change allows her to reshape the adults around her, even if they are simultaneously shaping her. The traits and even desires of the child subject become instrumental to the novel's happy ending. Thus, even though Marilla can warn Anne that she doesn't "believe in pampering vanity" and that her "serviceable dresses" should be sufficient for the little girl (127–28), and although Anne does suppress her longing for stylish clothes, Marilla and her brother actually change as much as Anne does. They learn to pay closer attention to her tastes and to act in accordance with them. By the time of Anne's graduation, Matthew and Marilla both have begun to buy things that will pamper Anne's vanity, as it were, and without being verbally prompted by the girl to do so (357). They do not become fashionable dressers themselves, but they do learn to seek out Anne's desires and change their own habits to flatter, even protect, those desires.

This reorganization of adult behavior and shopping around a girl's tastes is a cunning fictional representation of an important phenomenon in the period: the adaptation of the market to the presence of girlhood spending. This trend began at least as early as the Victorian age, when allowances were "considered valuable training in self-discipline" (Hunter 5), but during the Progressive Era—one of the early high points of consumer culture in U.S. history—girls' shopping and buying became increasingly important as both an economic and a cultural phenomenon. As retailers learned to appeal to this new buying force, they encouraged a sense among shoppers that they were individually important, that their desires and tastes were valid motivation for public actions such as buying. In this context, recall Jane H. Hunter's assertion that "middle-class girls, who were learning to discriminate in what they read, found shopping as well to be an arena in which they could demonstrate taste and through taste, *self*" (274). The store was just a local example of a national phenomenon in which the heretofore adult culture of production and consumption reorganized itself to cater to girls as equal citizens of a buyership whose only requisite for membership was money to spend.[2] Although, as Hunter argues, "Victorian mothers had not yet learned to defer to daughters' tastes" (275), early twentieth-century mothers were either learning just that or being circumvented by daughters who shopped for themselves. And it is no coincidence that this representation of shopping occupies such a memorable position in Montgomery's novel, which was after all a runaway best seller in the early history of a literary market aimed at girls. By this time, children knew well how to recognize literature marketed for them as well as how to earn and spend to obtain that literature.[3] Therefore, *Anne* not only contains a glimpse of the changes taking place in the shopping but is itself an example of how the formerly adult market began targeting the kinds of child spending that endorsed a conception of children as individuals.

The revisions to consumer identity offered by *Anne* and other classic orphan girl novels are revisions uniquely nuanced by affection, discipline, sentimental individualism, and perhaps their specifically North American contexts. Oddly enough, these novels often construct commodities in a way that emphasizes a pleasure in shopping that is subtly different from that emphasized elsewhere in Anglo culture. For example, Erika Diane Rappaport has convincingly argued that as nice as things in themselves were, shopping women in turn-of-the-century

London also and perhaps primarily enjoyed the *publicity* of shopping, the being in a marketplace, the experience of being courted to buy. But the public dimension of shopping is noticeably not a feature of enjoyable consumption in novels such as *Anne*, novels that are fundamentally antiurban. Acquiring is still pleasurable, as are the goods themselves, but the emphasis is now—novel-like—on a private pleasure, on the receiving of the goods and treasuring their significance in private. The point for these girls is not shopping for themselves, but training a man to know what goods the girl desires and teaching him to long to please her. The girl's desires are not exactly displaced onto the man, since the narrative makes plain the origins of the desire and since the grateful climax takes place when the *girl* receives the gift, not when the man buys it. Instead, the man is brought into resonance with the girl's desires, made to want what the girl wants—if only so he can give it away. If Rappaport is right that much of the shopping pleasure for London women was the thrill of shopping publicly in urban spaces, then the shopping imagined in nostalgic, rural novels such as *Anne of Green Gables* is strikingly private, driven by adults' self-effacing love for a girl whose individual tastes instruct their eager spending.

This is, again, not an unqualified advancement of the individual. Anne's arrival at adulthood is instead a mixture of successes and reversals with respect to her status as an individual. She is successfully disciplined, which means that the borders of herself are penetrated and the characteristics by which she is recognized are changed. But she also successfully disciplines, exporting her own traits and wielding her recognizable desires in such a way that she changes the people around her. Her performance outside of Green Gables, too, is marked by a pursuit of her own goals, and she does not submit to the boy who will become her husband in later novels but competes against him throughout her education for top marks in class and even the province's top academic awards. When, at the end of the novel, she chooses to return to Marilla to help maintain the family farm rather than pursue her own career, one could certainly argue that she chooses to efface herself and serve her family, just as a child educated in the Lockean system might. But her decision also keeps the farm in the family, and with no siblings, Anne's sacrifice also protects her future investment: Anne will almost certainly inherit Green Gables and become its sole proprietor when Marilla dies. In short, although the novel is very much the story of Anne becoming "of Green Gables," this is also the tale of Green Gables becoming of Anne: its owners become more like her, and the farm itself is maintained for her future assumption of its ownership.

CHAPTER SEVEN

The Secret Garden
and the Rajah's Master

Classic orphan girl novels regularly reflected the broader culture's ideas about loving discipline and the shifting subjectivity it engendered. At various points in their history, such books demonstrated a preference for shaping spirits rather than bodies, a tendency to invest citizens with rights that could be owned like tangible commodities, and even a concern that affective discipline might work *too* well. Novels in the mold of Susan Warner's breakthrough best seller therefore help us understand the history in which they participate. But there are just as many instances in which the history is a tool for better understanding the fiction, and nowhere is that clearer than in the case of Frances Hodgson Burnett's second orphan girl novel, the book on which her contemporary reputation is built. *The Secret Garden* has become one of the key texts of the field of children's literature in part because its secrets are so hard to tease out. One of those secrets, the mystery of its conclusion, can best be understood by placing it against the backdrop of the rich history of discipline in the sentimental mode.

Following on the success of *A Little Princess*, Frances Hodgson Burnett published *The Secret Garden* in 1911. It begins in India, with a spoiled, self-absorbed Mary Lennox still in possession of her father and mother until both are carried away by cholera. After much travel and multiple opportunities for Mary to earn her nickname of "Mistress Mary Quite Contrary," the orphan girl arrives at Misselthwaite Manor, the sometimes-home of her uncle, Mr. Craven, as well as, she discovers late one night, her invalid cousin, Colin. Left to her own devices, Mary builds strength and character, solving the twin mysteries of a hidden garden and Colin's long-dead mother. In the secrecy of the garden, Mary heals Colin, delivering him hale and hearty to his chastened father, who watches in delight as Colin beats Mary in a footrace they run in the secret garden.

This ending to the novel, in which Mary seems to disappear in favor of the restored Colin, has evoked a great deal of frustration in contemporary readers, frustration that is, frankly, understandable. Although the novel begins with petulant, spoiled Mary and follows her private character arc through most of its chapters, in the final pages, Mary's transformation from pouty to self-sufficient takes a back seat to Colin's transformation from physical and emotional invalid to strong, confident heir. That ending provokes no end of anxiety for readers today, as evidenced by Lissa Paul's important essay about feminist theory and children's literature. One of the centerpieces of her inquiry is the question of "why the story continues to resonate so strongly in me, even though I intensely dislike the way it turns from Mary's story into Colin's (a feeling I know I share with other readers, especially women)" (195). One such woman is Deborah O'Keefe, whose book is a catalog of girls' fiction that fails the young women it supposedly nurtures. As she complains,

> The Secret Garden created a wonderful group of equals supporting one an-other—Mary, Colin, the nature boy Dickon, Dickon's wholesome mother and sister, and the old gardener—until Burnett's devotion to the male aristocracy caused her to destroy the nurturing group, deify Colin, and abandon Mary. (138)

For readers such as O'Keefe, Burnett's betrayal means The Secret Garden must be rejected. Paul tries—"reluctantly"—to rescue the novel through an argument that "Burnett ends the story in accordance with the social and economic truths and values of her particular time and place" (197). From a feminist perspective— one that is clearly appropriate, given the centrality of gendered constructions of power in The Secret Garden as well as its postsentimental tendencies—the end of the novel is difficult to salvage, if indeed it deserves to be salvaged at all.

But read in the history of the debate over affective discipline, the conclusion reveals a much subtler meaning. According to common interpretations of the novel, the fact that it ends with a boy restored to health and reunited with his emotionally distraught father instead of with a girl growing up to become a capable lady is evidence of "Burnett's devotion to the male aristocracy." At this point in the story of girls' novels, however, many of the most popular books in the genre no longer focus the balance of their energies on shaping girls but rather on shaping men. To put it another way, at this point in the history of the orphan girl formula, the novels are figuring out how to discipline the male aristocracy.

Mary's physical absence from the end of the novel does not represent a capitulation to male dominance; although the story begins with Mary alone and follows her adventures in a mysterious place, *The Secret Garden* is never precisely a novel about what Mary does. Instead, it is a novel about how Mary, the novel's representative of girlhood, teaches men how to rule. *The Secret Garden* takes as its project the narration of the education of manhood. It continues the genre's debate over affective discipline, this time demonstrating how *good* it can be when a girl uses it on men. Through careful attention to Colin's moral being, Mary heals his physical body and teaches him how to use his power. It is a novel that explains what femininity should do with redirected masculine privilege, the father's law, his affection, and his wealth.

Key to the novel's project of masculine rehabilitation through affective discipline is a drastically revised version of the republican mother Linda K. Kerber describes. Like the mother in the domestic and sentimental periods Kerber studies, this mother is concerned with the boy child's body, training it up to be the body of a good man, and it is still clearly her responsibility to educate the boy who will inherit the legal power of the nation.[1] Kerber's republican mother is a pointedly American figure, and *The Secret Garden*, not unlike its author, is both British and American: the novel was probably written between the time Burnett left England in the fall of 1908 and returned in April 1910 (Gerzina 259–61), but its famous setting is widely regarded to be inspired by her cherished—and British—Maytham Hall (Gerzina 260). Thus, if one might expect to find echoes of the American republican mother in this novel about sick children, one might also expect to find traces of the Victorian mother preferred by the likes of Karl Pearson—who argued against the advancement of women's rights for fear of "the physical degradation of the race" (371)—or Arabella Kenealy—whose essay "The Talent of Motherhood" protested against a mother "forgetful of that grave trust[,] the welfare of her children, and, through them, the progress of the race" (458). But Colin has neither a republican nor a Victorian mother. Instead, motherhood separates from a biological mother and settles on the figure of the orphan girl. Because Colin's mother has died long before the novel's opening, there is no republican mother in residence to watch over the development of his body or morality. In many of the other novels in this genre, the father's body is stripped away by death, leaving only the privilege associated with his masculinity to be manipulated by effective affective girls, but *The Secret Garden* leaves the father incarnate—in his shape as both wealthy father and ailing son—and instead strips away the body of the mother. Her spirit, techniques, and obligations are therefore free to descend on Mary.

First among those obligations is Colin. He is a pale and despicable creature when Mary first hears him, howling hysterically down the long halls of his father's empty house. His father takes every opportunity to leave Misselthwaite, unable to countenance his wreck of a son, leaving in his stead a host of medical professionals and servants who cater to the boy's every whim and unwittingly reinforce his hysteria. Mary, however, is able to make an immediate improvement in Colin's health. Whereas the caretakers in place when Mary arrives focus their attentions on Colin's body, keeping it from stress and coddling it in order to heal him—something they doubt they will be able to do—Mary turns her attention to Colin's spirit. Although the most visible change in Colin's health throughout the novel is his strengthening body—culminating in that controversial footrace—Colin's corporeal improvement is an effect of his improving noncorporeal health. His doctor completely fails to attend to this dimension of Colin's well-being, in fact harming Colin further through his mishandling of Colin's spirit. Early in the boy's recovery, Mary overhears the doctor leaving the nurse with very specific instructions about Colin's mental diet. "He must not talk too much," the doctor warns, or "forget that he was ill" or "that he was very easily tired." Mary, however, "thought that there seemed to be a number of uncomfortable things [Colin] was not to forget." The doctor's precautions follow on the heels of a sudden improvement in the boy's health after Mary's first overtures of friendship, but the doctor does not make the connection between the two. Colin spells it out for him. "I *want* to forget [my illness]," he informs the doctor. "She makes me forget it. That is why I want her" (115).[2] Nonetheless, throughout the story, adults try to make Colin concentrate on his limitations. They do not intend to cause Colin pain, but by mishandling his interior health, they are frustrating a healing process that only Mary seems able to master. As he improves, Mary begins to think of him as a little Rajah, finally growing into his power. Colin makes plain the relationship between that improvement and Mary, despite the adults' conviction that he should remember his illness:

> "I don't want to remember," interrupted the Rajah, appearing again. "When I lie by myself and remember I begin to have pains everywhere and I think of things that make me begin to scream because I hate them so. If there was a doctor anywhere who could make you forget you were ill instead of remembering it I would have him brought here." And he waved a thin hand which ought really to have been covered with royal signet rings made of rubies. "It is because my cousin makes me forget that she makes me better." (151)

Here, the orphan girl protagonist is not the object of discipline but rather its only successful practitioner. Her efforts stand in opposition to those of adults, and the novel's happy ending rests on Mary's success in spite of the bumbling discipline of adults. As the novel's one good parent says, "It was a good thing that little lass came to th' Manor. It's been th' makin' o' her an' th' savin' o' him" (195).

Colin, the nurses, the doctor, their neighbors, and even the servants in the house all attribute Colin's improvement to Mary, the little disciplinarian; but Mary herself complicates things by crediting something else. After she has shared her secret, the garden Colin's mother tended before her death, with Colin, the two arrange to go visit the garden in private. It has been closed off by Colin's father, who finds its associations with his lost wife too painful, and the years have hidden its presence from the outside. It is in this private space that Colin can exercise his muscles without the adults finding out what he is doing. When one adult, the old gardener Ben Weatherstaff, accidentally discovers what they are doing and where they have been hiding, Mary begs him not to let the secret out. "The chief thing to be remembered," she implores, "was that Colin was getting well—getting well. The garden was doing it. No one must let him remember about having humps and dying" (178). Although everyone else gives credit for Colin's improvement to Mary, she herself credits the garden. In truth, both play a role, and they aren't as contradictory as they first appear. Mary, after all, is given responsibility for the garden by Mr. Craven himself, although he doesn't realize that the garden she is asking for permission to tend is the garden he has forbidden anyone to enter. In a telling speech, Craven grants her complete power over the garden, saying, "You can have as much earth as you want." He remarks that she reminds him of his wife in her desire to garden and tells her that "when you see a bit of earth you want . . . take it, child, and make it come alive" (93). Craven speaks here of literal earth, but his injunction works in the novel as carte blanche not only to bring life to the secret garden but also to the "bit of earth" who is his son. In granting Mary a right that seems small and unimportant to him, Craven gives her a responsibility that the novel plays out to its logical ends. The literal garden is Mary's responsibility, but that garden is heavily overdetermined in the book. Her care of the garden entails guardianship of the physical plot of land, the mother whose memory is inextricably bound up with the garden, the boy who so desperately needs to come alive, and the intangible friendship they build in the private—one might even say domestic—space of the garden. Therefore, it is true that Mary, Colin's mother, and the garden all three heal Colin: the latter two are the responsibility of the girl herself.

But Mary does not just heal Colin; she also rules him, and this is one of the main triumphs celebrated by the novel. The happy ending of the novel comes about when Colin is given full health by Mary, but the terms of her treatment have always made clear that Mary is in charge of the emerging Rajah. Mary's impact on Colin after she first discovers him becomes quickly obvious. As Mrs. Medlock, the chief caretaker, puts it, "The nurse was just going to give up the case because she was so sick of him, but she says she doesn't mind staying now you've gone on duty with her" (117). From the beginning of the children's relationship, the novel makes clear that there is a very particular "duty" in Mary's hands. The servants, for example, comment that Colin "had found his master, and good for him," and the butler, "who was a man with a family, had more than once expressed his opinion that the invalid would be all the better 'for a good hiding'" (154). But he doesn't get a hiding, he gets an orphan girl from India. And her jurisdiction over him will not end with his recovery; it won't even end with the close of the book. "If he does live," Medlock theorizes, "and that Indian child stays here I'll warrant she teaches him that the whole orange does not belong to him. . . . And he'll be likely to find out the size of his own quarter" (162). Mary's responsibility, like that of republican and Victorian mothers, is to train boys to be good men.

And there is good reason to think that Mary will maintain her affectionate grip on Colin past his boyhood—after all, Mary also manages his father. Like A Little Princess, Burnett's second orphan girl novel tells the story of a father restored to the family. The rat father that Sara tames through kindness and provides with food he then takes to his rat family is the first example in A Little Princess of a father's relationship with his family enabled by the little girl, but the happy ending of that novel relies on Sara's reconnection with her own father's inheritance, which is itself made possible by Sara's stories. In The Secret Garden, the garden is the means by which Mary restores Mr. Craven to his family. As Colin's strength grows in the private demesnes of Mary's garden, Mr. Craven is suddenly struck while abroad with the conviction that he has failed as a father. At the precise moment Colin is standing in the garden professing that he is not just healed but will live forever, Mr. Craven experiences an unbidden moment of understanding and resolves to return home. Craven arrives just in time for the fully healed Colin to come crashing into him as he wins the race that Mary cheerfully loses. The healed son and repentant father collide in Mary's private space and enjoy the happy reunion that closes the book.

Along the way, Mary also reunites father (and son, for that matter) with mother, marking her power over the one remaining familial position. Colin has always been marked by similarities with his mother's body, but until Mary comes along to heal his spirit, he cannot live up to her inheritance. Throughout the novel, various characters comment on the physical similarity between mother and child, as when Dickon hears of Mary's first sighting of the boy. When Mary describes "the small ivory-white face and the strange black-rimmed eyes," Dickon tells her that they are "just like his mother's eyes, only hers was always laughin'." This is the reason Mr. Craven stays away from the house: Colin is and yet isn't his beloved wife. People say, Dickon tells Mary, that "Mr. Craven can't bear to see him when he's awake[,] an' it's because his eyes is so like his mother's an' yet looks so different in his miserable bit of a face" (124–25). What this means is that in order for Colin to be fixed, he must be both endowed with masculinity (strength, confidence, and the other attributes he develops as his hysteria falls away) through Mary's attentions *and* feminized into the position formerly held by his mother. Mary sees the similarities between mother and son easily, and as he heals, she tells him, "You are so like her now . . . that sometimes I think perhaps you are her ghost made into a boy." Colin is intrigued by her insight and tells her he believes that "if I were her ghost—my father would be fond of me" (209). His hopes are well founded, as Dickon's mother tells him. She says that he is "so like thy mother tha' made my heart jump," and Colin, with endearing awkwardness, asks her if "that will make my father like me." She answers, "Aye, for sure, dear lad" and gives his shoulder "a soft quick pat" (215). Colin's feminization comes through Mary's kindness, and Mr. Craven's return to the family is secured by its completion. Mary already knows what Mr. Craven desires: his wife. She also knows that Colin has the physical makings of the deceased wife, but what he lacks is her spirit. This is what she revives, making him a manly man and a feminized man at the same time. It is at the moment of this success that the novel ends.

As Mary manipulates the men around her so that they either return to the families who need them, shape up into better prospective husbands, or just learn the extent of their own privilege, there is remarkably little exterior discipline enacted on the little girl herself. Mary's biological parents ignore her to the point of negligence, and when she arrives in Misselthwaite Manor she is clearly an unwanted burden. As such, she is left largely to her own devices. The story is filled with forbidden spaces and actions, but Mary doesn't know most of the taboos. At any rate, she obeys few of them. After all, as the narrator explains, Mary "had never been taught to ask permission to do things, and she knew nothing at all about authority," and as a result she never even considers asking Mrs. Medlock for permission to range around the house or its gardens (42). Medlock does contend that Mary needs looking after (45), but no one ever arrives to see to Mary's rearing. Instead, Mary receives bits of advice from Dickon's mother and sister, who are too busy to spend much time on her, and fixes herself. She asks for a jump rope when she needs it, asks for the "bit of earth" that changes the direction of the story, and generally improves herself while the adults go on with their business. *The Secret Garden* is a novel about how a little girl can successfully discipline herself when she needs to and then discipline the men around her. Even Mary's bad traits, the ones she disciplines out of herself, figure in the novel as good things. The novel's happy ending, for example, is enabled by Mary's lack of appreciation for authority, since it is while Mary is wandering where she shouldn't that she discovers Colin moaning in his sickbed. Further, although she gets permission from Mr. Craven to care for her garden, she never tells him that the garden she has discovered is the precise garden he has forbidden anyone to enter, so both crucial discoveries—the hysterical Colin and the overdetermined garden—come when Mary is *not* obeying. Medlock herself, usually the voice of conservative order in the novel, agrees that Mary's unintentional disobedience has been a blessing. "You are a sly young one to listen and get out of your bed to go following things up like you did that night," she says of the night Mary discovered Colin. "But there's no saying it's not been a sort of blessing to the lot of us" (117). Thus, even Medlock's half rebuke turns into gratitude. Mary is rarely the object of other people's discipline, but she does transform in the course of the novel from an insufferable brat to a joyful child on the verge of beauty. The discipline that works this change in her is one wrought as she heals Colin. And as the novel goes on, she stops doing naughty things and does only what is right, even scrupulously so. By working on the earth—meaning both the secret garden and Colin—she sees to it accidentally that everything else she does is right, too.

The most important question remaining for this novel is this: what are the limits of Mary's power? This question, too, has clear implications for a feminist approach to the novel, and it, too, can best be answered by turning to the history of child-centered discipline that informs Burnett's story. Karen Sánchez-Eppler's observation of how power in nineteenth-century temperance fiction passes through the child en route to reforming the father without granting the child any agency is again relevant. In Burnett's novel, although Mary has gotten what she wanted, her discipline and the novel's happy ending leave the basic power structures unaltered. Neither temperance novels nor those in the tradition of the sentimental orphan girl novel brought about any real change for actual children, but Sánchez-Eppler's point is that even the fictional children lose; although they are conduits for power, they are not truly wielders of that power, and it does not serve them except insofar as their wishes coincide with the father's needs. In these girls' novels, however, especially toward the end of the genre's history, the girls themselves do get what they want in addition to what the father needs. And what they want is no longer just a father who won't beat them. They do get a returned, feminized father, his masculinity assured by the affective discipline to which he subjects himself, as in the case of Colin's father. They also get boys, future husbands, and fathers who will be good to them. The accomplishment here is not quite the same as in nineteenth-century temperance novels, because there the victory is that the father will stop his negative behavior. In the late orphan girl novels, the victory is that the father will not only give up his former bad ways—absence, neglect, hysteria—but will begin behaving in accordance with the girls' needs and wishes. More than guaranteeing the absence of negative behavior, the affective discipline in all its various forms throughout these later novels guarantees a father who will do good things.

In *The Secret Garden*, disciplining—"reforming," in the parlance of the temperance novel—the father and future father is the main focus of the book, so the benefits given the girl are easy to miss, but Mary transforms her miserable new home into a place she enjoys, she gets to play where others are forbidden, and she gains dominion over the garden, the son, the father, and even the mother. These victories look false to a readers today because all the property is still in the hands the male subjects, but there has been a significant change from the children of temperance fiction—who erased themselves in order to keep from being beaten—and the girls in the final phase of this genre, who increasingly have personal needs that the people (and places, in Mary's instance) they discipline manage to meet.

CHAPTER EIGHT

Pollyanna and
Anxious Individualism

Because *The Secret Garden* and novels like it descend from the sentimental novel, they traditionally keep the mother out of the crosshairs of affective discipline. After all, the sentimental novel detailed the empire of the mother, and she guided rather than absorbed disciplinary intimacy. But, as *The Secret Garden* demonstrates, the mother can be stripped of her body just as can the father, allowing the spirit of motherhood to descend on the girl herself, with all its attendant rights and responsibilities. This trend is first explicit in *The Secret Garden*, but its origins go back at least as far as *Anne of Green Gables*, in which Marilla learns to laugh through Anne's discipline and comes to prize the girlhood she has lamentably disciplined out of Anne. In *Eight Cousins*, too, the genre is already toying with how to change the symbolic mother when Alec selects from a variety of possible feminine modes of discipline—as represented by the various aunts— in his experiment with Sara. In the next novel in the genre's history, Eleanor H. Porter's 1913 *Pollyanna*, the mother becomes the chief object of discipline, and the disciplined, disembodied father takes on a new role, one that dramatically extends the power at the command of the disciplining girl.

Pollyanna opens on the titular orphan's Aunt Polly, who is reluctantly but dutifully preparing her home to receive the only offspring of a marriage Polly tried to prevent. When Pollyanna does arrive, she is desolate in the wake of her beloved father's death, but she displays a remarkable ability to concentrate on what is good. Indeed, Pollyanna herself frequently remarks on this ability: to the cook, another orphan, a fallen woman, her mother's former lover, an invalid, a doctor, and just about anyone else who gives her an opportunity. In so doing, she teaches her adoptive town to love her and enjoy their lives despite their personal sorrows. Pollyanna's infectious joy, she reveals, is her only inheritance from her father, and it is with this power that she is able to discipline the people who, in very short order, come to love her.

The central conflict of the novel is built out of the extraordinary resistance one person, Aunt Polly, shows to Pollyanna's discipline. Polly begins the novel with a thin existence characterized by routine and repression. She ends it smiling, cheerful, with her libido again in bloom as she opens herself to a romance that she had forbidden years before Pollyanna's arrival. Delaying her rebirth is her edict against Pollyanna's favored disciplinary technology: the glad game. Pollyanna's efforts to heal her aunt repeatedly fail because Polly will not hear of the game in which Pollyanna attempts to find something, no matter how minor, to be glad about in the face of disappointment. To overcome Aunt Polly's resistance, Porter's novel expands the explicit scope of disciplinary intimacy to extents rarely seen in the domestic venues of previous orphan girl novels. In order to change her aunt, Pollyanna must first discipline the entire community in which they live.

The glad game opens the hearts of the community to the orphan girl, who makes some dramatic changes in even the most trenchant misanthropes, chief among them John Pendleton. Pendleton is a confirmed bachelor and miser, and the other members of the community have grown accustomed to his condescending airs. Pollyanna, however, forces him into conversation, and, when he is incapacitated following an accident, begins a friendship with him that allows her to teach him the glad game and win his heart. Before long, Pendleton has been so drastically changed that he asks—or rather begs—Pollyanna to let him adopt her. As he makes his case, he tells her straightforwardly that if she would join him, all his privilege would be at her disposal:

> How do you suppose I'm going to be "glad" about anything—without you? Why, Pollyanna, it's only since you came that I've been even half glad to live! But if I had you for my own little girl, I'd be glad for—anything. And I'd try to make you glad, too, my dear. You shouldn't have a wish ungratified. All my money, to the last cent, should go to make you happy. (146)

Although Pollyanna chooses to remain with her aunt—after all, she hasn't finished disciplining Aunt Polly yet—she does manage to redirect Pendleton's affection to an object she considers more suitable. When she encounters an orphan boy who has run away from the orphanage rather than live out his childhood in a home without "folks," as he puts it, Pollyanna uses her influence with Pendleton to make him take the boy. As Pendleton tells her aunt, "I have seen Jimmy Bean and . . . he's going to be my boy hereafter. Tell [Pollyanna] I thought she would be—*glad* to know. I shall adopt him, probably" (191). Pollyanna's unique form of affective discipline not only reforms Pendleton but restores him and his affection to the community, turning his depressing bachelor's house into a home for both Pendleton and Bean. Near the novel's close, Pendleton tells Pollyanna "what a fine boy Jimmy was getting to be, and how well he was doing. Jimmy had told her what a first-rate home he had, and what bang-up 'folks' Mr. Pendleton made. And both had said that it was all owing to her" (208). Porter's novel invents a new form of disciplinary intimacy and makes a point of showing how its successes can be credited to the little girl herself.

Pendleton's reformation is a microcosm of the changes Pollyanna makes throughout the community en route to the climactic transformation of Aunt Polly. By introducing this game and its strategy of finding a silver lining, Pollyanna changes the frustrated adults, who then go and share their new happiness with other members of the community. Paul Ford, the new minister in town, is one such disciplinary object. Pollyanna finds him taking a walk while he composes his next sermon, and she changes his relationship with his parishioners as a result. Ford is struggling with mounting frustration over his flock, who have long-standing habits of squabbling over minor disagreements, pointing out motes in one another's eyes while ignoring the beams in their own. The sermon he is in the process of composing is full of the anger he has been nursing over this church full of failures, and although he seems uncomfortable with his plans to browbeat his congregation, he can conceive of no other way to discipline them. Pollyanna, whose father was a minister himself, is well familiar with the kinds of squabbles that can derail a church body, and she suggests to Ford the kind of sermon her father would have preached. The plethora of "rejoicing texts" her father discovered in the Bible—the hundreds of verses in which the reader is enjoined to be glad—seem to Pollyanna a much better choice of text for a sermon to a squabbling congregation, and by the end of their talk, Ford agrees (160–61). Rather than use his pulpit to denounce his congregation, a form of discipline that even Ford senses would not succeed, he abandons his first sermon and pens another grounded in gladness:

> Thus it happened that the Reverend Paul Ford's sermon the next Sunday was a veritable bugle call to the best that was in every man and woman and child that heard it; and its text was one of Pollyanna's shining eight hundred:
>
> *Be glad in the Lord and rejoice, ye righteous, and shout for joy all ye that are upright in heart.* (163)

Pollyanna touches many hearts with her form of affective discipline through personal contact, but the spread of that discipline through the community is enabled by the eagerness with which her students communicate it to one another. In a very short time, the community as a whole has been disciplined to be glad like Pollyanna.

Pollyanna's discipline needs to have a wide scope in order to convert her aunt and, in a surprising twist, Pollyanna herself. Near the end of the novel, when Aunt Polly still resists Pollyanna's ministrations but after the community has been indoctrinated, Pollyanna suffers a horrible accident that leaves her bedridden. Her aunt calls in a famous specialist to consider her case, but the doctor has only bad news: Pollyanna will never walk again. Although they try to shield the girl from this dreadful news, she accidentally overhears it and—not unlike Colin Craven, who overhears his pessimistic diagnosis and reacts by making himself more ill—is overwhelmed by depression. Now, Pollyanna rejects her own game and sinks into a gloom from which there is no hope of recovery because she can find nothing to be glad about. The news of the little disciplinarian's defeat spreads across the town in a flash, from one of her converts to another, and one by one they come to convince Pollyanna to be glad again. Pollyanna's aunt prohibits these visitors from seeing the little girl, so they are forced to leave their messages with Aunt Polly. The result is that Polly hears, over and over again, of the very game she refused to entertain from the orphan girl herself. One such instance comes with the visit of Mrs. Payson. Payson is, for some reason darkly hinted but never fully explained, a shunned woman, but Pollyanna has struck up a friendship with her, her children, and her rowdy husband. Aunt Polly is predictably stunned to receive this woman in her own house, and Payson herself is uncomfortable there, but she is willing to cross class lines in order to make an attempt at making Pollyanna glad again. She says,

> Well, we've heard now that she's fretting her poor little life out of her, because she can't play [the game] no more—that there's nothing to be glad about. And that's what I came to tell her today—that maybe she can be a little glad for us, 'cause we've decided to stick to each other, and play the game ourselves. I knew she would be glad, because she used to feel kind of bad—at things we said, sometimes. Just how the game is going to help us, I can't say that I exactly see, yet. But maybe 'twill. Anyhow, we're going to try—'cause she wanted us to. Will you tell her? (201)

Polly will admit no visitors to Pollyanna's sickroom, but she does convey these messages. Each message includes some allusion to the glad game, a game the visitors assume Polly knows herself. The affective discipline Pollyanna has sown throughout the community comes back to her home, and the messages in which it is communicated "stirred Miss Polly to action" (191): to track down the meaning of these messages.

Polly's action is the long-deferred climax of her own slow change. She begins the novel attending to Pollyanna only out of "duty"—a word Polly uses throughout the novel to explain her reluctant care for Pollyanna.[1] Even when Pollyanna tells her aunt how happy her days are—surely a remarkable statement considering that her beloved father has just died—her aunt "wearily" replies that "I am gratified, of course, that they are happy, but I trust that they are profitable, as well—otherwise I should have failed signally in my duty" (75). Slowly that grudging attitude yields to one marked by genuine care, as Nancy points out when Polly is worried about Pollyanna's prolonged absence one day. This worry is an important sign, Nancy argues, because "it means she's at last getting' down somewheres near human—like folks; an' that she ain't jest doin' her duty by ye all the time" (150). During Pollyanna's convalescence, Aunt Polly hovers over Pollyanna, and Nancy sobs to the gardener that "ye didn't need ter mor'n look at her aunt's face ter see that 'twa'n't no duty that was eatin' her. Yer hands don't shake, and yer eyes don't look as if ye was tryin' ter hold back the Angel o' Death himself, when you're jest doin' yer *duty*, Mr. Tom—they don't, they don't!" (166–67).

Polly's growing affection for Pollyanna works a great number of changes in the once-cold aunt, but Pollyanna's final victory is forced by the child's inability to play the glad game and the community's efforts to make her play it again.[2] The action to which the repeated messages stir Polly is pulling aside Nancy, who was one of Pollyanna's first affective targets, and asking her for an explanation of this mysterious game. Once Nancy explains it, Polly resolves to play it herself. This is the final victory for the orphan girl's disciplinary project, and at last Pollyanna is glad again:

> Miss Polly sternly forced her voice to be cheerfully matter-of-fact. "Nancy told me. I think it's a beautiful game. I'm going to play it now—with you."
>
> "Oh, Aunt Polly—*you?* I'm so glad! You see, I've really wanted you most of anybody, all the time." (206)

Her aunt's transformation is total following this conversion. She allows the local doctor, who has heard of a breakthrough that will eventually heal Pollyanna, to examine the child, and in the process the spinster heals an old rift between the two of them that has prevented the marriage they both desire. Polly shows the doctor in, then slips out of the room, blushing, and the doctor tells his patient that "one of the very gladdest jobs you ever did has been done today." Following the examination, Polly confides to her niece that her long-delayed marriage is finally at hand. She says, "Pollyanna, dear, I'm going to tell you—the very first one of all. Someday I'm going to give Dr. Chilton to you for your—uncle. And it's you that have done it all. Oh, Pollyanna, I'm so—happy! And so—glad!—darling!" (216). The ebullient aunt at the end of the novel is the product of Pollyanna's discipline. As with the story of Mary and Colin, the orphan girl has brought life to a spiritually dead mother—in this case, the adoptive mother.

Aunt Polly's word choice in her marriage announcement at Pollyanna's bedside encapsulates the nature of the relationship of the father to the orphan girl here in the late period of the genre. Although Dr. Chilton's imminent marriage to Pollyanna's adoptive mother means that he will soon have full control over Pollyanna, Polly represents that marriage as a gift of the father *to* the daughter: "Someday," she says, "I'm going to give Dr. Chilton to you." He will be a gift to her in the sense that these novels increasingly promote, which is that the father represents a locus of privilege that can be repositioned by the disciplining daughter.

But the novel first presents the idea of a father as a gift long before Chilton's entrance. The father's body in its form as the soon-to-be uncle is controlled by Pollyanna, or more accurately by the affective discipline she wields, because it is not until everyone has submitted to her discipline that Chilton is able to come into the home. But from the very beginning of the novel, another father's body has been manipulated for the sake of this discipline: that of Pollyanna's biological father. Unlike Chilton, Pollyanna's father is never permitted into the Harrington home during Pollyanna's life. Because Aunt Polly's sister disobeyed her family's wishes and married a poor minister, the young couple was abandoned to its fate, one that turned out to be very harsh indeed. Pollyanna's mother dies long before the novel's opening, without reconciling with her family, and Pollyanna's father dies a few years thereafter, still in poverty. When Pollyanna departs the only home she has known, she leaves behind her father's body, but she takes with her his ideology. Porter presents the glad game as an inheritance from her father. It is a representation of his personal philosophy in that it is the strategy by which he both lived his life and reared his daughter.

The book insists on this close relationship between the game and Pollyanna's father, particularly through the twist of logic that keeps Pollyanna from telling Polly about the game herself. Her aunt tells Pollyanna from the very beginning of their acquaintance that "I do not care to have you keep talking of your father to me" (29), but when Pollyanna tells others about the game, she is careful to mention its association with her father. To one person, she says, "Why it's a game. Father told it to me, and it's lovely. . . . We've played it always, ever since I was a little, little girl" (38). Like Chilton's body, Polly has forbidden the entrance of this father's spirit into her presence. The game can't even be spoken of in Polly's presence because Pollyanna is unable to conceive of the game in language that could avoid his mention. Nancy spells out precisely this relationship when she explains why Polly is one of the very few people in the town who doesn't know of the game, even though she lives with its prophet: "Miss Pollyanna told me long ago that she couldn't tell [Polly], 'cause her aunt didn't like ter have her talk about her father—an' 'twas her father's game, an' she'd have ter talk about him if she did tell it. So she never told her" (181). When Polly finally approaches Nancy for an explanation of the game, Nancy says the same thing to her mistress's face: "Beggin' yer pardon, ma'am, you told her not ter speak of—her father; so she couldn't tell ye. 'Twas her father's game, ye see" (204).

Thus, although the father has been stripped of his body by the narrative, there is something of his power remaining, and every conflict in the novel revolves around how the orphan girl will wield the suasive tool identified with this bodiless father. To some degree, this is just another instance of a conservative narrative finding a way to reinstate the father: even when the patriarch is dead, he is still present. But it is vital to remember that this is a father who has been reduced to an affective discipline that is deployed either by the girl herself or those who work in service of that girl's needs. Through the glad game, Pollyanna makes available to herself Pendleton's extensive wealth, she changes the disciplinary tactics of the town's chief religious figure to tactics of which she approves, she places the orphan Bean where she wants him, and most dramatically of all, she takes possession of her aunt, the tyrant who at the beginning of the novel ruled over Pollyanna. As Pollyanna herself says, "Oh, Aunt Polly, I'm so glad you belong to me!" (171). This is the latest iteration of a struggle for control over the father that has been taking place throughout the novels in the genre. When Capitola and the other women of *The Hidden Hand* used their moral prerogative to instruct their men, when Sara conjured her father's friend into fulfilling her dreams in *A Little Princess*, and when Kate Douglas Wiggin imagined a wealthy young man spellbound by a woman's story, they were pondering how to discipline men. And even in the most conservative text of the genre, *The Wide, Wide World*, the formula dreams of killing off the father to see what happens to authority next. By stripping away the body of the father but retaining his power, these novels make conceivable a way of placing some agency in the hands of the imaginary child. Earlier novels did not explore this possibility, and in *Pollyanna* it is possible only because the novel constructs a version of privilege that is not defined by the body in which it is contained. The father still lives, but his privilege is worked at the whim of the orphan girl.

In this way, *Pollyanna* defines the role that bodies will play in the powerful technology of affective discipline. By making the protagonist herself an invalid, Porter's novel revises the motif of child invalids with which the genre has earlier experimented, raising its stakes. In *Eight Cousins*, the first novel in the sentimental orphan girl tradition explicitly published for girls, Louisa May Alcott introduces this motif with the figure of Mac, one of Rose's many cousins. Through sunstroke and overexertion of his eyes, Mac falls so ill that he must remain in bed and is not even allowed read the books he loves so dearly. Not unpredictably, considering the theme of self-sacrifice inherited from the sentimental novel, Rose volunteers to tend his sick bed and read to him. Through this act, "Rose, quite unconsciously, won not only the respect of her cousins, but their gratitude and affection likewise" (110). She later uses these emotional attachments to discipline them into better habits. In fact, nearly every novel in the genre following *Eight Cousins* features some scene, no matter how short, in which an invalid is cared for. In *The Secret Garden* and *Pollyanna*, invalidism is a major problem.[3] These scenes often have the predictable effect of developing sympathy between invalid and caretaker, as between Rose and Mac, but they also develop a more important point: moral suasion not only controls morals, it controls bodies. Porter's novel refines this scene and makes its resolution crucial to the happy ending by making the protagonist herself the invalid. Pollyanna's illness is a test case in which the body is again subjugated to the spirit. This is the reason the novel explains at such length the efforts the community goes to in order to discipline Pollyanna with her own technology. Her body is healed as a result of a confluence of effects of her discipline: she has made the doctor care enough about her to risk initiating dialogue with a woman who spurned his love, her aunt is willing to listen to the man she spurned because of her love for Pollyanna, and Pollyanna recovers enough of her spirit to carry her through the long rehabilitation because the community—and most of all her adoptive mother—have turned her own affective discipline on her crippled psyche. Pollyanna's body, like those of the other invalid children in these novels, is healed because of a massively successful project of affective discipline. The body that was the affidavit of the spirit in the sentimental tradition becomes, as the genre nears its conclusion, the overpowered object of the spirit's own well-being.

With the reclamation of the body in this revised and significantly expanded version of moral suasion, *Pollyanna* also introduces expanded possibilities for the suppression of individuality, but in fact its handling of identity is much more nuanced than might be expected. *Anne of Green Gables* told the story of a few adults reorganizing themselves around the tastes of the orphan girl, tastes that helped define that girl, and *Pollyanna* is the same story writ very large. As such, it reveals the persistent ambivalence that postsentimental orphan girl novels felt about the very individuality they were describing for their protagonists. *Pollyanna* takes from *Anne* the notion that the girl's interiority can be described, upheld, and even celebrated as she expresses that interiority through taste. It magnifies the project of impressing the girl's character on the people around her, depicting that character as both impervious to change and irresistible as an instrument of change in other people. But the bizarre outcome of the novel's insistence on individuality for the girl is sameness for the people who surround her. The novel is therefore both a continuation of the logic of subjectivity as articulated by previous orphan girl novels and an acquiescence to the sentimental dissolution of individuality.

Like Montgomery's novel, *Pollyanna* uses the relationship between the orphan girl and the adoptive mother as the through line by which to record both the solidity of the girl's character and its ability to reshape people who love her. Early in the story, Aunt Polly is pointedly cruel as she endures her duty to care for the child. But even her aunt's most cutting attacks have no effect on Pollyanna. Indeed, these attacks are constantly reshaped by Pollyanna's whim. When Polly forbids her niece to talk about her father, for example, Pollyanna refuses to believe that her aunt is acting out of anger.

> *After all, I—I reckon I'm glad she doesn't want to talk about Father,* Pollyanna was thinking. *It'll be easier, maybe—if I don't talk about him. Probably, anyhow, that is why she told me not to talk about him.* And Pollyanna, convinced anew of her aunt's "Kindness," blinked off the tears and looked eagerly about her. (29–30)

Pollyanna's perception of Polly's kindness is a misperception, or at least it is at first. Polly has long been jealous of the romance her sister found with Pollyanna's father and shamed by what she considers a stain on the family reputation, and if she is forced by duty to take care of the child from that union, she can at least, she thinks, demand that she not have to hear the man mentioned. But when Pollyanna misses these reasons and decides that her aunt acts out of kindness, she begins a process from which her aunt, struggle as she might, will never be able to escape: she will actually become, like Pollyanna, kind. Thus, when Polly attempts to punish Pollyanna for a perceived sin, her petty cruelty loses its effectiveness because Pollyanna refuses to believe that Polly is anything other than kind. In this way, she transmutes punishment after punishment into a perceived reward:

> Miss Polly was stalking on ahead. Miss Polly, to tell the truth, was feeling curiously helpless. For the third time since Pollyanna's arrival, Miss Polly was punishing Pollyanna—and for the third time she was being confronted with the amazing fact that her punishment was being taken as a special reward of merit. No wonder Miss Polly was feeling curiously helpless. (56)

Similarly, when Pollyanna attempts to find homes for stray animals, she decides that the perfect place to take them is Polly's spotless home, "and again Miss Polly, to her dumbfounded amazement, found herself figuring as a kind protector and an angel of mercy—a role that Pollyanna so unhesitatingly thrust upon her as a matter of course, that the woman . . . found herself as before, powerless to re-monstrate" (81–82). And by the time Aunt Polly declares, in the novel's closing pages, that she is "so—happy! And so—glad!—darling!" she is finishing a long process through which she receives the impression of Pollyanna's hallmark trait, her willingness to look for something that makes her glad.

This philosophy of happiness is, as I have pointed out, closely identified with Pollyanna's father, but with his body safely out of the way, the glad game's strategy for organizing one's interiority becomes Pollyanna's calling card. The central image of the game is therefore always that of Pollyanna, reflected especially in her decision to be happy over receiving a disappointing Christmas gift instead of the specific toy she had requested.[4] When Polly gives in to the glad game, she is explicitly following the *model* of Pollyanna, even if the origin of Pollyanna's power is her maligned father. It is Pollyanna's behavior after which her aunt patterns her own newly disciplined personality.

Aunt Polly is the convert to the glad game to whom the novel pays the most attention, but surrounding Polly are many other people who also give up their individual desires, squabbles, and prejudices to conform themselves to the model of the little girl. Pollyanna reforms her physician, a resentful bachelor, her minister, the petty ladies of her church, an invalid, a fallen woman, a runaway orphan boy—the book hardly mentions a character who is *not* somehow transformed by and in the image of Pollyanna. This becomes dramatically evident when Pollyanna falls ill and her aunt "beg[ins] to receive calls: calls from people she knew, and people she did not know; calls from men, women, and children—many of whom Miss Polly had not supposed that her niece knew at all" (190–91). Again and again, these people confess to Aunt Polly their love for the little girl and how their lives have changed for the better since following her example. As Polly confides,

> everybody, from Milly Snow to Mrs. Tom Payson, send[s] word . . . that they're "playing it[.]" As near as I can judge, half the town are putting on blue ribbons, or stopping family quarrels, or learning to like something they never liked before, and all because of Pollyanna. (202)

The reorganization of adult culture that *Anne* described on a small scale is expanded in *Pollyanna* to fill every available corner of adult culture. Through Pollyanna's game, players learn how to desire, how to ignore that which does not please, and how to cherish instead whatever small aspects of life will make one glad. As such, those who follow the game are giving themselves over to Pollyanna's tastes and to the interior character that defines Pollyanna as distinct.

It is necessary, though, to read Pollyanna's individualism here as, in another echo of sentimentalism, disingenuous. The interiority whose intractable tastes protect it from correction by the unsympathetic Aunt Polly does define the orphan girl as a strident individual, but the work of the plot is, perversely, to destroy individuality, to break down the distinctions between the miserable people Pollyanna meets so that they will be glad like her. The result of Pollyanna's individuality is homogeneity: the formerly disparate citizens of Beldingsville are now all alike, even though there is an individual at the center whose template is privileged. If it is true that *Pollyanna* sharpens the potential of a dramatically individual girl in her book, it is also true that Porter's novel is *more* ambiguous about individuality than many of the books leading up to it.

There may be a historically specific explanation for *Pollyanna*'s heightened ambiguity. What the novel does is both embrace individualism for its girl protagonist—something that *Anne* indicates fit with changes in the conception of earning and spending in the early century—and offer the image of a girl who will soothe the boundaries between individuals. As Frank Luther Mott's classic study of best sellers notes, the novel was first published in book form in February 1913, and "new printings were called for weekly through March, and monthly or oftener for the next year" (222). Perhaps the novel's ambiguity was not a hindrance to that popularity but one of its most powerful enablers. I want to consider the novel's booming popularity in this time period alongside another trend: the turn-of-the-century explosion in private residences. Placed within the history of popular American architecture, *Pollyanna*'s ambiguous construction of individuality looks more like a strength than a handicap.

The Progressive Era is the site of one of the most dynamic periods in domestic architecture, a site in which housing changed in ways that allowed for distinctions between families and even members of a single family that had been previously unlikely. Although interior halls, as Patricia Meyer Spacks has demonstrated, emerged in the late eighteenth century, providing a means of "dependable separation of individuals from one another" (*Privacy* 7), architecture still did not allow for much long-term spatial distinction even within the same household. Thus, even in the last third of the nineteenth century, middle-class families shared bedrooms, with at least same-sex siblings sleeping in the same room. Spiro Kostof has shown, too, that upper-class homes in the East designed hallways and staircases to emphasize shared space rather than privacy, and "space flowed freely among rooms that were only minimally separated from each other by mere screen walls, for instance, or very wide sliding doors" (651). The larger families of the Victorian era, too, meant that "privacy for the Victorian family was still associated with short periods of time alone, in a special place in the house: a window seat, a cubbyhole under the stairs, a man's library, or 'growlery'" (Wright 112).

But at the end of the nineteenth century, important changes in the spatial arrangement of families offered to emphasize the boundaries between individuals and families. Formerly communal resources—public kitchens, laundries, refrigeration, water, energy—were either privatized in discrete domestic spaces or handed over to massive production and processing plants that provided these resources to individual houses privately, through "water lines and heaters, gas mains, and electrical wiring circuits in the basements . . . not visible to any guest or resident" (Wright 147). Houses themselves represented individuality and stable citizenship, which is why Herbert Hoover took a direct role in expanding the housing market. As Gwendolyn Wright explains, to Hoover "private homes encouraged individuality; and residential construction, together with real-estate investments, played key roles in the national economy" (193). Wright points out a "great migration" that "gathered momentum as the century wore on" (96), a migration from shared housing to individual houses with space around them to describe the boundaries between families. With affordable loans and improved transportation, the number of private houses exploded in the earliest part of the twentieth century. Rachel Carley has called "the first thirty years of the 1900s . . . a building boom for the small single- and two-family house" (212). During the Progressive Era, the "American bungalow," a cheap and quickly constructed private residence, proliferated across the country, making home ownership possible outside the middle class.[5] Further, popular magazines such as the

Craftsman and *Ladies' Home Journal* made blueprints by professional architects (including internationally famous architects such as Frank Lloyd Wright) available cheaply and widely. But homes away from the centers of commerce would not have been feasible without another technological-commercial change: the popularity of the automobile. Carley points out that "in 1900 there were 8000 cars on the road; just fifteen years later the number was well over two million." She suggests that this "automobility, along with improved railroads," meant that the demand for homes could be met by contractors who could build on the increased radius of travel supplied by the middle class's ability to reach their places of work from the new suburbs easily (212).

But if it is true that members of the middle class moved en masse to the suburbs, it is also true that they saw in this widespread move the potential for individuality. The move to the suburbs happened so quickly that there was no way for new home owners to miss the fact that they were part of a trend, but this fact was all but obliterated by the perception of the home as a symbol of uniqueness. "Ignoring the evidence of standardization," Wright argues, "people identified themselves with their homes." She identifies the "rhetoric of domestic bliss, so closely associated with detached houses and elaborate architectural ornament" as key to this bit of self-delusion. Thus, the amateur architect Eugene C. Gardner, whom Wright also studies, could easily market his book of *Illustrated Homes* in which "various archetypal clients—the poet, the parson, the philanthropist, the professor's wife—conferred with their local architect about their dream house. Each of the resulting designs was unique, Gardner claimed, intended for that particular family" (113). Part of a trend or not, the boom of private housing read to Progressive Era home buyers as an opportunity for individuality, for drawing economically and geographically the boundaries of the family.

It is in the suddenness of this real-world development that Porter deploys Pollyanna's fictional adoptive hometown. In this conflation of real and imagined living spaces, Pollyanna collapses the distinctions between families that the all-but-overnight housing boom described. Perhaps this dramatic change in housing resulted not only in anticipation of improved economy, privacy, and nationhood but also in anxiety over the change from the familiar and comparatively communal lifestyle of the previous generation. If so, Pollyanna is both a very strange figure in the history of individualism and a sort of figure that only the sentimental tradition could produce, for she demonstrates that a character can model individuality while simultaneously working to ease fears over individuality. Given the explosion of private spaces in middle-class culture, spaces that were defined by boundaries that emphasized the private differences between bourgeois families, *Pollyanna* seems to operate as an endorsement of individualism that assuages contemporaneous anxieties attending a dramatic shift in housing. Porter's novel and its central ambiguity therefore valorize a kind of individuality that will heal the fracturing of communities already in progress.

CHAPTER NINE

Emily of New Moon
and the Private Girl

The last of the novels clearly in the sentimental orphan girl tradition that I examine is *Emily of New Moon*, published in 1923 by L. M. Montgomery, who had already achieved international fame as the author of *Anne of Green Gables*. Written at the end of the genre's long history, *Emily* relentlessly examines the trends of the earlier novels. Whereas early girls' novels such as *Eight Cousins* balanced scenes of girls doling out discipline with scenes of girls receiving discipline, *Emily* confirms the genre's later argument that girls do not need discipline. However, it also argues that girls may need information, which can best be communicated in a relationship that is characterized more by equality than disciplinary affection. And although *Emily* expresses more pointedly the genre's growing unease with the power of affective discipline, it continues to imagine how girls can rehabilitate and direct the power of fathers. Finally, it highlights the gap between the final years of the orphan girl genre and the genre's origins by portraying a girl who is capable of emphatic resistance to her adoptive mother in scenes that celebrate her resistance and insist that the mother herself is in sore need of discipline.

Emily of New Moon is a story of a young artist in bloom. In the novel's opening pages, Emily displays a boundless imagination populated with animistic figures drawn from her nearly pagan view of nature, then focused through her constant journaling. When her widower father dies, the family of her mother arrives to scowl at Emily and decide who should be burdened with the little girl. They draw lots; Emily's aunts Elizabeth and Laura, who live on the family's ancestral lands at New Moon, lose, and Emily bursts into their lives with all the passion they have managed to erase from their daily existence. Emily grows physically and artistically, slowly winning over even her most reluctant relatives, healing old rifts along the way.

Emily's story directly echoes themes first laid out for the genre in *The Wide, Wide World*, extending the logic of some of the most pervasive themes and pointedly contradicting others. Among those first suggested by sentimentalism is the oddly replaceable father, whose body was casually discarded in Warner's text and whose authority becomes increasingly the tool of the genre's later disciplining girls. This works in *Pollyanna* to give the orphan girl the moral authority her minister father once had, but Pollyanna's father is hardly the greatest of tyrants. Rather, he is one of the genre's many feminized men, and his spirit is an easy one to inherit. *Emily's* relocation of the father's power is more dramatic, demonstrating that even cruel, manly fathers can be stripped of their bodies, leaving behind a power that the orphan girl can wield to satisfy her own desires, even over the protests of the adoptive mother.

The tyrant father whom Montgomery's novel disembodies is Archibald Murray, Emily's maternal grandfather, whom she has never met. Long before Emily comes to New Moon, years before her own beloved father died, Emily's grandfather left behind a family who wept for his passing—but only in public. When Elizabeth Murray, Emily's aunt and adoptive mother, recalls her father, she remembers "the ashamed, smothered feeling of relief when old Archibald Murray had died—the handsome, intolerant, autocratic old man who had ruled his family with a rod of iron all his life" (58). His relatives published "a long and flattering obituary," but Elizabeth doubts that "one genuine feeling of regret followed Archibald Murray to his tomb" (58).

Archibald is hardly the sensitive, caring father whose authority fit so easily in the hands of Pollyanna, but there is nevertheless something of Archibald's authority living on in Emily. In particular, his potent glare remains. Sometimes, Montgomery plays this for laughs, as when Emily records an incident involving the Murray look, as it is called, during a visit she makes to her great-aunt's home. She writes in her diary, "I just gave Aunt Nancy a *look*. She said 'Well, Saucebox, my brother Archibald will never be dead as long as you're alive'" (252). But more common than such light scenes are those in which little Emily uses the look as a devastating tactical weapon in her interactions with adults. In these scenes, the look is always read as an inheritance from her grandfather. When Elizabeth determines, for example, that Emily's hair must be cut, Emily's protests have no effect until she turns the glare on her aunt. Elizabeth, who has shown no inclination to coddle Emily's desires, is profoundly affected:

An amazing thing happened to Aunt Elizabeth. She turned pale—she laid the scissors down—she looked aghast for one moment at the transformed or possessed child before her—and then for the first time in her life Elizabeth Murray turned tail and fled—literally fled—to the kitchen.

"What is the matter, Elizabeth?" cried Laura, coming in from the cook-house.

"I saw—Father—looking from her face," gasped Elizabeth, trembling. "And she said, 'Let me hear no more of this,'—just as *he* always said it—his very words." (107)

Emily rarely uses this gift, but when she does, her will inevitably reigns over anyone else's. Later, as the look becomes an infrequent but familiar part of Emily's life and her resistance to Elizabeth's tyranny, her aunt learns to surrender "without a struggle, rage at herself as she might afterwards for her weakness. It was her one vulnerable point" (147). One of the implications of power in these novels has been its use over fathers, specifically its ability to bring their physical being back into line with domestic ideology. But here at the end of the genre, the patriarch's body is dispensable. It is his power that these authors are concerned with, and even the most frightening father can be peeled away, leaving behind a paternal privilege at the girl's command.

This is not to say that *Emily of New Moon* overlooks the father's return to the domestic space. Reuniting fathers with the domestic space is still an important project of the orphan girl, just as it was in *A Little Princess*, symbolized in Sara's reconnecting the rat father with his family. Emily's use of the look is an important variation on that theme. The look, repeatedly identified with the authority of the tyrant father, is what is left after a father who ruled poorly is relieved of a tool of power. That tool is then returned to the home and entrusted to someone— this time female—who can use it better. And in fact Emily only uses the look, in the words of the narrator, "when the deeps of her being were stirred by some peculiarly poignant emotion" (147). It also helps that Emily only uses the look in defense of arguments the novel endorses; in other words, the novel arranges for Emily only to have this power when she is both emotionally engaged and in the right. The authority of the father is thus reunited with the family in a way that serves it better and with greater kindness than did physical iterations of paternal authority.

Emily also reunites the rehabilitated father and loving family in more traditionally sentimental ways.[1] In a subplot that finally resolves near the end of the

book, Emily discovers that her closest friend, Ilse Burnley, is the survivor of a terrible family scandal, one that has alienated father and daughter ever since. When
Dr. Burnley's wife disappeared with a man one evening years ago and never
returned, Burnley took his grief and humiliation out on his daughter. Now he
hardly acknowledges her existence. In a letter to her father, Emily writes that she
wishes Burnley would love his daughter again (214), but with the mother gone
and no explanation for her disappearance other than scandal, there is no real
hope of such a reconciliation. The scandal tortures Emily for the rest of the book,
and although other conflicts come and go, Emily never gives up her hope that she
can someday reunite daughter and father. In the final pages of the book, Emily
falls into an illness during which the story of Ilse's mother will not let her rest.
She mumbles pieces of it in her fever, at one point starting awake long enough to
force Elizabeth into a promise that leads directly to the discovery of the missing
woman's body. Mrs. Burnley did not leave with a beau after all, the community
discovers, but was in all likelihood returning to her husband and daughter when
she died. Dr. Burnley is overcome with remorse for his behavior in the interven-
ing years, and he credits Emily alone with his transformation.[2] Emily reconciles
husband and wife, but she also restores the affectionate bond between Ilse and
her father. As she recovers her senses and is told the story of Ilse's mother, now
revised, Emily cries, "And Ilse—does her father love her now?" Her Aunt Laura
replies, "Love her! He can't love her enough. It seems as if he were pouring out
on her at once all the shut-up love of those twelve years" (327). With a body or
without one, the father is the responsibility of the orphan girl, who can both
wield his privilege and direct him back to the loving domestic space.

There is one more father, perhaps the most obvious, remaining to be ac-
counted for in Emily's history. Her biological father, Douglas Starr, dies in the
early pages of the novel, but there is something of himself that he leaves for
Emily, too, and it becomes her most important tool. The story of Emily's father
is familiar from the pages of *Pollyanna*. Like Pollyanna's father, Starr was a poor
idealist who offered his sweetheart love and affection instead of wealth, and like
Pollyanna's mother, Juliet Murray ignored her family's wishes, accepting his suit
rather than look for one that offered better financial security. Juliet dies young,
not long after Emily's birth, and again like Pollyanna's father, Emily's father is left
to rear the child on his own. The Murray family despises Starr; his housekeeper
warns Emily that the Murrays "have always hated your pa like p'isen" (9). They
regard him as a failure, though Emily denounces them for it, saying, "Nobody
who was loved as much as he was could be a failure" (40). It is her deep love for

her father that allows him to communicate to her what he calls "the only legacy I can leave you" (17), and the foremost prize of her legacy is the passion for writing with which he has imbued her.

Just as the glad game is identical, both in the girl's mind and the novel's logic, with Pollyanna's father, writing is something that Emily insists on associating with her father. The first of Emily's notebooks to play a significant part in the novel is sacrificed when Elizabeth discovers it and threatens to read what is inside. Rather than allow Elizabeth to read the book, Emily burns it, but when it is gone she misses it "next to her father" (89). For fear of allowing Elizabeth to read anything she writes, Emily takes up writing again in secret, sneaking up to New Moon's garret—a little madwoman in the attic—to write letters to her father. The love of her father and her love of writing intertwine in these scenes:

> Thereafter few evenings passed on which Emily did not steal up to the garret and write a letter, long or short, to her father. The bitterness died out of her grief. Writing to him seemed to bring him so near; and she told him everything, with a certain honesty of confession that was characteristic of her—her triumphs, her failures, her joys, her sorrows, everything went down. (94)

Elizabeth does eventually discover that Emily has been writing, but rage as she might, Elizabeth cannot prevent her from doing so. The reason and justification for writing frequently revolve around Emily's father, as when Emily responds to Elizabeth's charge "that it is wicked to write novels" with the simple explanation that Elizabeth must be wrong—after all, "Father liked novels" (305). Elizabeth orders Emily to desist, but in one of the very, very few times that one of these girls disobeys her parent, Emily explains that she cannot stop writing. In Emily's mind, this is truly an inability, not a willed disobedience. And not surprisingly, part of the reason has to do with her father. "You see, it's this way," she tells her aunt. "It is *in* me. I can't help it. And Father said I was *always* to keep on writing. He said I would be famous some day" (306).

As the memory of her father fades, Emily meets other men who step in to encourage her development as a writer. These men are not technically Emily's father—though one of them is named "Father"—but they serve to reiterate the theme of masculine energy used to further Emily's goal of becoming a writer. Emily's cousin Jimmy, for example, is instrumental in her early years as a writer. It is from Jimmy that Emily gets the idea of becoming a poet—a title she first learns from him. Before long, Jimmy becomes her sole source of paper, and she calls the notebooks in which she practices her craft "Jimmy-books." Like her father, Jimmy is intimately connected to Emily's life as a writer, sometimes in ways that are not easily explainable. A new Jimmy-book "always appeared mysteriously in her school basket when the old one was almost full," without Emily having to tell him that she needed another notebook. "Cousin Jimmy seemed to have an uncanny prescience of the proper time—that was part of his Jimmyness" (301).[3] Another man, Father Cassidy, humors Emily by helping her with an epic she is writing (198), then condescends to listen to some of her poetry. Although he has been disarming and funny throughout their conversation, on hearing Emily's poetry he becomes sincere. He correctly identifies the poetry as "trash," but he also detects something more:

> Of course, it *was* trash. Father Cassidy knew that well enough. All the same, for a child like this—and rhyme and rhythm were flawless—and there was one line—just one line—"the light of faintly golden stars"—for the sake of that line Father Cassidy suddenly said,
>
> "Keep on,—keep on writing poetry."
>
> "You mean?"—Emily was breathless.
>
> "I mean you'll be able to do something by and by. Something—I don't know how much—but keep on—keep on."
>
> Emily was so happy she wanted to cry. It was the first word of commendation she had ever received except from her father—and a father might have too high an opinion of one. *This* was different. To the end of her struggle for recognition Emily never forgot Father Cassidy's "Keep on" and the tone in which he said it. (202)

Again the narrator points out the connection between Emily's father and her talent for writing, but here the baton of fatherly approval passes from biological father to social father. Writing in this novel is therefore a power aligned with masculinity, a power left to and enjoyed by the orphan girl.

If Emily uses the power of writing happily, she also uses it successfully. One of the greatest successes to which Emily puts writing is as a shield against the traumatic events of her life. Many of those events are set in motion by her Aunt Elizabeth's rules, rules that are anything but fair, a fact Emily likes to point out. But as the smallest, youngest, and poorest person on the New Moon farm, Emily has little recourse against Elizabeth. Fortunately, in addition to the look inherited from her grandfather, Emily is also able to call on her writing. Thus, when Elizabeth gives Emily a "black look," Emily can ignore it if she concentrates on her writing (64). When another aunt is cruel to her, Emily feels hurt for a while, but then puts the whole experience behind her by exercising her ability to write. Her aunt's insult, the narrator confides, "rankled in her for several days until she thought of a sharp answer she might have made Aunt Nancy and wrote it down in her Jimmy-book. She felt quite as relieved then as if she had really said it" (276). In a further similarity to Pollyanna's glad game, Emily's writing serves as powerful protection against trauma.

Unlike Pollyanna, Emily outgrows her father. Whereas the glad game is always part of Pollyanna's life and her use of it always protects her in his name, Emily needs the image of her father less and less as the narrative progresses. For example, the letters she writes to her father are, through most of the novel, the clearest symbol of writing's connection with the paternal, up until a critical scene in which Emily refuses to allow Elizabeth the right to read her private papers. Elizabeth wants her to dispose of the letters, but, as Emily explains, "I *can't* burn those letters, you know—they belong to Father." Instead, she goes through the letters writing "explanatory footnotes," as she calls them, softening things she said about her aunt that were too cruel. But following this activity, Emily discovers that the act of writing to her father "no longer meant anything to her" (314). The narrator is unclear on the reason for this change, but in the novel it represents two important moments.[4] First, it marks the moment at which Aunt Elizabeth no longer has the right to dictate to Emily how she may exercise her desire to write. In this way, the father has once more served the orphan girl's desire, rather than the other way around. The second important moment comes when Emily no longer recognizes writing as something bound to her father. Thus, the closing lines of the novel show an Emily who retains the power of writing inherited from her father but places the agency for writing in Emily's hands: "She was so full of rapture that she must write it out before she went back from her world of dreams to the world of reality. Once she would have poured it into a letter to her father. She could no longer do that." Writing is still a source of strength for Emily—this time in the face of the sublime—and she does write, but the novel makes clear that writing no longer equals her father (339). His legacy lingers to enable her and serve her emerging personality, but that personality outgrows his memory. Emily, in an expression of the logical end of the arguments the sentimental orphan girl genre has been making for almost three-quarters of a century, is both able to discard the father's body and to strip away the label of "father" from the privilege that she inherits from him. The power remains. The father disappears.

Although the sentimental tradition often contrived to discipline the daughter through the memory of the dead parent, in *Emily* the child is the disciplining subject, and the novel makes it clear that on the whole, Emily does not require correction of any kind. In comparison with her "hawty" Murray relatives, for instance, Emily's incomprehension of adult codes of behavior looks charming.

In one early scene shortly after her father's death, Emily overhears the Murrays talking about her father and the disservice they assume he has done her by failing to make her a lady. Implicit in the dialogue is the argument that Emily must be disciplined; her habits are deeply ingrained by her "failure" of a father, and the Murrays are debating who among them will cure her faults. But Emily disagrees. "I don't *want* them cured!" she rages to herself. "I like *my* faults better than I do *your abominable* virtues!" (39). In novels of the mid-1800s or even the late 1800s, Emily's rejection of adult discipline would have heralded a story in which the child's will was broken and the penitent girl reshaped according to adult desire. But in this book, Montgomery argues that Emily is right: she does not need discipline.

Emily does, however, require something similar to discipline. Instead of the sort of discipline that occurs between a faultless disciplining subject and a loving object, Emily needs instruction, the kind of instruction that takes place between individuals who respect one another. When Emily finds out that a certain behavior is bad, she stops that behavior because it is wrong, not because she has been successfully manipulated by her parents, either through love or beatings (41). And when Elizabeth takes the time to explain a point of conduct to Emily, the girl is willing to change her behavior. For example, when Emily says that her neighbor Lofty John is "dod-gasted," her aunts order her not to use such language. Emily, bewildered, refuses on the grounds that her cousin Jimmy uses precisely that phrase—her aunts' coercion is ineffective. Elizabeth therefore has to change tactics:

> "Emily," said Aunt Elizabeth, with the air of one impaling herself on the easiest horn of a dilemma, "your Cousin Jimmy is a man—and men sometimes use expressions, in the heat of anger, that are not proper for little girls."
>
> "But what *is* the matter with dod-gasted?" persisted Emily. "It isn't a swear word, is it? And if it isn't, why can't I use it?"
>
> "It isn't a—ladylike word," said Aunt Laura.
>
> "Well, then, I won't use it any more," said Emily resignedly, "but Lofty John *is* dod-gasted." (140)

Even though her beloved cousin uses the word, even though the word is *accurate*, Emily abandons its use because she has had the logic of the demand explained to her. This is very different from Ellen Montgomery, who anticipated rules through the affective discipline she had imbibed; Emily behaves because she has had the rules explained to her, not because she has been manipulated. Indeed, there *is* no affection between Emily and Elizabeth on which the latter might draw to discipline the former. Emily disregards the silliness of Elizabeth's argument, but she accepts the argument nonetheless because it has been rephrased as an explanation, not a "demand." Similarly, when Emily uses a rude—and ineffective—form of blush to highlight the color in her cheeks, Elizabeth helps Emily to understand what she has done, and Emily changes her behavior on her own. After Emily tells Elizabeth of her failed cosmetic experiment, Emily writes that "I expected an awful scolding, but all [Elizabeth] said was, 'Don't you know that you have made yourself *cheap?*' I did know it, too. I had felt that all along although I couldn't think of the right word for it before. 'I will never do such a thing again, Aunt Elizabeth,' I said" (210). Here and elsewhere in the novel, the rare changes that are necessary to Emily's behavior come from discussion rather than discipline. Emily is not disciplined; she is educated.

This is not to say that discipline has no place in the book—it does, but the girl is no longer its object. In fact, the novel continues a trend in discipline that was developing in earlier novels in the genre's history: disciplining the mother. Emily's biological mother is dead long before the novel opens, and their relationship is a minor part of the novel at most. But the orphan girl's relationship with her adoptive mother is central to the narrative. Just as *Pollyanna* shows the reformation of the dictator mother at the hands of Pollyanna, it is Aunt Elizabeth's changes that *Emily of New Moon* narrates. Like the lifeless homes of Burnett's and Porter's novels, New Moon is, Emily's father informs her, a place of stagnation. The Murrays of New Moon "increased and multiplied and scattered all over, but the old stock at New Moon Farm is pretty well run out" (14). Emily's job is to restore vitality to this home, and her main opponent is Elizabeth, who insists on following old traditions and, in an echo of many orphan girl novels, regards Emily as a duty (43). The battle between girl and woman is waged on the field of child care; Elizabeth begins the novel with ideas of discipline of which the novel does not approve, and these must be driven out of her. This much is consistent both with the trend of the genre and its early twentieth-century iterations. But the point that *Emily* makes about affective discipline, the point that shows most clearly the break that the late orphan girl novel makes with its sentimental antecedents, is that affective discipline, even accidental affective discipline, is unethical.

Although the women who attempt to discipline Emily never use physical violence—a mode the genre has long since discarded—the nonphysical modes of discipline they use are just as roundly condemned by the novel as any scene of whipping might have been. The local schoolmaster, for instance, has developed a "reputation in Blair Water of being a fine teacher—due mainly to the fact that she was a strict disciplinarian and kept excellent 'order'" (77). Her favorite tool of discipline is a form of emotional violence: "Miss Brownell ridiculed her for her mistakes in spelling. Miss Brownell was very fond of ridiculing her pupils" (81). After Emily refuses to let her teacher have the poems she has been keeping in her school desk, Brownell resolves to go to New Moon to lay the matter before Elizabeth. Brownell is smug, secure in the presumption that Emily's defiance means she will be humbled, but even she is taken by surprise when Elizabeth commands Emily not just to apologize, but to "kneel down here before Miss Brownell and ask her pardon for your conduct to-day." The narrator breaks point of view in order to make perfectly clear what is at stake in this action: Emily will be forever humbled, inferior to Brownell not just in rank but in a way that will permeate their relationship:

> Never again, Miss Brownell felt, would Emily be able to look levelly at her with those dauntless eyes that bespoke a soul untamable and free, no matter what punishment might be inflicted upon body or mind. The memory of this moment would always be with Emily—she could never forget that she had knelt in abasement. Emily felt this as clearly as Miss Brownell. (170)

The teacher has until now been frustrated, as the lines about "what punishment might be inflicted upon body or mind" imply, by Emily's resistance to discipline, but this act of humiliation will permanently inscribe a differentiated power relationship between the two, and Brownell relishes the coming apology.

Fortunately for Emily, the novel cannot tolerate such a use of discipline. Just as Emily is about to follow Elizabeth's orders, her cousin Jimmy interjects that "a human being should not kneel to any one but God." Jimmy is a nominal authority in the home at best, but his words ring true to Elizabeth, who softens her tone of command and says, "Emily. . . I was wrong—I shall not ask you to kneel" (171). Emily does apologize, but Brownell leaves unsatisfied—a warning to readers who might long to use the tactics Brownell prefers.[5] Here and in other scenes in which Emily might be humbled, the novel condemns adults who would use their power to dominate Emily.[6]

It is modes of discipline such as this that Elizabeth must forego. The tools of affective discipline so important in earlier texts and throughout the sentimental tradition are rarely endorsed in this novel, which endorses instead a relationship between adoptive mother and daughter that privileges Emily's rights as an individual. As Elizabeth gives up these tools, she progresses through a character arc that is the genre's final iteration of disciplining the mother. The most dramatic example of Elizabeth's change is one spelled out in the scenes that concern Emily's writing, scenes that directly refute the kind of moral power of which Ellen Montgomery so longed to be the object in the pages of *The Wide, Wide World*. Whereas Ellen craved surveillance and contrived a way to maintain it even when an ocean separated her from her disciplinarian, Emily refuses disciplinary observation. Moreover, Elizabeth, unlike John, must come to accept the fact that discipline by surveillance will not be tolerated. While Elizabeth and Laura are shopping for clothes for Emily during their journey to New Moon, Jimmy foregrounds the importance of disciplinary scrutiny—and strategies for avoiding it. Jimmy wants to give Emily something special, but his options are limited. He decides to give her ice cream, saying, "No use my getting anything for you that Elizabeth could see. . . . But she can't see what is inside of you" (52), a telling phrase at the end of a genre that has been so concerned with allowing the loving multitudes to see inside. Emily agrees with this logic, particularly in regards to her writing. "No stranger eyes must behold these sacred productions," the narrator explains (90), and Emily goes to great lengths to make sure that her writing remains private, even inventing a private tongue in the hopes that "I will soon be able to write my poems in our language and then Aunt Elizabeth will not be able to read them if she finds them" (201).

Whereas observation—not just of one's body and actions, but even, as in the case of *A Little Princess*, of one's stories—was key to discipline in earlier texts, in *Emily* the orphan girl insists on the privacy of her writing. When Elizabeth discovers Emily's first notebook early in the narrative and threatens to read what Emily has written, the two characters argue over precisely this right:

> "You mustn't read that, Aunt Elizabeth," she cried indignantly, "that's mine—my own *private property*."
> "Hoity-toity, Miss Starr," said Aunt Elizabeth, staring at her, "let me tell you that I have a right to read your books. I am responsible for you now. I am not going to have anything hidden or underhanded, understand that. You have evidently something there that you are ashamed to have seen and I mean to see it." (47)

But Emily refuses to compromise, and rather than risk Elizabeth taking possession of her notebook, Emily stuffs it into the kitchen stove. As it burns, Emily weeps:

> She felt as if she had lost something incalculably precious. It was terrible to think that all those dear things were gone. She could never write them again— not just the same; and if she could she wouldn't dare—she would never dare

to write *anything* again, if Aunt Elizabeth must see everything. Father never insisted on seeing them. She liked to read them to *him*—but if she hadn't wanted to do it he would never have made her. (47–48)

The comparison between Elizabeth and Emily's just-dead father is not gratuitous sentimentality. Rather, he represents the parent who will respect the private nature of Emily's mind. Even if there is something in that mind of which the child is "ashamed," as Elizabeth puts it, whatever is in the child's mind is off-limits to parental observation. Because of the uniquely intimate nature of writing, to read Emily's writing is to look inside her. But the good parent will not use writing as a tool for keeping watch over the girl. Instead, the good parent will encourage writing as a means for the girl to protect herself and work through her desires. Emily's father knew this. Now Elizabeth must learn it.

Montgomery closes Elizabeth's character arc with a similar scene late in the novel. After Emily has filled pages with letters to her father, usually in an effort to deal with the pain of Elizabeth's injustice, Elizabeth stumbles across them and reads them all. The act is shocking given Emily's repeated assertions of her right to her own privacy, but Montgomery makes it clear that Elizabeth is not acting out of malice, only out of her understanding of discipline and personal rights. "Elizabeth Murray would never have read any writing belonging to a grown person," the narrator informs us. "But it never occurred to her that there was anything dishonourable in reading the letters. . . . Aunt Elizabeth thought she had a right to know everything that this pensioner on her bounty did, said, or thought" (309). Later, she summons Emily to the parlor to punish the girl for her letters, but as soon as Emily sees what is in her aunt's hands, the scene spins out of Elizabeth's control. Emily snatches the letters away and faces her aunt with outrage. Elizabeth demands that the girl give the letters back to her, but Emily refuses. "They are mine and Father's—not yours," she states. "You had no right to touch them. I will *never* forgive you!" (310). The two part, and Emily flees to her room. But before the chapter ends, Montgomery inverts this moment borrowed directly from *The Wide, Wide World*. In Warner's novel, when the cruel aunt reads the private letters the orphan girl receives, the point of the scene is that the child needs to learn to control her anger even in the face of injustice. In this chapter, however, titled "Sacrilege," even though Emily convinces herself that she must apologize for her outburst, the novel preempts her. Before Emily can render her own apology, Elizabeth comes to her room and apologizes. "Emily," she says, "I had no right to read your letters. I admit I was wrong. Will you forgive me?" (313).

This about-face over the issue of privacy is a recognition of discrete rights.

Emily's rights and thoughts occupy a space that the late genre will not allow to overlap with those of her aunt. The novel does not narrate Emily's disciplined journey from spoiled girl to stately woman but rather Elizabeth's path toward understanding that little girls have rights that may be owned privately. Earlier in the genre, discipline and morality were internalized. The space inside the girl represented an unassailable promontory from which the ideology of the disciplining parent could maintain dominion over the child's person. But here at the end of the genre, the child's private being signifies a space delineating the individual, her thoughts and desires, and her rights, to which she is not only entitled but that it is her duty as an emerging individual to exercise. The "discipline by interiority" developed by adults becomes an interior owned by the emerging individual, who is the only person with any right to its access.

This genre narrates a long, changing history in the relationship among gender, power, and discipline from the height of the sentimental novel to the granting of women's suffrage. Supporting their arguments on these subjects is an understanding that physical coercion, coded masculine, was insufficient to the task of discipline. But although the novels grow out of a sentimental tradition that endorses moral suasion, coded feminine, by the end of the genre's history the novels have come to give that endorsement less enthusiastically. Even when the characters at the end of the genre do use moral suasion, they either use it accidentally (Emily's father loves her, and therefore she loves him, which is not the same as making her love him; Aunt Polly stops looking at her niece as a duty not because Pollyanna uses stories or gazes but because she lives her life in accordance with the glad game), in which case it is successful, or they use it intentionally and the novel denounces them for humiliating or manipulating their disciplined objects. Even Emily's Murray look is a power that she uses reluctantly, one that she feels guilty for using (107). The girl herself needs discipline less often, and the novels increasingly become tales of mothers, not girls, who are successfully improved.

Montgomery's cunning revision of the sentimental structures of the orphan girl genre had pointed repercussions for her portrait of individualism. *Emily of New Moon* appeared in bookstores in the midst of several critical legal battles, resulting in waves of female enfranchisement (Canada in 1918, the United States in 1920, Prince Edward Island in 1922), and a lengthy debate that began with the appointment of Emily Murphy to the position of police magistrate in 1916. Murphy's appointment sparked more than two decades of national debate across Canada before the Persons Case, so called because it literally determined whether women were legally "persons," was settled in 1929. Montgomery, living in the suffrage hotbed of Ontario at the time she wrote *Emily of New Moon*, was keenly aware of these national—indeed, international—arguments about the legal status of women, and so were her readers. Thus, although *Emily* frequently struggles with the sentimental impetus to elide individuality in favor of types, it believes more fervently in the vision of individual subjectivity for girls than do any of the previous orphan girl novels. The ambiguity of *Pollyanna*'s portrait of individualism is virtually absent in *Emily of New Moon*, a book consistently dedicated to individualism.[7] Montgomery's novel urges an understanding of an individual's entitlement to her work and body. Key to both is a right that sentimentalism not only failed to recognize but actively worked against: privacy.[8]

The importance of privacy to Emily's individuality is tied to the work she treasures most, a kind of work in which her author also indulged: writing. For Montgomery, writing certainly resulted in a product that could be made public, yet from a very early age she considered her writing fundamentally private. Significantly, Montgomery not only recorded her opinions on the privacy of writing but wrote of the importance of keeping it safe from the prying eyes of a mother figure. When Montgomery moved west to live with her father and his new wife, a woman with whom Montgomery never managed to get along, she worried in her diary that her stepmother would "sometime find and read this journal, although I keep it locked up" (Montgomery, *Selected Journals* 33). In tandem with the change in Progressive Era reading habits Christine Pawley has noted, habits educators celebrated because they developed "silent, private reading" (59), Montgomery believed firmly that no one—proxy-mothers perhaps especially—could insist on the right to read what girls wrote.

That insistence would cause a major break with a precedent that had long been set in the sentimental tradition. From as early as Susan Warner's *The Wide, Wide World*, girls were called on to ignore, not defend, the privacy of their writing. In Warner's novel, little Ellen Montgomery finds that a letter from her parents has been opened and read already, before she even knew it existed. She confronts her aunt, whose conscience seems to have troubled her but "only for a second."

> "Who opened it?" she answered; "*I* opened it. I should like to know who has a better right. And I shall open every one that comes to serve you for looking so;—that you may depend upon."
>
> The look and the words and the injury together, fairly put Ellen beside herself. She dashed the letter to the ground, and livid and trembling with various

feelings—rage was not the only one,—she ran from her aunt's presence. She did not shed any tears now; she could not; they were absolutely burnt up by passion. (146)

For Montgomery, scenes such as this must have been very disappointing. Here Warner implies that Aunt Fortune has done something wrong, but Ellen's livid reaction notwithstanding, her aunt's incursion into Ellen's privacy is not the point of the encounter. Although privacy does have value in Warner's orphan girl novel, the point of the scene is that Ellen must learn not to express her anger, her "passion," even when she has a right to do so. Therefore, although Warner writing in the mid-nineteenth century may have indulged an intuition that Ellen is an individual entitled to ownership that is private in all senses of the term, the narrative does not pursue that entitlement. Instead, it looks at this moment of quite possibly warranted anger as an obstacle to be overcome as Ellen dissolves into Alice Humphreys' subject position, that of the self-effacing Christian lady who does not respond to injustice with anger. The child's right is a possibility for Warner's novel, but it is a possibility to be waived in order to allow the adult position to subsume the child. Such is certainly not the case in Montgomery's revision of this scene. Instead, the aunt receives the impression of the little girl, agreeing to respect the child's desires and recognizing her right to privacy—embedded in what Emily herself calls "my *private papers*" (310)—that the girl avows.

But privacy plays differently in different historical contexts, and turn-of-the-century Americans had important ideas about what privacy meant. As Moira Gatens has cautioned, privacy "cannot be understood independently of the historical specificity of the social and political contexts within which such identities are formed" (130). At the beginning of the Progressive Era, Alan Ackerman argues, "the injection of private experience into public space . . . became a crucial aspect of American life" (2). Deckle McLean points to a "broad privacy" at the close of the nineteenth century and argues that the early twentieth century saw an erosion of personal privacy:

> By the end of the nineteenth century, the casually accepted but broad privacy enjoyed during the period was swamped by swelling industrial bureaucracies, increases in the scale of government, police methodology modeled on the Pinkertons, meddlesome newspaper reporters, and the arrival of social science research. Calls for privacy protection started in the 1890s and continued into the twentieth century as expanded military bureaucracies, the draft, and income tax, broadcast mass media, electronic surveillance, computerization,

national security justifications, and the social science and market-research questionnaire took hold. (31–32)

McLean reads these phenomena as evidence that privacy bowed to public commerce in the early century, but if he is right, they are also evidence that fights *for* privacy became more, to borrow a term from Warner's contemplation of privacy, passionate. According to McLean, during this period

> most Americans were swept along from complacent enjoyment of privacy, to irritation at the increase of invasions, to insistence that privacy be explicitly protected—an insistence later satisfied to a degree by the privacy invasion torts, the constitutional privacy right, the Privacy Act, the Fair Credit Reporting Act, and other data-control legislation. (31–32)

I am not convinced by his argument that privacy did slip during this time—keep in mind the simultaneous boon to privacy in the expanding housing market—but even if he is right, the point remains that the public was very concerned about protecting privacy. If privacy did slip, it wasn't because the culture was any less interested in maintaining privacy.

But a commitment to privacy is not the same as wanting to cut one's self permanently off from others. Louis A. Renza has argued, for example, that to Americans "privacy most often appears synonymous with self-autonomy, or with the ability to control access to information about and surveillance concerning one's personal affairs" (xii). As though to demonstrate his point, Sandra Petronio has advanced a theory of privacy that "identifies ways privacy boundaries are coordinated between and among individuals" (3). In literary studies such as Patricia Spacks's inquiry into eighteenth-century privacy, this has meant that one can examine "records of imaginative energy focused on selves conceived as set apart, at least temporarily, from their kind" (*Privacy* 8). In cultural studies, those boundaries can define layers of privacy differentiating the kind of privacy the individual enjoys and "the classical locus of the private—namely, the family" (Rössler, "Privacies" 6). In U.S. culture, privacy is another right, which means that like other rights, it can be waived at the discretion of the individual. This is the form of privacy that informs *Emily*'s take on writing, and it is a form that plays into the interest in possessive individualism that girls' fiction inherited from sentimentalism.

The point in the privacy of writing scenes is not that Emily's work is good and must therefore be protected, but that it is hers, the product and reflection of her inner self, and only Emily has the right to circulate that self. Thus Emily would rather destroy her work than let it be circulated against her will. But she does not write just because she wants to keep her work private; rather, she wants to be able to decide when, where, and how it is circulated. One of the main things she misses about her father is the opportunity to share her writing with him (28). Although it is Emily's decision to burn the book and Emily herself who thrusts it into the fire, "its enforced burning was something for which she held Aunt Elizabeth responsible" (89) because it is Elizabeth's attempt to appropriate Emily's labor that prompts the book's destruction. The private space explored and narrated by writing is a space to which only the individual has legitimate access, and its export to the public space, Montgomery's novel argues, can only ethically be managed by the writer herself. Thus there is a private space whose borders coincide with the boundaries of the individual, and approval of movement across those borders must be the right of the individual as well.

But there is another reader with whom Emily shares all of her extant private writings: the reader of Montgomery's novel. In *Privacy*, Spacks documents the emergence of reading as a (troublesome) private experience between reader and novel during the eighteenth century and the private pleasure authors and readers anticipated from the act of reading at the beginning of the nineteenth century (53).[9] Elsewhere, she has argued that

> Jane Austen (and Charlotte and Emily Brontë after her) helped us to grasp the private way of reading. Of course, not only women thought or cared about privacy. But possibly early women novelists felt special impetus to imagine reading as temporary escape, a grateful interval of self-enclosure, and perhaps they in particular urged their readers toward a new way of reading. ("Privacy" 312)

Similarly, Nina Baym conjectures that "print's invisibility" allowed women new ways to circulate private ideas ("Women's Novels" 339). Since Montgomery had girl readers in mind at least some of the time she composed the novels, it can be eye-opening to consider the remarkable amounts of time girls spent in the secluded act of reading at the time Montgomery published *Emily of New Moon*. Henriette Walter's 1927 study of contemporaneous girl culture in the United States, published by the National Committee for the Study of Juvenile Reading, revealed that although movies and dancing—public activities shared with peers—were very popular, the majority of girls in senior high schools spent *at least* 2 hours per *day* studying outside school. The study also found that girls spent a combined 9.4 hours per week of their free time reading books and magazines; significantly, the girls in the study spent more of their spare time on reading than on any other activity except studying at home (97). Walter goes on to cite a Milwaukee study showing that 97.2 percent of girls read at least part of the newspaper (though too often, the study implies, only the comics or lifestyle sections) (135). This number is surely exaggerated, but the fact that Walter can present it with a straight face means she expected it to ring more or less true to her audience: girls read, and reading was private. The intimacy implicit in the act of Montgomery sharing Emily's emphatically private writings with the private girl reader works not so much to discipline the girl into a belief in privacy but to validate the private experience of reading that was so prominent in the lives of girls in the late Progressive Era.

Montgomery does, however, make writing into a site that threatens Emily's individuality in a decidedly insidious way, and in doing so, the novel reintroduces the sentimental trope of dissolving the individual into the image of her family. Specifically, although Montgomery goes to great lengths to portray Emily's writing as private, there is an element of that writing that also keeps it closely aligned with the spirit of her father. Elizabeth identifies Emily's longing to write with Douglas Starr, the dead father: "No Murray of New Moon had ever been guilty of writing 'stories' or of ever wanting to write them" (305). And Emily agrees with her, even defending both writing and reading novels by referring to her father's love of both (305–6). Writing is a skill Starr made sure to pass on to her, and the joyful moments father and daughter share at the beginning of the novel, as he lies on his deathbed, are almost the only happy memories she carries away. Therefore, as private as writing may be for Emily, it is also a cherished site of overlap between her own identity and that of her father's.

Writing is only the most obvious instance of this overlap between Emily's individual identity and the group identity of her family; another is that most visible representation of Emily's individuality: her own body. The presentation to a viewing adult of her body does not imply the presence of a unique person with physical boundaries that delimit her space; rather, her body is a collection of pieces that remind adults of her ancestors. This take on her identity is established from the beginning of the novel, even before her father dies. Starr himself maps out the similarities Emily's countenance has to those of other people:

> The smile [Emily's] began at the corners of her lips and spread over her face in a slow, subtle, very wonderful way, as Douglas Starr often thought. It was her dead mother's smile—the thing that had caught and held him long ago when he had first seen Juliet Murray. It seemed to be Emily's only physical inheritance from her mother. In all else, he thought, she was like the Starrs—in her

large, purplish-grey eyes with their very long lashes and black brows, in her high, white forehead—too high for beauty—in the delicate modeling of her pale oval face and sensitive mouth, in the little ears that were pointed just a wee bit. (4–5)

Because Emily's smile represents that which "caught and held" her father, it allows the novel to write his desire into Emily's face, an important contrast with the development of individual identity through the girl's desire that Montgomery explored in *Anne of Green Gables*. Other adults also spot the similarity of Emily's smile to that of her mother (27), and labeling Emily's physical inheritances is a frequent trope in the novel. Starr, who has reason to resent the Murrays, looks for evidence in her face that she is his, not theirs. The Murrays make similar efforts, though they are at the same time interested in finding reasons to recognize Emily as not-Murray. But Murrays who are less resentful toward Starr can see a mix of both families in her. Aunt Nancy, for example, sees Murray in Emily's eyebrows (240) and ankles but has to confess that although Emily "has more Murray points than Starr points," the girl "looks like the Starrs and not like the Murrays" (242).

In *Rebecca*, complicating the received projection of adults helped the protagonist assert some independence and choose which face she would bear, but a similar confusion over Emily's pedigree does not have a similar effect in Montgomery's novel. The reading of Emily's body can be complicated by which piece of her body recalls which ancestor, but these characters take for granted that her body signifies her ancestors and not herself. The novel never questions these interpretations of Emily's body, instead using this physical legibility to set up the strongest point against which the orphan girl's individuality will have to contend. Emily's physical appearance is natural: she looks like various of Emily's ancestors because she is Emily. The definition of "Emily" is not found in a set of unique characteristics but in a messy arrangement of overlaps between her own body and others', preventing her visual representation from signifying a unique individual.

If Emily's body is an ever-present threat to her status as an individual, at least her behavior—the quality of character that Pollyanna exported with such aplomb—is under her control. But in general her behavior does not serve to mark her off as an individual any more than does her body. Instead, the adults around her comment on her behavior as another inheritance. Aunt Ruth, for example, calls Emily's eavesdropping evidence of "Starr blood coming out—a Murray would never have done such a thing" (40). Naughty behavior is not the only behavior that signifies Emily's father. When Dean Priest, Starr's old friend, discovers Emily hanging off the edge of a cliff, he is amazed at her strong will and lack of prejudice despite his crooked back. "What a child!" he thinks. "I'll never forget her eyes as she lay there on the edge of death—the dauntless little soul—and I've never seen a creature who seemed so full of sheer joy in existence. She is Douglas Starr's child—*he* never called me Jarback" (272). Few of the people Emily meets have ever known Starr, though, and most of her behavior is read as Murray. When Emily expresses a respect for the exclusive burial grounds of the Murray family, Cousin Jimmy chuckles that Emily is more of a Murray than the rest of the family may care to admit (71), and when Emily saves the family from disgrace by baking a cake for visitors (177) or keeps her room neat, even Aunt Elizabeth concedes that "there is a resemblance to the Murrays I never noticed before" (226). Elsewhere, a neighbor calls Emily "a chip av the ould block" (234), and Elizabeth recognizes her great-grandmother Mary Murray in Emily's stubbornness (304–5). Emily's behavior is therefore no stronger an indication to the adults around her of Emily's individuality than is her body.

Part of the problem that Emily's behavior poses for her emerging individuality is that Emily herself agrees with these adult readings of her behavior as representations not of her unique self but of her families. Whereas the adults quibble over which part of Emily's body or actions most resembles which family, Emily struggles throughout to see that both are interpreted as Starr. Thus she informs the only aunt who is kind to her at the beginning—Aunt Laura—that "I'm not a Murray, you know" (44). When Jimmy argues that Emily's stubbornness is evidence that she is a Murray, after all, that "the Starr is only skin deep," Emily cries, "It isn't—I'm *all* Starr—I *want* to be" (46). As a result, Emily is cowed by the possibility that her behavior might not only reflect her father but that it might reflect on him poorly. Thus, though at first she feels no remorse for snubbing Aunt Ruth, she immediately changes her mind after she realizes that her actions signify a fault in her father:

> "You are a very ill-bred child," she [Aunt Ruth] said; "But of course it was only what was to be expected."
>
> Emily felt a sudden compunction. Had she cast a reflection on her father by her behaviour? Perhaps after all she should have shaken hands with Aunt Ruth. (26)

For most of the novel, this is Emily's concern. She accepts without argument the idea that her actions signify adults rather than herself, and her struggle is not to free herself of adult projection but to make sure that projection is the one that flatters her father.

The extensive attention the novel gives to the ways in which Emily sees and even pursues the overlap on which the adults insist does not set up not a pattern Montgomery endorses but a problem Emily must overcome. Emily argues that her body and behavior should be understood as Starr not because the novel endorses that erasure of individuality but because Emily has been pulled into the ongoing and ultimately profitless adult argument between Starr and Murray. She emerges from this never-ending conflict to realize that her body and actions must represent herself, not her father, even if her father's cherished memory is under assault from the cruel Murrays. Thus, although Emily can identify her love of writing with her father (305), she does not make significant progress toward mastering writing until she has divested even writing of her father's image and infused it with only her sense of self. Writing is the one act that can signify Emily as an individual in this book, and even though Elizabeth tries to blame "the Starr coming out in her—Douglas Starr especially" (305) for her desire to write, and even though Emily's writing habits did in fact start during her childhood with her father, by the end of the book Emily has had to disavow her father in order to keep writing. In the novel's climactic scene, when Emily and Elizabeth square off over the letters Emily has written to her dead father, Emily wins the right to keep the letters. But the aftereffects of the battle leave Emily unable to write to her father anymore. Until now, her letters to her father have been the most consistent and important aspect of her writing career,

> but when she again tried to write a letter to her father she found that it no longer meant anything to her. The sense of reality—nearness—of close communion had gone. Perhaps she had been outgrowing it gradually, as childhood began to merge into girlhood—perhaps the bitter scene with Aunt Elizabeth had only shaken into dust something out of which the spirit had already departed. But, whatever the explanation, it was not possible to write such letters any more. She missed them terribly but she could not go back to them. A certain door of life was shut behind her and could not be re-opened. (314)

In the end, writing is a solitary act that is performed by Emily and for Emily. This paragraph recasts the emotionally charged letters the orphan girl writes throughout the novel not as obeisances to the departed father but as psychological tools used for the daughter's benefit. Emily's writing is rooted in her relationship with her father, but her writing after his death is exorcised of his spirit; Emily has outgrown her father. Or perhaps she hasn't: perhaps he has been thoroughly subsumed, and the aspects of writing that formerly bore his name now exist solely for Emily's use and identification. The result is an individual Emily whose inner thoughts are no longer shaped by or in dialogue with her father, who has until then dominated Emily's ideology. The obstacles to individuality that Emily suffers are just that: elements of conflict in the narrative of the emergence of the individual. The girl's father and body are tools Montgomery uses to illustrate the difficulty of that narrative. The novel's rising conflict centers around her identification of roles, and the happy ending comes with her rejection of them in favor of a unique identity.

Emily of New Moon is far removed from the novel that birthed the sentimental orphan girl genre. It is far removed from *The Wide, Wide World* in sensibility, obviously, but it is also far removed in terms of sales. Although Warner's novel continues to attract attention in part as a result of its unprecedented popularity, *Emily* failed even to achieve the popularity of Montgomery's previous orphan girl novel. After *Emily*, the nostalgic, sentimental orphan girl genre gave way to stories about more modern, often urban girls.[10] Perhaps *Emily* revised the formula too drastically for public taste, drifting too far from the self-effacing model provided by Ellen Montgomery almost seventy-five years beforehand. Or perhaps the public's decreasing interest in the genre should be attributed to a different backlash. Rather than longing for the antimodern politics of sentimentalism, readers in the years following suffrage perhaps had no need for the strategies of power derived during the early days of feminism. Perhaps the new cultural realities of enfranchised women—of women with legally recognized subjectivity and property rights, of women with the ability to influence the public sphere directly rather than through affection—perhaps these realities made the story of sentimental-style discipline less relevant.

Oddly, *Emily of New Moon* may be more at home now than it was during the age in which it was written. Many of the articles in Irene Gammel's *Making Avonlea*, a collection of essays published in 2002, suggest this may be the case. Brenda R. Weber's reflections, for example, begin with nostalgia for *Anne of Green Gables*, Montgomery's most famous book by far, but end with a confession that she now prefers the Emily books. Similarly, Irene Gammel's essay finds itself irresistibly drawn to *Emily* as it explores sexual initiation stories. As both authors indicate, *Emily* has the darker, more existential qualities and moral complications that appeal to contemporary scholars. As this chapter has argued, *Emily* embraces both the charm of the sentimental narrative and the irony of the twentieth century through its pastoral tale of a Prince Edward Island enjoyed by a girl whose confirmed feminine subjectivity is yet modern. For many readers at the beginning of the twenty-first century, it is a book that successfully negotiates its nineteenth-century roots, evidently aware of the inadequacies of the genre's original story to the needs of its contemporary audience. Perhaps *Emily of New*

Moon, last iteration of a genre birthed almost a century beforehand, was too far ahead of its time.

The story of affective discipline recorded and provoked by classic orphan girl novels from *The Wide, Wide World* to *Emily of New Moon* reveals the changing shape of discipline and individuality. It also, however, necessitates revisions to terms that have been key to the study of the sentimental mode from which the genre emerged. "Sympathy"—the term that recent scholarship has considered definitional to sentimentalism—and mothers—the figures around whom sentimental writers themselves configured their ideology—have played key roles in our understanding of sentimentalism. But as women writers of the new century reworked the genre laid out by sentimental writers of the previous century, they also renegotiated the place of sympathy and motherhood. It is therefore to these two terms that the final chapters of *Disciplining Girls* turn. The previous chapters' exploration of the genre's slow changes lays the groundwork for a new understanding of the terms that have proved most central to sentimentalism and the discipline it championed.

CHAPTER TEN

Spinning Sympathy

When Katy Carr, of Susan Coolidge's 1873 novel *What Katy Did*, awakes on Christmas morning in her invalid's bed, she is delighted to discover three important gifts. From her cousin Helen, who is also an invalid, there is "a little silver bell." Tied up nearby is "a beautiful book . . . 'The Wide Wide World'" (203). These gifts and others adorn the third gift, a new chair from her father and the place in which she will spend many of her waking hours over the coming years. All three gifts will be important for the novel's happy ending. From this chair, Katy will assume a severely limited position in her family that allows her to find fulfillment and a measure of power. With the use of her bell, she will be able to summon siblings and servants so that she may exercise that power over them even when they are well beyond her physical reach. Armed with a strategy preached in *The Wide, Wide World*, she will make them eager to answer her summons, impatient to do her bidding. Together, these three gifts symbolize the promise and the threat of girls' fiction that follows the sentimental tradition.

Key to the power of affective discipline was a force that would later be called "sympathy." As Katy's broken body indicates, sympathy in the sentimental tradition offered power that came with pointed limitations. But the fact that Katy's body will heal before her story is finished demonstrates an important break that the new girls' fiction made with sentimentalism. Sympathy, so vital to the power of the affective discipline that girls' novels inherited from sentimentalism, changed in telling ways over the course of the orphan girl story between 1850 and 1923. Tracing this defining aspect of moral suasion through the history in which Katy appears at the middle reveals how turn-of-the-century novels for girls revised sentimentalism so that it would better fit the reality of girls during the first acme of consumer culture in America.

The history of sympathy in the classic orphan girl novel in many ways parallels the history of individualism, especially insofar as questions of power apply. For women writers as early as Warner and as late as Porter, sentimental individualism tended to be a hollow enterprise, as witnessed in the disingenuous individualism of *The Wide, Wide World* and *The Hidden Hand* as well as in the individual identity enabled by aggressive homogenization of the broader community in *Pollyanna*. Similarly, sympathy structured fictional relationships in a way that guaranteed power for girls—Katy's bell is a symptom of that promise—but also required of those girls a public display of cheerful disability—such as the performance Katy will give on a daily basis in her new chair. The changing value of individualism across the history of the classic orphan girl novel highlights the mixed results of sentimentalism's promises of empowerment. The changing uses of sympathy across that same history highlight the ways the genre simultaneously offered and undermined power.

The topic of sympathy therefore allows a close look at precisely what it means that these girls' novels descended from sentimentalism, at how exactly the terms of that heritage worked. First, it is important to note that the terms were controlled by sentimentalism: the formulaic plot in which a disempowered female protagonist uses sympathy to knit the people around her into a group bound by sameness was scripted for girls' novels by fiction of the early and middle nineteenth century. Second, although the terms were dictated by the previous generation, the new generation worked endlessly to revise those terms so they would be more suited to girl readers. Although it is true, as Claudia Nelson has argued, that turn-of-the-century orphan narratives demonstrated that sentimentalized children were required to tend to "the spiritual and emotional uplift of adults" (*Little* 7), that moral work did not preclude spiritual and material benefits for the imagined girls. These books were best sellers of their day in part because they appealed to adults and told traditional stories about the ways children could be useful to adults, but orphan girl novels at the turn of the century rejected the old model in which girls happily sacrificed themselves in order to fix the adults around them without any hope of reward for themselves. These girls did continue the work of improving the lives of adults who were sympathetic to them, as was their chief responsibility in sentimental novels. However, the performance of those duties in the Progressive Era promised—in forms and dimensions not possible in sentimental fiction—material and social comfort for the girls themselves.

In the last ten years, sympathy has become for scholars of American litera-

ture the identifying trait of sentimentalism, even for books that clearly predate
Warner's best seller or that take as their scope something much larger than the
domestic setting typical of sentimental fiction. Sympathy is, for current scholars,
that process by which people achieve a synchronicity of feeling. In other words,
sympathy can be recognized by its effects: where people are sympathetic to each
other, they strive to be and feel the same. But we can also recognize sympathy
by its characteristics as it is in motion. Sympathy is an emotion (which is why
it flourished in sentimental novels) made up of a potent concoction of guilt,
affection, and admiration. A person feeling sympathy feels an obscure guilt over
his or her revulsion at the person who is ill or weak in addition to a certain
amount of guilt at being happy, wealthy, or mobile. But affection and admiration
are also key to sympathy: without them sympathy becomes pity or even disgust.
Thus, sentimental fiction and its descendants make a point of instructing their
weak characters (and readers) in the art of being pleasant, of being *good* invalids,
orphans, or waifs. Children, women, and invalids who bear up well under the
weight of their affliction (which can range from illness to financial hardship to
*un*sympathetic relatives) are admired for being unlike all those other children,
women, and invalids who have become embittered. Sympathetic girls will make
being around them as pleasant as possible and will allow visitors every opportunity not to think about the inequity that has made those creatures weak.

The irony is that by doing so, the girls of stories in the sentimental tradition
make it impossible for the people around them to think about anything else. Sympathy therefore creates a network of guilt and affection that forces the healthy
and powerful to obsess over the weak, which allows—in sentimental fiction—
moral instruction to flow out from the object of sympathy to the people wringing
their hands around her sickbed. Such a network conveys a certain power to the
girl around whom the network is arrayed: the girl attains a moral position from
which she can instruct and improve the people around her. Orphan girl novels of
the turn of the century revise the story of sympathy to offer Progressive Era readers a version of sympathy more relevant to the new consumer culture: girls at the
center of a sympathetic relationship are still able to improve sympathizing adults,
but the later novels offer girls a centrality ensured by consumerism.

BEGINNING IN THE MIDDLE

Rather than beginning my survey of sympathy in novels about girls in midcentury, when these ideas were enjoying their first exposure through popular sentimental novels, I begin with *What Katy Did*, which, published in 1873, figures as

a transitional book between the midcentury high point of sentimentalism and the turn-of-the-century Progressive Era. *Katy's* scenes clearly sum up the steps required for establishing sympathetic power, which made it instrumental in the transmission of the sentimental model to Progressive Era children's fiction.

Coolidge's novel tells the story of Katy Carr, a natural leader who is imaginative and hot-tempered. A half-orphan, she obeys her aunt when she chooses and adores her often-absent father. The narrator makes clear that Katy is essentially a good girl who has a great deal of trouble controlling herself, and although she is always genuinely sorry for her indiscretions, her plans to be great and good are rarely sustained past an initial swell of promise. But when Katy disobeys her aunt and plays on a broken swing, she suffers a terrible fall that leaves her an invalid for most of the rest of the novel. From this point on, the novel becomes a record of Katy's successes and failures in learning the lessons of sympathy. Katy's happiness, the maintenance of her home, and her relationship with those she loves depend on how she negotiates the sympathy they feel for her.

Fortunately for Katy, she has had an excellent tutor in the figure of her cousin Helen, who is also an invalid and whose example Katy follows carefully. The first phase of sympathy, however, is not pretty. Before Katy's accident, Helen has had to expend a great deal of effort in order to become a favorite of the children at the Carr house. One of Katy's siblings "backed away with his hands behind him" on first meeting Helen, "staring hard for a minute or two" (125). Secretly, Katy and others worry that Helen might envy and even resent their healthy bodies (137–38). Sympathy can only exist between the weak and the strong, and although many sentimental stories about the relationship between the weak and strong often choose to ignore the potential for resentment on the part of the former or guilt and aversion on the part of the latter, *What Katy Did* makes the original state of sympathy clear. One party must be weak, the other must be strong, and there is good reason to think the inequity will wedge the two apart.

And yet even Philly, the boy who held himself back from Helen, somehow comes to cherish her caresses. The means by which the original state of sympathy is overcome is absolutely key to the model of sympathy sentimental novels (and novels, such as Coolidge's, that follow in that tradition) espouse. "There was something in Cousin Helen's face and manner," the narrator explains, "which made the children at home with her at once" (125). That "something" is more carefully constructed than Katy first realizes. Helen later tells Katy, "sickness is such a disagreeable thing in itself, that unless sick people take great pains, they soon grow to be eyesores to themselves and everybody about them" (185). Helen is no fool. Keenly aware of the aversion and guilt that can fill the well on sight of the ill, she repeats a lengthy conversation she once had with her father when she first fell ill:

> "My daughter, I'm afraid you've got to live in this room for a long time. Now there's one thing I want you to do for my sake."
>
> "What is that?" she asked, surprised to hear there was anything left which she could *do* for anybody.
>
> "I want you to turn out all these physic bottles, and make your room pleasant and pretty for *me* to come and sit in. You see, I shall spend a good deal of my time here! Now I don't like dust and darkness. I like to see flowers on the table, and sunshine in at the window. Will you do this to please me?"
>
> "Yes," said the girl, but she gave a sigh, and . . . she felt as if it was going to be a dreadful trouble.
>
> "Then, another thing," continued her father, "I want *you* to look pretty. Can't night-gowns and wrappers be trimmed and made becoming just as much as dresses? A sick woman who isn't neat is a disagreeable object. Do, to please me, send for something pretty, and let me see you looking nice again. I can't bear to have my Helen turn into a slattern." (179–80)

This exchange again makes plain the threat behind sympathy: the weak can become an eyesore, in which case they will be lucky to have any friends. Therefore, it is incumbent on them—as Helen, her father, and the novel argue—to be pleasant and pretty. This passage demonstrates that some people will visit the ill out of duty—Helen's father is resigned to spending "a great deal of time" in Helen's room even though he is fed up with the conditions of the place—but other passages make clear that the ill themselves have a duty. "A sick person," Helen tells Katy, "ought to be as fresh and dainty as a rose" (177), both for those who must visit and for those who might be induced to visit. When Katy protests that she can no longer get up to interact with her siblings and friends, Helen says, "But you can make your room such a delightful place, that they will want to come to you! Don't you see, a sick person has one splendid chance—she is always on hand. Everybody who wants her knows just where to go. If people love her, she gets naturally to be the heart of the house" (185).

Becoming the heart of the house is the goal of the weak party in such a sympathetic relationship. Helen's phrase introduces the idea that girls in sympathetic relationships must be the center of those relationships. They will be the sentimental heart of the home, radiating daintiness and delight. They will be the moral center of the home, as Katy becomes when she teaches her siblings to be kind to a horrid relation (253). They can even become the organizational center of the home, as Katy does when she takes over the duties of managing the house after her aunt dies; the narrator remarks that "Katy, sitting up stairs in her big chair, held the threads of the house firmly in her hands" (234). Getting "naturally to be the heart of the house" is the essence of the promise inherent in the sympathetic relationship, for it means that the powerful no longer need to feel guilty and that the weak can find power.

In the sentimental model there is another important social obligation for the weak party in the sympathetic relationship, an obligation that can be carried out successfully because of the new centrality possessed by these girls. The weak must use their position at the heart of the house to change the powerful so that the latter become more like the former. This is not to say that the powerful must become weak but that the powerful must become humble, charitable, kind, industrious, joyful, or whatever other characteristic now defines the girl at the heart of the home. Helen certainly uses her sympathetic power in this way, to the approval of Katy's father (138), most remarkably in the transformation of Katy, who consciously sets out to mimic Helen even before Katy has her accident (143). Later, Katy—again following Helen's model by becoming a model of behavior herself—uses her own sympathetic ties to change her able-bodied siblings. Well into her invalidism, Katy becomes the only person who can effectively discipline Philly, the boy who was once so disturbed at the sight of Helen. When the boy has done something naughty and refuses to take correction from others, Katy calls him to her now charming room, holds him in her lap, speaks to him gently, and asks him to behave better. "I will!" says Philly. "Only kiss me first, because I didn't mean to, you know!" "Philly was very fond of Katy," the narrator explains. "Miss Petingill said it was wonderful to see how that child let himself be managed" (247).

Katy thus not only manages the house from her big chair but also the other members of her family, especially her siblings. She molds them into her own image: they become obedient like her, sweet and approachable like her, and they acquire any number of other traits that the new moral center of the house has acquired. When she rings her silver bell, the children race each other to see who can reach her big chair first (239), and the influence she shines on them is guaranteed by the sympathetic arrangement proposed by *The Wide, Wide World* and the sentimental philosophy of the decades leading up to *Katy*. When Helen returns to the Carr house, she makes a point of recognizing Katy's success:

> And Katy, darling, I want to tell you how pleased I am to see how bravely you
> have worked your way up. I can perceive it in everything—in Papa, in the

children, in yourself. You have won the place, which, you recollect, I once told you an invalid should try to gain, of being to everybody "The Heart of the House." (273)

Katy has indeed worked her way up. Helen probably means this compliment to convey how impressed she is that Katy has shed her depression, but it is also true that Katy has ascended—upstairs in her big chair—to a position of influence. She is still weak in body, but, following the rules of sentimental sympathy, she has parlayed that weakness into an opportunity to become the center of her household. Her success in becoming the heart of the house is documented by her success with Papa and the children as well as herself. Without moving from her room, she has made her father and siblings happier and better, and if she has gained some power along the way, all the better.

SENTIMENTAL ORIGINS

But there are important limitations on the power a girl such as Katy can wield, and these limitations become more dramatic with a look back at the girls of mid-century sentimental novels, girls who made the terms of sympathy clearest. Consider, for example, Eva St. Claire, the girl who plays so prominent a role in Harriet Beecher Stowe's *Uncle Tom's Cabin* (1851). The immense popularity of this novel—and its publication during an era when family time often involved adults reading novels to the family, with the result "that children often heard stories that were far beyond their reading abilities" (Murray 53)—means it is extremely likely that middle-class girls outside the South knew the story well. As such, it is an important predecessor in the emergence of later girls' fiction. The doomed Eva similarly makes herself the moral center of her household, in the process drawing a disobedient slave and both her uptight aunt and disappointing father into sympathetic relationships. She makes herself charming and lovable, eventually correcting the faults of those around her through the sympathy her pitiful state, charm, and boundless love enable. Topsy's willfulness, Ophelia's heartlessness, and Mr. St. Claire's devotion to the bottom line all lose their sharpness, and the characters become, through sympathy for Eva, more like the little girl: obedient, kind, and loving. Eva is able to remake the people around her according to her own tastes, and because she is so adept at the game of sympathy, they do not resent her interference. Indeed, they are grateful for it.

Clearly, this is an important kind of power, but at what cost does Eva gain her power? Studies of sympathetic children in midcentury fiction have been skeptical of the power such fiction pretends to offer girls, noting how "the child's love works to enforce a bourgeois patriarchal order that leaves the child as vulnerable as ever" (Sánchez-Eppler, *Dependent* 3). This is in effect what happens in Eva's story. As Bridget Bennett points out in her work on *Uncle Tom's Cabin*, the sacred fetishes little Eva leaves for her new converts in the form of locks of hair serve to highlight the disappearance of everything *but* Eva's bodiless message. It is as though the heart of the home only has power when she acts as a centrifuge: Eva radiates influence outward, losing her body in the process.

Therefore, the terms of sympathetic power offered by midcentury literature were conflicted at best. Girls could have power, but at a horrible personal cost. As girls' fiction borrowed the story of sympathy from sentimentalism, it faced the difficult task of revising those terms in order to leave its protagonists happy and intact. Still, from early in the history of fiction explicitly for girls, that revision was already taking place. Consider again *What Katy Did*, in which Helen and Katy figure as effective sympathetic centers without dying. Coolidge's novel is firmly aware of its origins, and Coolidge makes clear her link to novels such as Stowe's when, for example, Helen gives one of the children "a cunning little locket" holding a bit of her hair (141). Helen, it seems, is already feeling the pull of the centrifuge. And yet she resists dissipation, and her student Katy not only avoids death but learns to walk again. The genres of "woman's fiction," as Nina Baym famously dubbed it, and girls' fiction were bound to each other, but girls' fiction tested those bonds from the very beginning.

PROGRESSIVE ERA REVISIONS

An obvious heir to Eva and Katy is Pollyanna, who would not appear until 1913. Pollyanna arrives at her aunt's house as a burden that, Polly takes pains to make clear, is both unwanted and a perpetual reminder of the "silly" choices Pollyanna's mother made (Porter 13). Pollyanna is not an invalid—not yet—but she is weak, wracked with grief, penniless, and left with no relatives but the everfrowning Aunt Polly. Because she has been thrown on Polly's charity, the power relationship necessary to sympathy is a given from the beginning. Because Polly sees her niece as an imposition and an heirloom of family shame, the requisite aversion is also in place. The novel's project is to narrate the story of how Pollyanna manages to become the heart of the house and to show what she does with the power her new position gives her.

Porter's novel endorses the old model with minor changes. The story follows

Pollyanna as she trips gaily through the town, across social barriers, and into the hearts of the disparate, stagnant townspeople. The glad game she preaches is the perfect philosophy for a standard tale of sympathy from the previous century. It is activated when things are bad—as when Pollyanna receives a crutch instead of a doll one Christmas—and requires the sufferer to ignore what is wrong, to focus only on what will make her pleasant and happy. By finding something to be glad about in any situation, Pollyanna is able to mitigate the various pains of the people in the town and bring them all into a synchronicity of, to borrow a phrase from Stowe, right feeling. Pollyanna's effect on her community is similar to Katy's effect on her father and siblings; Pollyanna forces pain and joy to commingle, which causes the secret grudges, petty jealousies, and moral inadequacies of the townspeople to evaporate. Their unenviable situations—loneliness, lameness, fussiness—are refitted with happy faces because of the glad game, which means they can become sympathetic heroes in their own right. Pollyanna's cheerful response to her own pitiable situation—not only is she an orphan but she also has to live with Aunt Polly, a fact that inspires great pity in the book (27)—makes her the cheerful sufferer necessary for the sympathetic structure. As a result, Pollyanna ends up at the center of the new community. Like Katy in her big chair upstairs, Pollyanna has a moral vantage point from which to keep the town in order. There are variations on the old theme in that Pollyanna has created new, limited sympathetic centers throughout the town. But the basic plot is still in place: Pollyanna has taught the people of the town to be sympathetic toward her as well as sympathetic *like* her. As Eva did, she uses their sympathy to help push her moral code onto them.

It is significant to note that one of the revisions girls' fiction proposed to the sentimental model of sympathy was a broadening of its scope. Karen Sánchez-Eppler has indicated that this potential was always implicit in sympathetic models, particularly those tied to children, as in Sunday school stories that used sentimentality to endorse an imperial right to impose white, bourgeois, American Protestantism through missionary work.[1] Alice Mills has argued that *Pollyanna* and its sequels tell the ongoing story of how the orphan girl is able to use her pathos to spread her philosophy of life to ever wider circles, and Laureen Tedesco has revealed that Girl Scout handbooks in the Progressive Era enabled girls to enforce bourgeois American codes on the tides of immigrants who reached America during these decades. Although these scholars do not connect girls' literature of the new century with midcentury fiction, they do indicate that the imperialist, hegemonizing potential of sentimental sympathy was always latent in children's culture.[2] They further indicate that sympathy was used on broader stages as a means of knitting people together. The scope of sympathy, therefore, expanded, working its way ever outward as the decades passed.

But sympathy also developed a tendency to turn toward its center, even as the heart of the house spread her influence wider, and it is *Pollyanna* that makes this innovation clearest. When Pollyanna is struck by a car, the accident leaves her seriously wounded; although the accident is not fatal, it becomes quickly apparent that Pollyanna will never walk again. Yet the physical blow is not so great a danger as the new spiritual wound that most threatens her: Pollyanna's faith in the glad game is uprooted when she overhears the doctor's gloomy diagnosis. Bereft, Pollyanna, like Katy before her, enters into a deep depression from which there is no sign she will emerge. In her reading of novels such as *Pollyanna* in the broader context of the history of childhood, Gail Schmunk Murray argues that what happens next feels very similar to what might have transpired in a mid-century sentimental novel:

> [Porter] used the accident only as a device to complete the transforming power of Pollyanna's positive thinking. In Porter's hands, the suffering caused by the accident does not bring redemption in and of itself, but it multiplies the number of persons drawn into "the glad game" as they seek to comprehend the tragedy that has befallen the heroine. (109)

For Murray, this fallout from the quasi-deathbed scene is similar to what one might find in midcentury portrayals of perishing daughters: midcentury sentimentalism knew well how to turn an ailing child into an opportunity to influence adults. Murray's reading, too, is consistent with the novel up to this point: this has been a story of how Pollyanna drew more and more people into the glad game, radiating influence with a gusto that would have been the envy of any of her predecessors.

But for all that, this reading is not exactly accurate. I want to emphasize that this reading *makes sense*, given everything leading up to the accident, including the events leading up to it from other novels clearly in the same tradition. But Pollyanna's illness does not, in fact, allow her to convert masses of adults to the glad game. A string of people do stop by the house but not to gaze on the child's wilting body and thereby draw inspiration from her (noble bearing of) pain. Pollyanna does not serve the adults of the community after her accident; she is still the heart of the house, indeed of the town, but she is no longer directing the people around her and dispensing moral instruction. Instead, this stream of people comes to serve the little girl herself. As Polly's servant Nancy puts it, what the line of people dropping by the house during Pollyanna's illness means is unambiguous: "It means that ever since last June that blessed child has jest been makin' the whole town glad, *an' now they're turnin' round an' tryin' ter make her a little glad too*" (202, emphasis added). The first part of the novel forecasts a further widening of the glad game, but the conclusion provides no such thing. It might multiply the number of sympathizing characters *of whom we are aware*, but these people come to the house—that is, present themselves in a space where the reader can see them—because, as they say one after the other, they are *already* grateful to her for the changes she has *previously* wrought in them. Those people have already been helped, and their visits to Pollyanna are made with the intention of working for Pollyanna. This ending significantly revises the traditional use of sympathetic communities centered on ailing girls: this is not a widening but a tightening—a reversal from centrifugal to centripetal—in which the adults remain in the sympathetic structure built by the little girl but turn to her to heal her body and shine her own influence back on the wounded child.[3] The purpose of the sympathetic relationship now becomes, to paraphrase Nancy, to make the child glad.

As a direct result of this sustained adult attention, Pollyanna's mood does in fact improve, and—to complete the bargain—a specialist in Pollyanna's specific ailment is located, invited, and successfully engaged to heal the little girl. To be sure, the adults around Pollyanna benefit from her influence, but the change in this story of sympathy is dramatic. Not only does Pollyanna avoid the fate of sentimental girls in the mold of Eva St. Claire, girls whose deaths cemented their life's work in building the sympathetic network, but Porter's novel goes so far as to suggest that the point of sympathy is to construct a community of adults who will provide for the child. From the vantage of *Pollyanna*, even *What Katy Did* looks old-fashioned in this sense. Certainly a weak, sympathetic girl will make a point of directing the moral and mundane lives of the people around her, Porter's novel suggests, but her real power lies in making the people around her want to make *her* happy.

And whatever good these sympathetic adults may do Pollyanna's spirit, it is significant that one of the services they offer her is improvement of her body. Although Eva distributes bits of her body at the end of her life in order to help those around her remember, her body is a barely necessary conduit through which the people standing around her deathbed or fingering bits of her hair access her message. When Katy spins influence from her big chair, she retains her body and regains her health but only accidentally; the sympathetic arrangement offers her power and distraction from her illness until her invalidism disappears of its own accord. In Pollyanna's story, however, the body is a major reason the adults come together. Healing it, serving it, and providing it with pets and trinkets is the reason adults surround Pollyanna's body. Right feeling and morality radiate from Eva's bed, and like her bits of hair, Eva and her message dissipate from the bed outward. Pollyanna's wounded body, however, becomes the magnetic center of adult attention. Although she has lived her life previous to this moment ranging far and wide in her personal outreach program, at the end of the novel she has stopped radiating and begun consuming the fruits of her labor: adult attention. It is significant that this attention leaves the girl with a body that is more solid, that is healthier, stronger, and that is more attended to than before.

REFLECTING ON THE TRANSITION

The changes taking place in the sympathetic model borrowed from sentimentalism are most dramatic when viewed through high points in the overall narrative—a sentimental story published in 1850, a transitional story in 1873, and a late–Progressive Era novel in 1913—but they were changes that had been taking place all along. *Eight Cousins*, for example, clearly arranges its male cousins around the orphan girl, and a major turning point of the novel is Rose's discovery that she can and should influence the boys. She is a pitiful, morose, sickly child at the beginning of the novel, and only when she ignores her sadness—à la Katy—in service of influencing her cousins does she become stronger. By helping rid the boys of their vulgar habits and instilling in them a love of bourgeois lifestyle, she reshapes them as girls on either end of the historical spectrum might. There is some promise of reward for the girl herself—recall the promise that disciplining the boys will produce "fit friends for an innocent creature like yourself" (183)— but the reward is delayed and slots Rose for the kind of "second-class citizenship" Alcott herself found so unsatisfying (Strickland 162). The orphan girl of this novel, situated at the opening of the period, uses sympathy as a sentimental girl might; there is only a hint that there might be some significant reward in this relationship for herself.

Later orphan girl novels of the period use sympathy with uneven results. One such novel written just after the turn of the century, *Rebecca of Sunnybrook Farm*, shows a movement toward Pollyanna and away from Eva. Like Rose in Alcott's novel, Rebecca sets up a sympathetic network, this time of neighbors, teachers, and peers. Recall by way of example Jeremiah Cobb, the old man who delivers Rebecca to her aunts' home, the man whose "mental machinery is simple" except when, as the narrator tellingly puts it, "propelled by his affection or sympathy." As

Rebecca tells him she has decided to run away, Cobb finds that "these were both employed" (Wiggin 86), and Cobb finds exactly the right words to keep the girl in the home where her education and social mobility will be provided for. Here, sympathy guides an adult to see to the girl's needs rather than guiding the girl to see to an adult's needs. But reading further in the scene, it becomes clear that the benefit to the girl is not so neatly defined as it will be ten years later for Pollyanna. Following the successful conversation with Cobb, the narrator sighs that Rebecca "had been saved from foolishness and error," which should be read as a benefit for the child, but the sentence goes on to explain that she has also been "kept from troubling her poor mother; prevented from angering and mortifying her aunts" (92). On the same page, the narrator reveals that Rebecca's "heart was melted now," which is to say that she has become the target, not the dispenser, of sympathy, "and she determined to win Aunt Miranda's approval by some desperate means," which is to say both that she will attempt to act in accordance with *Miranda's* moral code and that she will do so in order to repair the sympathetic relationship that will give *Rebecca* a happier life in Miranda's house. This sort of ambivalence about the direction of sympathy continues throughout the novel until the end, at which point another man, the wealthy Adam Ladd, is moved by love for the girl and pity for her family's dire financial situation (the mixture of the two yielding sympathy) to negotiate a business deal that will finally relieve Rebecca of the financial burdens under which she has suffered throughout the narrative. In this way, the novel seems to be leaning toward but not fully committed to the process of forging sympathetic communities that will grant the girl benefits.

When sympathetic communities do shift from centrifugal to centripetal, they tend to do so in terms such as these, terms emphasizing real, financial gains, not just the spiritual rewards awaiting the girls upon marriage or death. In *A Little Princess*, for example, the suddenly destitute Sara creates a sympathetic community around herself first by telling compelling stories, then by being seen (and overheard) bearing up admirably under harsh circumstances. Sara's visibility, as I emphasized, is part of her ability to move people, and in the context of other temporarily unfortunate orphan girls such as Katy, Pollyanna, and Rebecca it becomes obvious that key to the successful forging of affectionate links is Sara's ability to create sympathy in those who witness her gracious bearing during a time of profound misfortune. The attorney who will be instrumental to Sara's restored social status, for example, joins with his family to watch and discuss the pitiful—yet somehow still noble—girl they see on the street. For the Carmichael family, Sara is a reminder of the hideously precarious nature of wealth. But because Sara is so noble and kind, because she is so lacking in resentment—think of Cousin Helen's cheerfulness toward the able-bodied—the Carmichaels can look at her with pity and admiration; they can sympathize. In addition, Sara's neighbor, Tom Carrisford, who knows what happened to her father and who will one day take his place, devours stories about the girl who holds up so well in her misery, and his servant—Ram Dass—secretly watches Sara, eavesdropping on her dreams of luxury. Anyone at all susceptible to sympathy falls for Sara, and just as Adam Ladd provided Rebecca with financial ease and Aunt Polly showered trinkets on her young charge, these sympathetic adults go out of their way to give the orphan girl the money and goods her heart desires. Carrisford and Dass conspire to fill the poor girl's room with furniture and treats for which they have overheard her longing, and when he discovers that she is none other than the daughter of his deceased business partner, Carrisford bestows the wealth of bursting diamond mines on her. In the last half of the novel, after the sympathetic network has been established according to sentimental guidelines, the people who feel sympathy for Sara come into a synchronicity with her: they learn her desires and desire those things for her. The novel's happy moments come with a little girl receiving material goods after a long period of knitting together a sympathetic community.

As did Eva, Sara spins her influence out, but as with Pollyanna, the purpose of that influence is to arrange adults around her so that she can draw in from them worldly satisfaction. The direction of sympathy is still mixed, as the novel ends with a scene that emphasizes the good influence Sara has had on the adults who watch her, whether that be in the form of Carrisford's suddenly improved health or the charity of a baker inspired by Sara's own charity during her days of poverty. So even here, in a novel whose conflict is that the right adult (Carrisford) has yet to pay the right kind of attention (passing on her father's wealth) to an orphan girl, the influence of the sentimental model is heavy.

But there is a pattern emerging in these later texts. When sympathy turns to seek its center—namely, the girl who has been radiating influence in the tradition of sentimental narratives—the adults who have been forged into a community of likeness through their devotion to the girl can now show their conversion not just through good deeds directed to heaven or one another. Now they can tell the girl they love her by bestowing her heart's desire, which is no longer a father who will be less alcoholic or give up his slaves; instead, the promise is of diamonds, decorations, pets, clothes, property, and cash. These sympathetic communities were designed by a sentimental project that deferred satisfaction to the afterlife and insisted on the importance of sympathy because of the good that girls could do for the people around them. In the popular heir to the sentimental novel at the turn of the century, sympathetic communities still existed to make adults, cousins, and siblings feel right, but increasingly, adults feeling right meant that children gained. And that gain was not a happy surprise, a positive side effect of pleasing or healing adults. The *goal* was to make sure children were happy, and happy adults looked increasingly like a means to that end.

THE PRICE OF BEING A CONSUMING SUBJECT

Girls were central to the sympathetic communities imagined in novels in this tradition from at least 1850, but their centrality took on different forms. In the earlier novels, that centrality only guaranteed them an opportunity to provide services, moral or mundane, for people around them. As they influenced the people connected to them through sympathy, they also ran the risk of losing their bodies and lives to the sympathetic process. When the sentimental model of sympathy migrated to novels featuring orphan girls, that process changed in such a way that it confirmed rather than eliminated the body of the girl at the center of the relationship. The result was a validation of the girl as a subject. Rather than a vessel for a message, the girl existed in happy endings as a solid, well person. One of the favorite ways these novels demonstrated that their girls were valid subjects was through the concentration of material goods on these able bodies.

But this is not to imply that the protagonist of Progressive Era novels was necessarily more liberated or subversive than her sentimental predecessor. The cost for midcentury girls at the center of a sympathetic relationship was dissolution in the needs of those who sympathized with her. That cost was no longer necessary for girls after the heyday of sentimentalism as a genre, but the very centrality that enabled the sympathetic relationship also placed profound limitations on the girls wielding power through sympathy. These girls became consumers of the goods the sympathetic adults showered on them, and in doing so they achieved a historically appropriate subjectivity that required them to remain in a position of weakness.

The subjectivity offered to girls in these novels was one marked by the ability to consume. That consumption was accomplished in a variety of ways, usually passively and often with the aid of—this should be no surprise—sympathy. Jane H. Hunter has said that the Progressive Era sought to produce girls who "found shopping . . . to be an arena in which they could demonstrate taste and through taste, *self*" (274). The protagonists of these orphan girl novels very rarely purchased things themselves, but they did find ways to manipulate adults into purchasing for them—indeed, into purchasing in accordance with the girls' tastes.

This pattern had already emerged in scenes in which the sight of a pathetic but brave Sara Crewe inspires Carrisford and Dass to give her exactly the gifts of which she dreams, but a Canadian novel written in this tradition during this period that became an enduring best seller in America contains an example more clearly motivated by the emotional synchronicity enabled by sympathy. *Anne of Green Gables* features a shy, withdrawn man who pities the poor girl he has accidentally adopted, and when the brave girl overwhelms him with affection, Matthew is transformed into what Anne would call a "kindred spirit," a sure marker of sympathetic synchronicity. Anne declares that "Matthew and I are such kindred spirits I can read his thoughts without words at all" (Montgomery 203), and Matthew is evidently similarly keyed into Anne's thoughts because he buys a dress for her that she has longed for without her even asking him for the gift. When Marilla remarks with amazement on Matthew's sensitivity to Anne's wishes (270), she is flagging the results of Matthew's sympathetic identification with Anne. One of the most important kinds of influence these sympathetic girls exercise—and Anne's influence on Matthew is a prime example—takes the form of them teaching the adults around them to desire what the girls desire so that the adults can exercise the girls' taste. Here, Matthew knows exactly what dress to buy for Anne. She does not shop, as Hunter implies she would if she were to express her position as a consuming self, but because she is such a skilled wielder of sympathy, she hardly needs to. She can express her taste and therefore self through the choices Matthew makes under her unspoken direction.

Consumption at the turn of the century thus promised girls a sense of self, a confirmed subjectivity, and it did so in terms that went to the heart of the sentimental ideology that drove the classic orphan girl novel. Although American children provided crucial supplemental earnings to the household budget—and in some circles girls contributed more of their earnings than did boys—a significant amount of girls' new earning power went to the private delights of fiction.[4] Consider for example the conflation of sentimentality and selfhood in the popular children's magazine *St. Nicholas*, which both flattered its readers as individuals (Rahn 109) and used sympathetic pleas to the reading children to influence their spending patterns, urging them not just to buy the magazine itself, which it certainly did, but to buy the products advertised in its pages as well (Van Horn 126). Thus, again, sympathy, subjectivity, and consumption intermingle. That pattern continued in advertising copy as well, in a trend during these years that seemed to take for granted that children were key participants in consumer culture. For instance, although Catherine Van Horn recounts how consistently the majority of *nineteenth*-century advertising in children's magazines "addressed mothers and families more than it did children" (122), she indicates that at the *close* of the century that pattern underwent a very quick change: "As they worked to make their advertising pages pay, publishers of children's magazines became pioneers in casting children in the role of an advertising class" (122). This mission, she suggests, largely had been achieved well before the end of the Progressive Era. Therefore, Van Horn's study demonstrates that a new emphasis on the child at the center of the process of consumption came into being during the period of the sympathetic plot I have been following. As these fictional girls were becoming consuming subjects at the center of their sympathetic networks, the girls reading those stories were being assured of an important role as a consumer at the center of the new economy.

Seen this way, the new foregrounding of consumption (passive or shopping by proxy) as a sign of successful sympathy is also liberatory—probably. The question of whether participation in consumer culture is empowering or debilitating has spawned a debate that crosses into nearly every arena of literary studies, and a brief survey of that debate will demonstrate just how muddied it has become. For Peter Stoneley, for example, the question can be summarized easily: "Is the girl buying, or is she sold?" (5). But, even for Stoneley, the question cannot be answered so easily. A girl reader might, he suggests,

> be flattered by her own centrality to the world of the novel and her ability to smooth the contradictions [between class, leisure, and consumer culture] that adults seem unable to manage. There is even a sense that the girl has an aptitude for the new world of consumerist exchange. But all the while, the child-reader is being informed of what she is needed to be: naïve, innocent, and available to the world of commerce. (70)

Other studies of girls' culture and their participation in the world of consumption often produce similarly ambivalent answers. Kelly Schrum's analysis of the origins of *Seventeen* magazine, for example, demonstrates that the magazine is, first, a good example of how consumerism forces the broader culture to put girls at its center and, second, an example of how consumer culture both dominates and is casually shrugged off by the consuming girls it addresses. Sherrie A. Inness has made *both* a case for the possibility that girls can "shape market-place commodities in ways that might or might not have been intended by their adult creators" (introduction 4) *and* that specific bits of girls' consumer culture (such as the American Girl franchise) can serve to keep girls focused on being part of consumer culture, thereby ignoring inequity and sexist discrimination ("Anti-Barbies"). Others, such as Rhona Justice-Malloy, have argued that even when girls take an active role that allows them some agency over the images of consumer culture, there is something inherently coercive, something that cannot be resisted, in the images consumer culture feeds them.

In scholarship on sentimentalism, the conclusion is no clearer. Gillian Brown has made the point that American literature often conflates spending with citizenship and subjectivity. Read at face value, then, the role of girls in real and fictional models of consumption guarantees girls citizenship and a subject position in which to absorb the goods of consumer culture. Compared with the dissipation that usually awaits girls in sentimental narratives, this is a tremendous improvement. But critics such as Ann Douglas have been skeptical of the subjectivity consumerism offers. As a new wave of leftist criticism has come to dominate discussion of American sentimentalism, scholars such as Lauren Berlant have revived a criticism originally leveled by Douglas: sentimentalism uses consumerism and other tools to make its reader passive and happy in subordination. Right feeling heads off the need for action, allowing inequity to persist.

Certainly, the same problem of contented inaction presents itself in even the most liberatory of these orphan girl novels. Through sympathy, the protagonists win an important place in their communities. Through consumption enabled by sympathy, they mark out a subjectivity. But that process is predicated on a power relationship that insists on one party's weakness. Sympathy cannot exist without an inequity of power. By wielding sympathy to gain some kind of power—call it subversive—these girls have accepted the terms of sympathy—namely, that they will be weak. Do they gain power? Of course.[5] Are they as powerful as the people who feel sympathy for them? The definition of sympathy says not. If they exceed or even match the power of the people around them, sympathy must end. The technology of sympathy requires a disappointing limit on the power sympathy can offer.

And yet it would be hasty to dismiss these novels as complicit, to say, in an echo of Berlant's criticism of woman's fiction, that girls' fiction is not revolutionary enough. The bodies—marked out by consumption—that these girls manage to retain will become the site of arguments about women's rights for the twentieth century, and the fact that the happy ending in *Pollyanna* coincides with the community celebrating the girl's healthy body will have crucial implications in the coming decades. The terms by which she is given the tools to achieve that solid, valid—as opposed to invalid—body impose awful limitations, but the ability to spin sympathy without being dissipated by the centrifuge is an important improvement.

This paradox will not be easily resolved, but perhaps such a realization becomes easier to stomach with the realization that readers at the turn into the *current* century are not the first to try to resolve it. The weighing of power and cost that becomes necessary on analyzing these novels in retrospect was also taking place—much more quietly—as the writers of the new girls' novels revised the plot their literary foremothers had given them. The integrity of the individual and her ability to dictate her personal boundaries through taste and ownership were constantly under threat by sympathy and the sentimental rules of affective discipline, and the women writing in the new century understood both the implications of sympathy and the resistance to its limitations that their readers would have.

Girls' Novels and the End of Mothering

When postsentimental orphan girl stories used mother figures as antagonists in plots about girls achieving a more robust subjectivity, they performed a stunning revision of the sentimental model of discipline they had inherited from nineteenth-century sentimental novels. That mothers could be antagonists at all was a fundamental shift: in the mode from which this girls' fiction borrowed its central plot, mothers were the benevolent heroines, not the villains. The domestic spaces over which they presided and the fiction about the importance of those spaces were, in the words of Mary P. Ryan, "the empire of the mother." But between *Eight Cousins* and *Emily of New Moon*, that empire was utterly conquered by the orphan girls of popular fiction. The project of protecting and healing the home space switched from mother to daughter. The responsibility of using the power inherent in affective discipline to rule over the people within that space was displaced from the mothers of the sentimental mode to the girls who followed. As I have demonstrated, such power came with significant restrictions on the girls wielding it, but girls were not the only ones who would pay the price for changing structures of sentimental-style discipline. In order to lay solitary claim to the power of disciplinary intimacy, the protagonists of the postsentimental orphan girl novel played to turn-of-the-century fears about motherhood gone awry, imagining ways for girls to take control of other little girls, the men and boys around them, and even mothers themselves.

SENTIMENTAL MOTHERS TAKING CARE OF BOYS

The origins of sentimental ideology were steeped in a dedication to a disciplinary role for mothers, a disciplinary role that spelled out clearly the inclinations and expectations of good mothering, specifically good mothering of sons. Jan Lewis has argued that "by 1830, the feminine social role had been redefined: women were to prepare their children, and especially their sons, for membership in society" (214), and Ryan has said that a "tight, indeed controlling, bond between mother and male child was at the very core of the cult of domesticity" (58). In his study of conflicts within midcentury philosophies of motherhood, Ken Parille has maintained that "as essays in mothers' magazines and advice books repeatedly remind[ed] readers, 'good mothers alone make *good men*'" ("Medicine of Sympathy" 105). This was a heavy responsibility indeed, considering that domestic writers "believed the mother-son relationship was the affective familial bond most crucial to domestic and national stability" (Parille, *Boys at Home* 44). Mothers were of course to nurture and even shape both sons and daughters, but midcentury mothers had a special duty to the republic to develop boys into men who would be excellent husbands, fathers, and citizens.

The means by which mothers would discipline their boys was as widely discussed as was the fact of mothers' responsibility for boys. Recent scholarship troubles the notion that this period was univocal in its support of the theory that mothers were perfect disciplinarians, but it also observes that the first two-thirds of the nineteenth century tended to attach to motherhood a particular brand of discipline founded on affection, sympathy, and the boy's identification with his mother.[1] Such identification is central to the project of affective discipline, especially as discipline is imagined in novels before the twentieth century. Claire Chantell has recently made the observation that a careful reading of midcentury novels reveals that sentimentalism itself argued for the necessity of other influences in shaping children, but she confirms the point that mothers in the sentimental mode were assumed to wield affection and sympathy as their chief disciplinary tools. In *The Wide, Wide World*, for example, the mother "uses an exclusively emotional tutelary method, focusing on Ellen's heart, specifically its susceptibility to religious penetration. She exploits Ellen's adoration and her desire to please as a conduit for her moral lesson" (135). For mothers, both those within the covers of a novel and those within the boundaries of real domestic spaces, the use of sympathy and affection was understood to be an ingenuous exercise: "In these texts, maternal instruction appears as an instinctive, spontaneous reaction rather than a reasoned, deliberate choice" (131–32). Although Parille has notably added that writers of the period often worried that such discipline would not be adequate to the challenge presented by boys, he too argues that in sentimental texts—the texts from which the later orphan girl novels descended—"the ability to sympathize is seen, like mother love itself, as 'unquenchable' and inherent to women" (*Boys at Home* 46).

When mothers brandished this affective form of discipline, the effect often hoped for was one that had direct implications for the subjectivity of the disciplined son. Mothers were to use their natural instinct for affective discipline to shape a child who was moral because he was *similar to his mother*. Affection would create the channel through which a mother could—indeed was assumed to—stamp her own image on the malleable child. Such an idea appeared in many of the venues where writers of the first part of the century proclaimed the role of the mother:

> The mother's child became, as Lydia Sigourney put it, her "twin-soul." Although most advisers alerted mothers to the "great diversity in the natural dispositions of children," they never seriously considered that the child should become anything other than the mother writ large, in Dr. Joseph Hanaford's phrase, "a mental and moral daguerreotype of herself." From the mother's perspective, then, the child was self, rather than other. That is why Lydia Sigourney, in another remarkable turn of phrase, could instruct [a] mother to regard her baby as "a fragment of yourself." (Lewis 216)

The boundaries between child and mother were ignored in the ideal mother-child relationship under sentimentalism, leaving their identities "merged. . . . [T]he very process of loving would obliterate the distinctions between—the separateness of—mother and child" (Lewis 216). In her reading of Warner's sentimental orphan girl novel, Chantell declares that "the logic of sentimental maternalism as articulated in this novel defines the mother's greatest triumph as the implantation of her image in her child's mind, so that he or she may carry it throughout life as an emotional and spiritual touchstone" (136).

The mother whom sentimentalism celebrated was not just a loving mother. She was a mother whose love allowed her to imprint her son with her own image. She was a mother, indeed, who was expected thus to mold her boy so that he would think as she did. When sentimental novels slipped from the best seller list to be replaced by novels for girls, the new novels took notice of this mother and the way she marked her loving son. The hallmark of the good mother in sentimental ideology, the natural affection that allowed mothers to write themselves onto their boys, was too powerful, too useful a narrative to be ignored by the next generation of women writing about orphan girls.

WHAT GIRLS—NOT MOTHERS—ARE FOR

Prominently situated at the turn from the midcentury tradition into the Progressive Era, Louisa May Alcott was an indispensable figure in the history of fiction for girls. Her successful two-part novel *Little Women* began appearing on shelves in late 1868 and confirmed for the children's literature industry the marketability of the domestic novel to girl readers. Following on the heels of the sentimental tradition, Alcott's story still takes for granted the necessity of disciplining girls: Jo must learn repeated lessons in mastering her passions, and the pathetic death of Beth lingers over the novel in ways similar to the ways the fetishized deaths of children overshadow *Uncle Tom's Cabin* and other midcentury novels. Although *Little Women* would prove crucial to the new girls' novel as a marketing category, in most of its characteristics it is a midcentury novel about girls learning at the feet of their mother, not about orphans becoming the disciplinary heart of the home.

Alcott makes the first move in separating the genre from its predecessors with her next series of novels for girls. Although *Eight Cousins*, published less than a decade after *Little Women*, represents only an incomplete revision of sentimental novels, the extent to which it is able to break away from sentimentalism depends on the subtly changing disciplinary role of mothers. A contrast between *Little Women* and *Eight Cousins* illuminates the separation clearly. Most significant to the history of the change from sentimentalism to novels such as *Eight Cousins* is the shift from Marmee, the exemplar of sentimentalism's beloved and moral disciplinarian in *Little Women*, to women of the setting of *Eight Cousins*, a setting so replete with mothers and would-be-mothers that it is patronizingly referred to as the "Aunt-hill."

Most obvious in the change from one novel to the other is the simple diversification of women who would be mothers: they range from mothers Alcott all but condemns (Aunt Clara, who is blamed in the sequel for the death of Rose's one-time sweetheart) to mothers who frequently figure as the *opponents* of good discipline (the hypochondriac Aunt Myra and lecturing Aunt Jane) to mothers who are well intended but frequently ineffective (Aunt Plenty) to, in recognition of the historical proximity of Alcott's novel to the empire of the mother, two genuinely good mother figures (Aunts Peace and Jessie). In Alcott's earlier novel, Marmee's is the didactic and infallible voice of reason, her insights on vanity, men, and domestic economy a guaranteed bet to resurface as the moral of any of the girls' subplots. But in *Eight Cousins*, the mothers remain notably absent from the center of the disciplinary narrative of the novel. Even the two best mothers lack Marmee's omnipresent authority. Aunt Peace, for example, bears all the hallmarks of sympathy—she has survived a personal tragedy with "an atmosphere of repose" that "soothed whoever came to her" (41–42)—that would normally indicate a primary disciplinary figure, but the novel spends very little time communicating Peace's character to Rose, apart from a three-page montage in which Peace teaches her niece womanly skills such as needlework (167–69). Aunt Jessie, of whom Rose, Alec, and the novel approve immensely, provides a successful lecture against boys' novels in the vein of Oliver Optic's tales (176–82) and supports Rose's good choices (105, 140), but even she is rarely part of Rose's immediate world.

One of Jessie's most important roles is as an ally for Alec, one who acknowledges the rightness of the novel's premise, which is that responsibility for the little girl passes from the aunts to Alec, but even here, the plot requires that Jessie exist on the periphery of its tale of good discipline. And although Jessie has significant successes with her boys—one of her nephews notes with jealousy that "Aunt Jessie and her boys have capital talks" (198)—she has neither the centrality nor the extraordinary résumé of Marmee. She and the other boys' mothers have tried, for example, to stop their sons from smoking, but the boys laugh off their efforts—"Fiddlesticks!" says Charlie (172)—even though Rose thinks their mothers lovely and inspiring (182), the sorts of qualities that would have given them affective leverage in *The Wide, Wide World*, or, for that matter, *Little Women*. The mothers are not wrong, the novel indicates, and they do not lack any of the affective tools of previous novels, but the boys that the aunts—according to the precepts of sentimental maternalism—are to mold into their own moral image seem suddenly invulnerable to the discipline of mothers. Frustrated that the boys won't follow their mother's wishes, Rose then remembers "something Aunt Jessie once said—'You have more influence over the boys than you know. Use it for their good, and I shall thank you all my life'" (173). Rose is up to the task of influencing the boys, and it is this scene of correction, this scene in which Rose acts in place of the mothers, over which the novel dwells. Mothers *can* be successful in *Eight Cousins*, but whereas *Little Women* made Marmee's influence key to nagging conflicts, *Eight Cousins* presents a much more fractured vision of motherhood.

Eight Cousins also provides a bizarre interlude in the story of transferred motherhood in the figure of Uncle Alec, the man who disciplines Rose as she learns to discipline boys. At the opening of *Eight Cousins*, Rose is a sickly and depressed child, recently orphaned and pining for her father, and the aunts have not been effective in helping Rose regain her health and good spirits. After a china tea set, needlework, and a drafted playmate have failed to distract Rose from her troubles, Aunt Plenty literally throws her hands in the air and retires "to tell sister Peace that she never *should* understand that child, and it was a mercy Alec was coming soon to take the responsibility off their hands" (27). The novel therefore produces two surrogates for maternal discipline—Alec and Rose—and the first surrogate prepares the second for her duties. Just as Rose has avowed that her duty is to take care of boys, Alec declares that his is to take care of Rose and that his intervention is necessary to contradict the effects of mothering by women. He says of one of the aunts,

> Aunt Myra is a—ahem!—an excellent woman, but it is her hobby to believe that everyone is tottering on the brink of the grave. And, upon my life, I believe she is offended if people don't fall into it! We will show her how to make constitutions and turn pale-faced little ghosts into rosy, hearty girls. That's my business, you know. (32)

Alec is not speaking metaphorically about his business: he is a physician, and it is literally his business to manage constitutions. Rose responds with pleasure: "I had forgotten you were a doctor. I'm glad of it, for I do want to be well" (32–33). Alec's profession marks him out as a historically significant character. Not only is he a man taking over the role of mothering a girl; he is also a scientist who will set Rose on a regimen that will compensate for the well-intentioned (Aunt Myra *is* an excellent woman) but imperfectly executed disciplinary strategies of women.

Uncle Alec is virtually unique in the history of this orphan girl story, and his appearance is indicative of where the novel falls in the history of motherhood in America. In the introduction to *"Bad" Mothers: The Politics of Blame in Twentieth-Century America*, Molly Ladd-Taylor and Lauri Umansky sketch a history of motherhood that took a strange turn toward the end of the nineteenth century. "While earlier generations viewed mothering principally through a religious lens," they argue, "middle-class families increasingly saw child nature as a matter to be investigated, quantified, and studied by psychologists, doctors, and others" (9). This new approach to mothering did not advocate shutting mothers out of the process of mothering; rather it indicated that mothers should remain primary but could do better if they followed the advice of professionals with scientific credentials: "Scientific knowledge (usually provided by men) combined with women's mother love to form the ingredients necessary for successful childrearing in the modern age" (9). The result was a strategy dubbed "scientific motherhood," and Uncle Alec is its perfect image. With his status as a physician, he is the ideal person to dictate a new strategy for rearing the orphan girl, but he also exudes the tenderness that scientific motherhood assumed was inherent in the love of an actual mother. When Alec proposes porridge as part of Rose's rehabilitation, the girl first balks at the "wholesome" dish, then gives in because of the softness with which Alec offers it to her (37). When Alec later witnesses Rose disciplining a little girl by threatening the child with the wrath of God, Alec intervenes, saying, ""Come, Rose, it's too bad to tell her little tricks before everyone and preach at her in that way—you wouldn't like it yourself." He then coddles the weeping child and begins "administering consolation in the shape of kisses and nuts" (157–58). Alec embodies both the tenderness of the mother and the rigor of the scientist. As a representative of scientific motherhood, his appearance fits easily in a novel published at the moment of highest popularity for scientific motherhood.[2]

At this historical moment, Alcott could make the argument that the scientific motherhood theorized by men and here symbolized by a male physician would offer a good substitute for traditional maternity. She could make that argument alongside an argument for a revised orphan girl, who would learn from a man first by paying careful attention to how he rehabilitated her. From this, she would learn how to be a better disciplinarian herself; she would learn how to mother with a mixture of rigor and love. But in the decades to come, Uncle Alec would disappear from the narrative. This brief-lived highpoint of scientific motherhood would allow for an Uncle Alec, but as that philosophy lost currency, the manly mother would be stripped away, leaving only his little charge—not the mother he himself seems to replace—to manage boys.

GIRLS TAKING CARE OF GIRLS

Inspired by Alcott's new vision of girls directing discipline, orphan girl novels of the early century confirmed the disposability of mothers and the efficacy of discipline wielded by girls. They expanded the scope of girls' authority beyond boys, in fact, to include girls. As the genre ripened, its novels more explicitly placed girls in the roles of mothers as they took responsibility for the girls around them—and for themselves.

Consider in this context A Little Princess, published thirty years after Eight Cousins. Sara Crewe, a half-orphan at the beginning of the story, has never known or, the narrator explains, even missed her mother (Burnett, A Little Princess 6), so the novel takes as its premise an orphan girl who only knows of the emotional centrality of a mother by observation, not personal experience. As a result, Sara is untouched by the affectionate discipline of a mother and indeed seems to be a good argument against the necessity of parents at all. Her first few years at Miss Minchin's boarding school offer her easy indulgence because of her father's wealth, and, the narrator observes, "If Sara had been a different kind of child," the indulgence

> would not have been at all good for her. She was treated more as if she were a distinguished guest at the establishment than as if she were a mere little girl. If she had been a self-opinionated, domineering child, she might have become disagreeable enough to be unbearable through being so much indulged and flattered. If she had been an indolent child, she would have learned nothing. (36)

Sara, however, establishing what would quickly become a typical pattern throughout the genre, does not *need* discipline. She regulates the abundance of the gifts her wealthy father gives her in the novel's opening scenes despite his eagerness to shower her with toys, and in his absence—but not the absence of his wealth—she resists becoming spoiled simply because that is her nature, because she is not "a different kind of child." This is not to say that all the girls in the novel can do so readily without discipline. Rather, Sara is clearly the exception to the rule, and her exceptional nature allows her to deal with the other children remarkably well. Untouched by the need for a mother herself, Sara is able, even casually able, to replace the mothers of other children. Sara initially announces herself as a mother to her newest doll—she has new clothes fitted for the doll by a tailor who specializes in children's clothing—and seems to learn the tricks of mothering almost instantly. When Lottie, one of the girls at Miss Minchin's boarding school, throws a tantrum, Sara speaks of the wishes of Lottie's mother so convincingly that the child comes to heel (43–44). Subsequently, Lottie asserts that Sara "is my mamma at Miss Minchin's" (49).[3] As Elisabeth Rose Gruner has noted, "Orphaned Sara can not be expected to know much about mothering, but in fact it is her primary talent, her original skill" (176).[4] Whereas Rose of *Eight Cousins* could do the mother figures around her the favor of ridding their boys of bad habits, Sara and the girls who followed her could take the place of mothers altogether.

Even when these orphan girls were not replacing mothers in name, they were replacing them in position. In *Little Women* and novels of the midcentury sentimental tradition, girls orbited around their mothers, using solid maternal morality as a reference point, making mistakes and returning to mothers for correction. But as the orphan girl story took on its new form in the twentieth century, the new mothers slipped out of a position of moral dominance, instead orbiting—often in a dazed, haphazard trajectory—around the girls they mistakenly assumed they were required to educate. This pattern is clearest in *Pollyanna*. As the titular orphan approaches the spacious home of her aunt, Polly speaks only—and endlessly—of her "duty" to the child. When one of Polly's servants exclaims how "nice" it will be to have a child in the house, Polly replies, "Nice? Well, that isn't exactly the word I should use. . . . However, I intend to make the best of it, of course[;] I am a good woman, I hope, and I know my duty." When the servant argues that Pollyanna might brighten her aunt's life, Polly answers, "I can't say, however, that I see any immediate need for that" (13). But Polly is quite wrong about her needs, as the novel demonstrates. Polly's heart has hardened, and she has neither joy nor romance in her life. Fixing her aunt's problems is Pollyanna's duty, and the orphan girl manages that duty with skill that is as ingenuous and inherent as the discipline a midcentury mother was expected to use on her son. Each time Polly misunderstands Pollyanna's actions and tries to discipline her new charge, Pollyanna transforms that discipline into a special treat, leaving her aunt feeling "curiously helpless" (56). Polly will come to be grateful for her helplessness in the face of the orphan girl's innocent machinations, for it is directly through Pollyanna's actions that Polly rediscovers love, first for the child and subsequently in the form of a lover she dismissed many years ago. Because of his deep affection for Pollyanna, Dr. Chilton—another physician, this time benefiting from the orphan girl's influence rather than directing it—dares to brave the house from which he was expelled as a suitor, and the novel ends with the announcement that Aunt Polly is at last happy and has only Pollyanna to thank for it. "It's you," as Polly gratefully tells her niece, "that have done it all" (216). Polly's gratitude marks the success of Pollyanna's manipulations, which the girl brings about as naturally as would any sentimental mother, and marks the mother figure's joy at having become the object of the girl's manipulations.

In the orphan girl story emerging at the turn into the twentieth century, women such as Polly who might seem eligible for a position of maternal authority instead see their discipline shrugged away. But the result is not a bevy of willful orphan girls, spoiled and thoughtless; the new girl can take care of herself and the girls around her. Further, by allowing girls to replace them, these mothers are rewarded with loving, intelligent children who will give them their hearts' desire. Distracted by their joyous new circumstances, they either fail to notice or fail to complain about having been relentlessly relocated away from the heart of the disciplinary relationship.

THE PROBLEM WITH MOTHERS

What cultural shifts could possibly justify this transfer of power and responsibility from the disciplining mother—whose history dates back at least to the republican mother who, Linda Kerber has convincingly argued, forged the manhood of the Revolution—to the girl? The most fundamental of these changes was one that would have been unthinkable only fifty years earlier: there was at the turn of the century something inherently wrong with mothering by mothers, with the very instincts that characterized her indispensability to an earlier era. Up to and throughout the main part of the nineteenth century, mothers bore the burden of disciplining children, but very shortly after the turn into the twentieth century, parental advice literature shifted from considering mothers to be its main agents to considering them to be its main problems. As Ladd-Taylor and Umansky have documented, a child whose behavior did not fit the dominant (middle-class, white, heterosexual) mold became incontestable evidence of poor mothering in the private sphere, out of the control of public correction but with ramifications on the public character. "From the 1890s to the 1950s," for example, "independent-minded or overprotective women were thought to have 'caused' their sons' homosexuality" (5). Although the first of these kinds of mothers—the independent mothers who came from the ranks of the New Woman—elicited considerable attention, it was the second mother, the overprotective one, who was thought to threaten children most. Middle-class mothers were in an impossible position. Their class and sex dictated that they had to remain at home and care for the children, but the gendered logic of the age insisted that the affective skills of discipline, the modes of child rearing in which women were inevitably skilled, were the very traits that would incline women to overmother. Experts increasingly warned that the very nature of mothers led not to the rearing but to the depravity of children (Ladd-Taylor and Umansky 11).

Throughout the advice literature of the time, warnings continually sounded against this mother, quickly dubbed the "oversolicitous" mother. Even in texts that allowed some blame to fall on fathers, the ultimate fault was that of women. Douglas A. Thom made this clear in his 1927 *Everyday Problems of the Everyday Child* when he argued that "the unhappy combination of a rigid father and an oversolicitous mother," which he described as "not uncommon," "is brought

about by a feeling that prompts the mother to make up in some way for the father's attitude." Thus, even though a father's rigidness might predate a mother's
oversolicitousness, it is really the mother's reaction to his rigidness that brings
about the "unhappy combination." Thom does admit that fathers can be guilty
of coddling the child too much, of incurring too strong an affectionate bond,
but he cannot resist observing that a child's dependence falls "particularly upon
the mother," which leads him to argue that "it is important that this phase of
absolute dependency of the child upon the parent be terminated by the process
of gradually weaning him, not only from the breast, but from the incapacitating
emotional relationship existing between child and parent" (28–29). The physical
and emotional bonds between mother and child cannot be avoided, but they represent a threat to the child that must be eliminated as soon as possible. The very
affection that had previously defined maternal priority in the home turned her,
in the opening decades of the new century, into the greatest threat to the child.

By the end of the nineteenth century "scientific motherhood" had modified
the logic of child rearing, observing that women did indeed have a natural and
useful instinct for the management of children, an instinct that could be en-
hanced by science. But scientific motherhood proved to be more of a transition
than a lasting movement, as science shouldered motherhood aside. Sonya Michel
details the mood immediately after the turn of the century, by which point science so predominated over motherhood that "parent education and other fields
challenged the notion of maternal instinct and called for training and profession-
alization for those who dealt with children" (308). Kate Douglas Wiggin, writing
this time for adults, confirmed this opinion, urging feminist activists to agitate
"for the highest education, which shall include a specific training for parent-
hood" (*Children's Rights* 23), training that seems to take the place of maternal inclination. The affection and instinct that legitimated mothering before this time,
that ruled equally with knowledge in the brief era of scientific motherhood, lost
their place of privilege in the public estimation of mothering in the early years
of the new century. It would be a clear overstatement to argue that the importance of affection disappeared during this period, but it is nonetheless true that
the bonds of affection were considered more suspect, always doomed to failure
when confronted with professional opinion. Emily K. Abel traces one example of
just such a losing battle in the case of an immigrant family, the Germanis, who
in 1918 lost their argument to retain control of their tubercular daughter in the
face of the New York Charity Organization Society's scientific authority, which
determined that Maria Germani required hospitalization. Although the Germanis made what can only be regarded as a heart-breaking plea that the courts

ignore the organization's recommendations, "the Germanis' use of the language of emotion and family intimacy appears to have reinforced their reputation for irrationality and poor parenting" (64). In court as well as in public opinion, affection—hitherto the defining characteristic of a mother's authority—was actually a reason *not* to trust a given set of parents with a needy child.[5] Ladd-Taylor explains that although experts before the First World War would have "maintained that effective childrearing depended on both science and mother-love, authors of the 1920s insisted that it required only science" (*Mother-Work* 6). By the end of the period, popular psychologist John B. Watson would go so far as to beg the readers of his *Psychological Care of Infant and Child* to

> remember when you are tempted to pet your child that mother love is a danger-
> ous instrument . . . which may inflict a never healing wound, a wound which
> may make infancy unhappy, adolescence a nightmare, an instrument which
> may wreck your adult son or daughter's vocational future and their chances for
> marital happiness. (87)

The sentimental mother was, to put it mildly, out of fashion in the first decades of the new century.[6]

This distrust, even paranoia, over mothers and their influence on children had direct consequences in the literature and culture of children at the turn of the century. Claudia Nelson's work on British children's fiction between 1857 and 1917, for example, finds that boys' fiction of the time increasingly encouraged boys not to learn kindness and morality from their mothers but to try to be the opposite of their mothers. "Angelhood," Nelson's term for the status bequeathed on mothers who in a previous time would have served as the moral center of the household, "slowly grew antithetical to 'manliness' as mid-century definitions of the terms . . . gave way to new and vastly different versions" (30). Similarly, Kenneth Kidd's reading of boys' literature in America from 1869 to 1916 demonstrates that a new kind of fiction—"Bad Boy writing"—became popular during exactly this era of anxiety over maternal influence. In bad boy fiction and the culture surrounding it, "the feminine suffers a fate similar to that of the savage, imagined as a stage to be suffered through and then surpassed" (59). And although, as Kidd cogently observes, bad boy culture owed fundamental debts to the domestic logic of the mid-nineteenth century, "the Bad Boy writers saw themselves as rebellious, as challenging the tales of pious children authored by women such as Susan Warner, Fanny Fern, Maria Cummins, and Harriet Beecher Stowe" (61). By "declar[ing] boyhood's independence from all things feminine, including advice writing" (2), the literature for boys that developed during this era set itself up as

the direct opposite of the sentimental and domestic literature that had traditionally championed the centrality of mothers to boys' development.

It was during this same period that the sales of postsentimental orphan girl
novels began to flourish, but that literature, marketed primarily toward girls,
would face a very difficult task in defining itself. Between the Charybdis of
the Progressive Era's distrust of mothers—a distrust that these books would not
openly contest—and the Scylla of the genre's roots in the very women's literature
that championed mothers, the way was terribly narrow. Furthermore, considering that the new novels for girls still wanted to imagine precisely the project of
masculine reformation that turn-of-the-century culture and literature despised
in the hands of mothers, these novels would have to forge a disciplinary strategy that would use the logic of affection borrowed from midcentury fiction but
somehow disavow the oversolicitous mother who had become its very emblem.
Fictional girls would not only have to replace mothers at the helm of affective
discipline; they would also have to convince their own readers that they could
make up for the errors of their mothers.

COMPENSATING FOR MOTHERS

These observations about the declining disciplinary capital of mothers and the
new ability of girls to discipline boys and girls afford a vantage point from which
to read more carefully some of the classic girls' fiction from this period that remains popular with both children and critics today. One evocative example addresses all of these changes: it features a girl who disciplines herself and then a
boy, a boy who has proven remarkably resistant to scientific techniques and who
has been badly marred by his failed mother. The girl's success in healing this boy
reads as a direct answer to the concerns turn-of-the-century culture had about
those who would use the techniques of mothers to discipline boys.

Frances Hodgson Burnett had already contributed to the genre's separation
from mothers in A Little Princess, and she pushed that separation more vigor-
ously in her 1911 orphan girl novel, The Secret Garden. The first part of the novel
relates the story of Mary emerging from the wreckage of her own mother's influence, and the second tells of Mary's extended disciplinary project: the healing
of Colin. This novel retains a deep longing for the mother, but its conflict is
driven by the ramifications of the failures of mothers and how Mary can compensate for them without threatening the masculinity of Colin, the object of her
sentimental-style discipline.

There is, it must be noted, one very good mother in The Secret Garden: the mother of Martha and Dickon, working-class Susan Sowerby. Sowerby helps the children maintain the secrecy of their play time, helps them buy extra food to nourish their developing bodies, and allows Dickon to grow into a strong, nearly magical boy—albeit largely by leaving him alone. Sowerby does most of her on-screen good mothering, in fact, in this way, rarely remaining for long in the garden where Mary and Colin are healed. Sowerby's maternal success, in fact, does not spring from any sentimental attachments she fosters with the children or loving surveillance over them that she maintains. Rather, it comes from her role as representative of the simple people who, early twentieth-century England strove to believe, lived in the good, British countryside. Martin Wiener has indicated that during this period "the myth of an England essentially rural and essentially unchanging appealed across political lines both to Conservatives and Imperialists, and to anti-Imperialists, Liberals, and Radicals," and Burnett's sensibilities seem fundamentally similar. Britons with imperialist inclinations, for example, "saw a historic countryside . . . where officers and gentlemen were bred" (55), and this is exactly the mission at the heart of disciplining Colin, who is the feeble only child of a wealthy British man who spends more time abroad than he does at home. If the countryside was, as Wiener argues, "the repository of the moral character of the nation" (56), it is hardly surprising that the rural mother is an effective mother. But this makes it only all the more strange that Sowerby is not the central disciplinarian of the book: if she—and through her, rural England—is so good for young aristocrats, why isn't she the one exercising with Mary and, more to the point, Colin in the pure Yorkshire air? Perhaps she is absent because, for all of the novel's enthusiasm for a simpler England, Burnett's novel is at least as much a novel about class as it is about gender.[7] As Jerry Phillips has observed, Sowerby's parenting strategy "is very much a politics of fitting social elites to rule over their particular cultural domain" (178). Perhaps the reason Sowerby is so often absent from the disciplinary scene is also why she is so good at discipline: she is not a member of the elite class. She can, like the Yorkshire air, provide support for the improvement of Colin. But just as the bulk of his improvement takes place in the private, leisured, non-productive space of the manor garden, so too what Colin needs is a member of his own class to guide him through the process of self-improvement. Sowerby *is* a good mother. But she is evidently not what Colin needs.

With the limited exception of Mrs. Sowerby, *The Secret Garden* engages with its period's concern over mothers by agreeing with the broader culture that mothers themselves are dangerous things. Through its mothers of the ruling class, the book illustrates the double jeopardy of mothers, who can fail by being both too present and too absent. Further, it illustrates the crucial role girls should play in replacing and then regulating the mother. The novel's first mother, Mary's, is a lovely socialite who has no interest in her child, and, the novel makes clear, it is as a result of this neglect that Mary becomes "contrary." After Mary's mother dies, the only eulogy the novel gives her is a disappointed recollection at the hands of a minor character, Mary's very temporary foster mother, Mrs. Crawford. Crawford regrets the opportunities Mary's biological mother wasted, saying, "Perhaps if her mother had carried her pretty face and her pretty manners into the nursery more often, Mary might have learned some pretty ways too. It is very sad, now the poor beautiful thing is gone, to remember that many people never even knew that she had a child at all" (8). Obviously Colin's mother is guilty of the same crime, since she is not only absent, she's dead. In earlier novels this would have given her a kind of moral superiority that would allow her even in her absence to determine the path of Colin's spiritual success, but in this novel her death does nothing of the kind.[8] "She is my mother," Colin says when he first shows her picture to Mary. "I don't see why she died. Sometimes I hate her for doing it. . . . If she had lived I believe I should not have been ill always" (79). Colin's physical disability—which the novel repeatedly attributes to his psychological disabilities—is the novel's fictional fulfillment of the threats absent mothers posed to their children, but Burnett does not stop there. In fact, Colin's mother is a grotesque example of *both* of the worst kinds of mother. Because she is dead, she is the epitome of the negligent mother, but because she dominates his every thought, his physical appearance, and his health, she is also a smothering, "oversolicitous" mother. Even the hatred Colin's father feels for the boy is the result of her undue influence over him, a fact Mary realizes when she puts together the father's hatred for the secret garden (30)—which he used to tend with his wife—and the invalid child—who has "the great grey eyes with black lashes round them, so like and yet so horribly unlike the happy eyes he had adored" (168). Colin is horridly himself and his mother, an unbearable conflation.

The process of his healing puts his physician-disciplinarian, Mary, in a position to fix both an old and a new problem. Ken Parille's work on pragmatic writers of the mid-nineteenth century reveals that although sentimental literature may have praised mothers' ability to wield sympathy and affective discipline well,

> pragmatic writers offer two distinct objections to sentimental discourse: some claim that mothers are inherently unsympathetic towards boys yet can learn to use sympathy when managing them, while others argue that the use of sympathy with boys is at best ineffective (boy nature is such that they can't respond

to it) and at worst dangerous (boys will manipulate it to avoid punishment).
(*Boys at Home* 47)

Although pragmatic writers agreed, then, with sentimental writers that mothers could use sympathy and that they could use it well *on girls*, they disagreed with the best sellers of the midcentury over how well boys would respond to it. Mothers, they argued, simply were not very good at developing the affectionate connection with boys necessary to this model of discipline (*Boys at Home* 48). Moreover, when mothers tried to overwhelm the boys' natural resistance to sympathy, they set themselves up to be manipulated instead by the very boys they were trying to correct. To pragmatic writers, at least as far as boys were concerned, maternal sympathy was "an unreliable emotion" that could "negate discipline" rather than enforce it (*Boys at Home* 51).

This slipshod handling of sympathy, an old concern among women writers, is a major problem that Mary successfully overcomes in *The Secret Garden*. Mary forges an affectionate connection with Colin (Mary "has just bewitched him," according to one onlooker [111]) and then uses his dedication to her to motivate him out of his sickbed and on to the outdoors, where he recovers his health. But she is also able to withstand his tantrums, which no one else, not even the adults in charge of him, can do. When Colin first quarrels with Mary, demanding that she think only of him and not go outside unless he gives her permission, Mary flies into a rage that matches Colin's own, and Colin is so distraught that he acts in precisely the way pragmatic writers most feared: "He turned his head on his pillow and shut his eyes," the narrator relates, "and a big tear was squeezed out and ran down his cheek. He was beginning to feel pathetic and sorry for himself—not for any one else" (99). But Colin's pathos does not move Mary, who continues to argue with him, eventually storming out with a promise never to return. Her heart is later softened when one of the servants explains Colin's condition, and she allows that she might return to see the boy the next day. When Colin works himself into a fit, she does indeed return but not with soft caresses and a willingness to give in to the boy's demands. She slams open the door, rushes to his bed, and tells Colin that if he wants to "scream [him]self to death," he is quite welcome to do so. In a pointed phrase, the narrator argues that "a nice *sympathetic* child could neither have thought nor said such things, but it just happened that the shock of hearing them was the best possible thing for this hysterical boy whom no one had ever dared to restrain or contradict" (103, emphasis added). Mary is at times a sympathetic child, as her initial softening indicates. But Mary can drop sympathy when good discipline demands it of her.

Indeed, her impatience, even self-centeredness—characteristics that sentimental mothers were called on to suppress—serve her well in this scene as it sparks her correct response to Colin's tantrum. Unlike the mother over whom many mid-century writers worried, Mary is an extraordinary wielder of affective discipline: she can use it well on this boy, and she can ignore affection when the boy tries to use sympathy to manipulate her.

The result of this improved form of mothering by daughters will, the novel promises, have important benefits for masculinity. As earlier models of maternity promised she would, Colin's mother has impressed herself on her son. This means that he looks like her, but it also has the effect of ruining the boy's physical and emotional health. Colin suffers from, as his doctor puts it, "hysteria" (111). The result, as the medical professionals and gossipers around him confirm, is a warped body, whose minor real ailments are magnified through the lens of his hysteria into self-propagating major disabilities. Although Colin also bears resemblances to his father, his illness has a distinctly feminine cast. Mary reveals even that highly visible mark of his father's illness, the hunched back, to be a trick of Colin's hysteria, severing the most obvious similarity between Colin's illness and the image of his father. At stake is masculinity itself, both the boy's and the masculinity of the leisured class, especially since Colin is an only child of a wealthy estate. Hysterical and too much his mother, Colin needs to discover his strength, his confidence, his self-control, and his manliness. In the second half of the novel—after Mary, like Rose at Alec's knee, has learned how to wield this form of discipline accurately by practicing it on herself—the story recounts the successful project of restoring Colin's masculinity in the secret garden.[9] Colin grows stronger—standing for the first time in his life when he has only been in the garden a few hours—smarter, faster, and more confident while there under Mary's direction. In privacy arranged and safeguarded by Mary, the boy improves daily, dropping his initial conviction that he will develop a hunchback and die before adulthood and taking up instead dreams of being a scientist, lecturer, and athlete. The boy's transformation from hysteric to young man is a narrative of greater manliness that refutes the bad boy fiction being sold alongside Burnett's novels. The novel directly engages with the fear that children's novels by women will sap masculinity, instead mapping out a plan for the restoration of masculinity.[10]

The mother the Progressive Era was busy abjuring exists in Burnett's novel largely as a mother with a marvelous capacity to fail both as a deserter and a smotherer. Colin needs attention and affection. What Colin needs, to put it bluntly, is mothering, but the mother herself must be split off from it. Mothering therefore, to borrow twenty-first century terminology, must be outsourced to someone who can regulate affection carefully, who can make up for the mistakes that a mother's instinct leads her to make. It is through this disciplining girl that the new orphan girl novel separates itself from the sentimental mother to whom it owes so much.

THE DAUGHTERS OF WOMAN'S FICTION

These novels articulate a narrative that fits with the cultural prejudice of the historical moment. Boys need mothering, they argue, and mothers are no longer qualified for the role. As the novels are making this argument thematically, the genre itself—and here I mean the genre as a class at this moment in the history of mass publishing—makes it commercially. I have been demonstrating how these novels put girls in the place of mothers to do the work of domestic discipline; consider also how this new emphasis in the orphan girl story ascends at exactly the moment that woman's fiction has begun to recede. In the fictive space, girls have taken the place of mothers. A sentimental novel could tell the story, as did *The Wide, Wide World*, of an orphan girl who receives discipline from her mother, is successfully shaped by it in the name of her mother, and then stands up to a series of tests to demonstrate she is now ready to marry and become a mother. At the turn of the century, though, a descendant of Warner's novel marketed for girls tells the story of how a girl discards her mother's influence and then replaces another child's mother in a successful campaign of discipline. That change manifests itself at the level of individual text. And at the level of literary history, the story repeats: the girls' novel takes the place of woman's fiction as the genre with sovereignty over domestic discipline. Women writers tell a story similar to that told by the previous generation, but they tell it in a commercial category of fiction for girls that follows in the footsteps of, and yet replaces, the sentimental novels of the midcentury. As the fictional girl has taken the place of the fictional mother, the fiction of girls has taken the place of the fiction of mothers.

Finally, then, these novels represent an important resettling of domestic ideology. Clearly they are participating in feminist dialogues, reworking maternalist points borrowed from first-wave feminism and anticipating second-wave feminism's interest in gender role reversal. But there is in them a sense of advancing and retreating, calling for more power for girls but sacrificing mothers to the turn of cultural opinion, renegotiating gender roles in a cultural moment that disavowed mothers but could not do without mothering.

Affection, Manipulation, Pleasure, Abuse

Although standard readings of the history of affective discipline in the United States stop with the close of sentimentalism, women writers of the next several decades continued to fictionalize and test new strategies of discipline through love. They did so in novels that borrowed a narrative formula about orphan girls, revising such key terms of sentimental suasion as sympathy, individualism, and even the motherhood that had once been affective discipline's clearest marker. The story of affective discipline did not end with the close of sentimentalism but continued in turn-of-the-century novels for girls.

Two points remain to be made about sentimental-style discipline in the classic orphan girl novel. The second has to do with what became of such discipline in the century after the highpoint of the genre. But before we search for contemporary descendants of affective discipline, it is necessary to look more closely at how the pleasures of discipline complicate the structures of gender that inform moral suasion. Doing so reveals how the classic orphan girl novel is not only girls' fiction, not only a replacement for woman's fiction, but, because of the pleasures of discipline, also, in a limited but profound way, fiction for men.

FICTIONAL GIRLS DISCIPLINING REAL MEN

I have been documenting throughout this study how gender played a critical role in the negotiations of power that surrounded sentimental-style discipline. I have therefore been emphasizing the importance of gender distinctions despite a recent scholarly tendency to downplay those distinctions. There is, however, one aspect of affective discipline, particularly in its literary representation and consumption, that I want to argue can better be understood by looking at how readers of the classic orphan girl novel have *refused* to obey gender categories.

As the classic orphan girl novel learned to strip fathers of their bodies—something for which the genre had shown considerable adeptness ever since *The Wide, Wide World* disposed of Ellen's biological father in what amounts to an afterthought—it fulfilled sentimentalism's dream of guaranteeing the influence of feminine domesticity over masculine authority. Such a notion was not an invention of sentimental fiction but a mainstay of nineteenth-century U.S. culture. "The home," as Mary P. Ryan contends, "was only the imperial center, the mother country, from which women launched their vast social influence" (145). By combining moral superiority with submissiveness, women discovered a "convenient method of castigating social evil without encouraging overt rebellion" (134). Although, as Ryan points out, the logic of domesticity maintained that women must marry and must submit to their husbands, it also demanded that the wife "must find some range of power and action within her apparently inferior position" (120). Specifically, the ideal wife both must submit and, as Cathy N. Davidson puts it, "take greater control of her life and must make shrewd judgments of the men who come into her life" (113). The real power of sentimental women lay in their ability to socialize "adult males as well as children" (Ryan 144), and it was the bond between mother and child—particularly male child— that "was at the very core of the cult of domesticity" (58). Sentimentalism and other aspects of the gendered culture of nineteenth-century America took for granted that women would control men.

Here I am straddling a line between the imaginary world of fiction and the real world of adult men who married and were socialized by disciples of the cult of domesticity. However, what I want to demonstrate is that the print culture of the nineteenth century itself repeatedly blurred the line between fiction and reality. In the novels, women disciplined men. In the real world, women struggled to do the same. A fascinating middle ground developed when the novels, written by and supposedly for women and girls, began to work on men themselves. The tales of discipline imagined by these novels did not have to go through women to get to the men of the real world; men of the real world sought out these novels on their own.

Recent studies of readership in the nineteenth century bear this point out. Although then as now women and men were supposed to have very different reading habits, the public library records in both a metropolitan and a rural area demonstrate that historically they did not. In his analysis of the midcentury records from the New York Society Library, Ronald J. Zboray shows that "the reading patterns of men and women differed little" (163). "Not only," he points out, "did men and women charge similar titles, but their rates of withdrawal conformed throughout the year" (167). In looking at the records of a library in Osage, Iowa, Christine Pawley likewise found little evidence that separate spheres of reading maintained in the real lives of nineteenth-century Americans:

> Adult men disproportionately read books by Elijah Kellogg, Charles Dickens, Oliver Optic, James Fenimore Cooper, and C. A. Stephens—all writers designated as "male." But adult men's most frequently borrowed authors were Pansy and Miss Mulock—the same as those of the women. Like women, men read the books of these authors in strict proportion to their numbers. This mixture of "men's" and "women's" authors suggest[s] that neither adult men nor women readers in Osage made clearly gendered choices. (109)

To be more specific, then, men and women did have slightly different reading habits—women rarely checked out books, for example, pertaining to the fields from which they were prevented entrance—but sentimental literature crossed over from one group of readers to the other with no difficulty. Davidson recalls a similar history told by the inscriptions in one copy of *Charlotte Temple*, recording both the transference of the book as a gift from sister to brother and the brother's inscription in the back, recognizing his ownership of the novel, one of the most famous sentimental novels in U.S. history. "Men," Davidson concludes, "obviously, were not excluded from Rowson's community of readers nor were they reluctant to claim membership in that community" (75, 7). In fact, Zboray's research indicates that in some instances men were considerably less than reluctant to participate in sentimental reading. "Just as many men as women charged classic 'feminine' novels like *Chestnut Wood* and Mary Jane Holme's [sic] *Tempest and Sunshine*," he notes. "*More* men than women withdrew the romance *Magdalen Hepburn*" (164). According to traditional notions of reading in the nineteenth century, there should have been a clear demarcation between what men and women read. So far as sentimental novels go, that line did not exist.

The same is true to a large extent of books marketed for children. This should not be surprising, considering the staggering contemporary popularity of J. K. Rowling's novels, and Pawley's research demonstrates that a similar phenomenon occurred in the nineteenth century. She asserts that readers made neither "clearly gendered choices" nor "clear choices based on age" (109). This is directly relevant to the historical period in which the postsentimental orphan girl novels were published:

By the end of the century, publishing books specially targeted at young people was relatively new, and while the 1880s and 1890s may have been the formative period of the "golden age" of children's literature, clear lines separating adult's and children's reading had yet to form. After all, six of the ten best-sellers in the United States between 1875 and 1895, including F. H. Burnett's *Little Lord Fauntleroy*, had been written for children, which suggests a considerable adult readership of these ostensibly children's books. (106–7)[1]

During this time, publishers and authors both were aware of marketing categories, so it would be an exaggeration to say that contemporaries could not conceive of a difference between books written for adults and children. Nonetheless, it would be true to say that that difference was seriously undertheorized even by the people most invested in it. "In the 1880s and 1890s," Pawley asserts, "some publications displayed both an awareness of gender and a more prescriptive designation of what constituted 'children's' books. However, publishers made these assumptions with little reference to actual data beyond sales figures and anecdotes" (106). Moreover, the experience of private reading was very likely not so all-consuming as it is today. Instead, people of multiple modern demographics frequently experienced books together. Zboray points to an 1855 letter reporting a leisurely afternoon spent over a shared book as well as a passage from Alcott's diary in which she remembers sewing with her sisters while their mother read to them aloud (160). The boundaries that we today take for granted between readers were not a matter of course for nineteenth-century readers.

Other scholars have demonstrated that adults—both men and women—and children frequently read the same books, and my own research confirms that men read and enjoyed these girls' novels themselves. This research hasn't been difficult, because scholars of girls' and women's fiction love to point to instances in which men read the books under discussion, perhaps themselves operating under the assumption that men only rarely read "woman's fiction." Jane Tompkins, for example, in her afterword to *The Wide, Wide World*, cites a letter to Susan Warner from "a man from Philadelphia" who writes, "When I say that your books give me exquisite pleasure, I deny them their highest and truest praise. They have done me good. They have made me a wiser and a better man—more strengthened to duty, more reconciled to suffering" (qtd. in Tompkins 584). Peter Glassman, in his afterword to *Rebecca of Sunnybrook Farm*, cites a similar letter written to Kate Douglas Wiggin by Jack London:

> May I thank you for "Rebecca"? *Penelopes Experiences* [another novel by Wiggin] whiled away the hours for me the other day, but they appealed to my

head, while Rebecca won my heart. Of course, I have laughed, but I have wept as well. She is real; she lives; she has given me many regrets, but I love her. I would have quested the wide world over to make her mine, only I was born too long ago and she was born but yesterday. Why could she not have been my daughter? Can't I adopt her? And, O, how I envy "Mr. Aladdin"! Why couldn't it have been I who bought the three hundred cakes of soap? Why, O, why?" (qtd. in Glassman 291)

Glassman comments that "a legion of men—young and old—have echoed Jack London's pleas" (291), pleas repeatedly marked by pleasure in the effective use of affective discipline that crosses the border between fictional girl and real man. Mollie Gillen's juvenile biography of L. M. Montgomery records a host of examples of men similarly affected by Montgomery's girls' novels, including "the venerable 73–year-old Mark Twain" (28), "the governor general, Earl Grey" (30) and "Britain's prime minister, Stanley Baldwin," who commented that "I've read every Montgomery book I could get my hands on two and three times over" (45). Gillen goes on to report that Montgomery followed the success of *Anne* with visits to "the homes of Emerson, Hawthorne, Thoreau, and the Alcotts." She claims that Montgomery's life was filled with fans such as the prime minister, as attested to by Montgomery's recollection of letters from "men and women who are grandparents, boys at school and college, old pioneers in the Australian bush, missionaries in China, monks in remote monasteries, and red-haired girls all over the world" (qtd. in Gillen 55). Thus, although Montgomery may have confessed that "I thought girls in their teens might like it but that was the only audience I hoped to reach" (qtd. in Gillen 27), her books reached much, much further.[2] These novels reached far beyond their original audiences, and, as the testimonials suggest, they evoked the kind of affectionate response in their male readers that the sentimental novel and its descendants strove for throughout their history.

Nineteenth-century literature used children in various venues to discipline male readers, and this genre fits into that tradition, though its life extended into the next century. The genre of nineteenth-century fiction in which children discipline men that has attracted the most critical attention in the last twenty years is temperance fiction. Charles Strickland's book on Alcott, for example, makes mention of Alcott's use of her own fiction to address "the notion that males have a fatal weakness for tippling and that they must be saved by the influence of good women." But Alcott did not make this argument only in her adult fiction, according to Strickland. "Long before the rise of the Women's Christian Temperance Union," he notes, "Alcott used her juvenile fiction as a forum to promote the tem-

perance cause" (142). The transformation of men is the central project of temperance fiction, as Glenn Hendler points out in his article on the Washingtonian
temperance movement. That transformation is narrated by their changing bodies: as drinkers, they are "grotesque, bloated, red and brown monsters"; in their
reformed state, they return to "their proper white 'manly forms'—pale, respect-
able, docile" ("Bloated Bodies" 135).[3] These men would be reformed not through
their own desires—those desires had spun out of control, and clearly men could
not be trusted with them any longer—but by a web of sentimental discipline. "In
these tales," Karen Sánchez-Eppler claims, "disciplinary intimacy cannot simply
uphold patriarchal rule since it is the wife, and even more the children, who
must bring the erring man under discipline" ("Temperance" 6).[4] Although, as
Sánchez-Eppler correctly points out, the power structures of these relationships
remain fundamentally unaltered, in borrowing this sentimental child, the orphan girl genre at the same time borrows its belief that affective discipline can
actually revise the law of the father.[5] Sentimental literature imagined a mother
who could change the father into something that served the domestic sphere,
and the temperance novel extended that dream to a child who could do it even
better. But the postsentimental orphan girl novel made the final change by introducing girls who could get a masculine force to serve their private desires without
the father's body around to complicate matters. If the temperance child could
transform the father's body, the orphan girl could dispose of the body altogether.

It doesn't take much work to infer why, then, the classic orphan girl novel
was immediately popular with girls and women and has remained so—these are
happy narratives about how femininity is a route to power over the men who rule
the public sphere. But these are also narratives about the empowerment and improvement of men. These novels are power fantasies for an oppressed cultural mi-
nority *and* an endorsement of the status quo all at once, and, oddly enough, both
facets of the novels can provide pleasure to *both* girls and men. I have already re-
counted the ways in which these girls practice power over men, and in that story
their reification of the status quo is perhaps obvious: Mary takes a boy who might
have died and teaches him how to rule as good men ought, Anne comes back
to Green Gables when the farm needs her, Pollyanna teaches her community to
live the way her father said they should. With the exception of Capitola, none of
these orphan girls habitually disobeys even the most despotic of adoptive parents,
and even Southworth's novel ends with wedding bells that reaffirm the proper
distribution of property in accordance with the patriarchy. What is important
here is not which happens more often, more finally, or more subversively, but
that both happen alongside each other. There is pleasure in the slippage between

master and servant, a slippage that can be countenanced because it happens in a fictive space that does not call for revolution, only the secret, personal pleasures of alternating between dominating and being dominated.

I am hardly the first to notice this pattern, and in fact its most eloquent expression comes in another work of fiction by a woman. Only a few years after the publication of *Emily of New Moon*, Virginia Woolf articulated the same pleasures in the thoughts of the character prototypical of gender slippage: Orlando. In one of the scenes in which she is a woman biologically, Orlando takes on the role of a woman sociologically and determines, as a possible suitor offers her a slice of beef, that the pleasures available to women in this way are superior to the pleasures of men:

> Then she had pursued, now she fled. Which is the greater ecstasy? The man's or the woman's? And are they not perhaps the same? No, she thought, this is the most delicious (thanking the Captain but refusing) to refuse, and see him frown. Well, she would, if he wished it, have the very thinnest, smallest shiver in the world. This was the most delicious, to yield and see him smile. "For nothing," she thought, regaining her couch on deck, and continuing the argument, "is more heavenly than to resist and to yield; to yield and to resist. Surely it throws the spirit into such a rapture that nothing else can." (155)

When Mark Spilka argues that Frances Hodgson Burnett "identifi[es] with young Fauntleroy" (54), he is pointing to a source of pleasure in the classic orphan girl novel determined by the same blurring of boundaries that Orlando cherishes here. *Little Lord Fauntleroy*, after all, tells the story of a rift between father and son healed so a patriarchal line of aristocracy can be continued, but it also explains that the ideal male ruler—and there seems to be no more question here than in *The Secret Garden* that men can be made into ideal rajahs—will not forget his mother. For Spilka, Burnett in *Fauntleroy* is both the boy ruler and the mother over whom he will rule, both the restored male aristocrat and the subject of the mother from whom he learns how to rule.[6] In the classic orphan girl novel, both the disciplined man and the disciplining girl resist and yield, yield and resist. Little wonder that for both men and women, such stories could throw the spirit into such rapture.

The popularity of the classic orphan girl novel with girls, women, and men speaks directly to the gender politics of sentimental and postsentimental fiction. It makes clear that although readers are themselves examples of how the mid- and turn-of-the-century separate spheres of masculinity and femininity were illusory, those readers were nonetheless invested in the illusion. The pleasure of slippage, after all, is not possible unless one acknowledges the hierarchy that is being temporarily displaced, and hierarchy is *defined by* separate spheres. The documentable popularity of the classic orphan girl novel with male readers is not evidence that readers of that time—or for that matter of this time—did not believe in separate spheres. It is evidence that male readers enjoyed the consumption of both disciplinary narratives and fictionalized discipline. It also strongly suggests that the women who read, revised, and wrote sentimental-style discipline into their fiction had some idea of just how broad the range of readers was for whom they were producing.

Why, then, did it disappear?

AFFECTIVE DISCIPLINE IN THE CONTEMPORARY HOME

The orphan girl formula that worked so well for sentimentalism provides a clear path by which we can follow the history of affective discipline out of the nineteenth century and into the twentieth. But children's literature did eventually abandon the nostalgic tale of an orphan girl in a rural setting, and at that point in literary history, the trail of affective discipline again disappears. To paraphrase a point I make in my introduction, although discipline was, as novels at the turn of the century demonstrate, a provocative topic worked over and revised endlessly in popular stories of orphan girls, by the mid-1920s, evidently American readers and writers had lost interest.

But just as the idea that American readers got bored with sentimentalism doesn't hold, so too the notion that they lost interest in the sentimental orphan girl story doesn't stand up to scrutiny. From the victory of suffrage to the beginning of the twenty-first century, the venue of the debate over affective discipline perhaps can't be pinpointed, but there is ample evidence that the debate has been taking place. Further, that evidence becomes clearer when considered in light of the trends in the debate that were taking shape during the final years of the postsentimental orphan girl novel. As a body, the orphan girl story from 1850 to 1923 demonstrates that women writers in the sentimental tradition outlined, refined, and, at least until the new century, endorsed a markedly feminine form of power that could rechannel masculine power. Implicit in that fact is the idea that most of these novels believed the power of affective discipline to be valid and appropriate.

However, as novels beginning with *Rebecca* and continuing through *Emily* attest, there was a growing sense that there might be something *in*appropriate about the power of affective discipline. That seed of discomfort would grow in the decades following the granting of women's suffrage, and today it is difficult for us to talk about suasion and other forms of affective power in the unironically positive terms authors such as Southworth and Alcott used to describe them. Therefore, although it is difficult to determine exactly in what arena the post-suffrage debate about affective discipline has been carried out, the orphan girl novel does provide clues about where to look for it. One of the places evidence of that invisible debate becomes visible is not in fiction but in politically minded scholarship about fiction. The reaction to moral suasion by contemporary readers of the fiction that featured suasion makes the point repeatedly: although the nineteenth century believed strongly in the difference between coercion and suasion, contemporary U.S. culture argues that there is no significant difference between the two.

Throughout this study, I have made a point of noting the power that is implicit in affective discipline. Considering the ongoing interest in subversion in literary studies in general and children's literature specifically, one might expect contemporary readers of sentimental-style fictions to find such feminine modes of power appealing. Instead, they reject it. Deborah O'Keefe, for example, in her sarcastically titled *Good Girl Messages*, dismisses any such insurgent power: "Since many well-loved books did offer cop-out plots and only token strong females, if any, I cannot agree that—before the late twentieth century—*most* children's fiction tended to subvert a repressive status quo" (23). She comes to this conclusion despite tracing a parallel trend of refashioning masculine privilege to feminine ends. O'Keefe is uninterested in a historical reading of the books, focusing instead on the effects such conservative texts will, she believes, have on the little girls reading them. "The idea that a girl can entirely change a hostile adult without really doing anything," she claims, "is one of the most dangerous notions in these books. It's not bad for girls to learn that they should be loving and helpful, but it's disastrous for them to learn that there is no way to cope with hostility except by sitting around exuding virtue and good cheer" (109). What O'Keefe deplores is not girls being nice but girls being told that being nice will ensure that they will be happy and safe—in short, being told that there is power in affective discipline.

Sánchez-Eppler makes a similar point in her analysis of temperance novels, which frequently end with the loving, yielding children realizing their dreams of a father doing what they want—namely, giving up alcohol and taking up the mantle of pater familias once more. As she makes her point about the illusory nature of the power these children exercise, she puts a name to the fundamental crime of such fiction: abuse. To ensure the happy ending, she argues, the narrative "figures the child as simultaneously victim of abuse and agent of discipline" (*Dependent States* 86). Sánchez-Eppler expresses frustration with "the vehemence with which they define this hardly veiled erotic contact not as abuse but as the surest and best antidote to abuse" (*Dependent States* 70). To a nineteenth-century reader, this caressing father would likely have appeared sufficiently feminized, tamed and brought under control, his caresses both evidence of that taming and part of the technology that makes it possible. To a contemporary reader, though, the effects of disciplinary intimacy are inherent in the abusive acts of the drunken father.

Sánchez-Eppler's extensive work on the symbolic weight of the child in nineteenth-century culture returns to this argument again and again, and as a result she gives us an excellent glimpse of how contemporary culture understands a form of discipline that was once considered appropriate. No matter how much effective discipline the fictional children are able to carry out, "in reforming their fathers, they do not empower themselves" (*Dependent States* 100). Instead, disciplinary intimacy provides a false sense of efficacy to its proponents, and "the child's love works to enforce a bourgeois patriarchal order that leaves the child as vulnerable as ever" (*Dependent States* 72). This is the central problem for Sánchez-Eppler and other contemporary scholars: in relationships that are healthy according to contemporary definitions, the child must be empowered, not merely serve to empower a stronger man to her own benefit.

In her work on Sunday school tracts and sentimental evangelism, Sánchez-Eppler finds a similar pattern. Here, she echoes Jacques Donzelot's concerns that children act as conduits through which a nondomestic force can control the family, because the ideal sentimental child reader will see to it that parents who do not conform to the evangelical enterprise are brought back into line. "The task of disciplining one's parents," writes Sánchez-Eppler, "of producing the Christian and domestic order of the family, epitomizes the double bind of the child in didactic fiction: however much these children may appear as disciplinary agents, they themselves remain without agency" (*Dependent States* 213). The stories imagine and model a sentimental power for which the nineteenth century's version of the child (playful, malleable, innocent) is especially well suited, but they make sure this power is only used in the direction approved of by the church. She even extends her critique of this form of power from its inherent abuse of children to an imagined abuse of women. Although she points out that the sentimental evangelical movement expands the borders of domestic power beyond the home and into foreign, heathen lands, its repeated stories of "violence by and against heathen women" just provide new opportunities to figure women as subservient to men (*Dependent States* 218). For a nineteenth-century reader, the extension of feminine spheres to out-of-control men and unsaved nations might have represented significant power for women and loving children, but to contemporary readers they read as empty promises, even in stories that show such power as effective.

A new kind of child helped to make children better characters in stories that figured their own abuse. Here I am not thinking of a new kind of actual child but of an imaginary child whose attributes were increasingly being defined by absence: the child was that which was not sexual, not speaking, not endowed with personal rights, not required or even allowed to work.[7] By defining childhood through absences, the nineteenth century created a symbolic child who was emptied of anything except the symbolic weight with which authors chose to load it.

Sánchez-Eppler considers artifacts of this child in her essay on visual and literary images of dead children, focusing on Harriet Beecher Stowe's famous use of dead children as a sympathetic link between adults. Stowe fetishizes the open bureau drawer, charging it with representations of the child's death, of lost aspirations, and other emotional dynamite in a culture plagued by the frequent death of children. Sánchez-Eppler explores the use of the dead child in these texts, deciding that "if the dead child serves better than the live one, it may be because of the ways that a child is imagined like a bureau drawer, a receptacle for parental aspirations and feelings" ("Clutch" 70). The artifacts of the period are only reflecting a widespread cultural belief that children were blank slates on whom could be scribbled the kind of person a parent—particularly a loving mother—desired. When nineteenth-century citizens discussed such a child, it was with the understanding that a good mother would make a good child, that indeed it was her responsibility.[8] But when contemporary scholars comment on that relationship, as does Ryan, they argue that the child was to become "the emotional marionette of its parents, in a warm and morally salubrious environment devoid of all cause for rebellious self-expression" (52). Zboray can even trace this pattern out from the private relationships of children and adults to sentimental literature and its adult readers:

> The feminization of reading education, which had replaced the earlier external classroom discipline (i.e., physical force) with internalized forms of social control, may well have contributed to the nineteenth-century reading public's taste for sentimental literature by the notorious scribbling women. The psychological manipulations of formulaic fiction found ready acceptance from former

students conditioned to respond to pedagogical ploys developed for classroom control. Some teachers, like Louisa May Alcott, went on to become popular fiction writers, but the effects of pedagogical feminization often played more subtly: for upon schoolmistresses devolved a constricted but publicly expressed form of cultural authority that easily translated into a greater receptivity, later in a student's life, to women writers. (104)

The former students / future readers of whom Zboray speaks are people who have had sentimentality inscribed onto them by careful methods of education. What contemporary scholars note in these sentimental relationships is that children were expected to be blank and ready for inscription. Once children received this education, they would carry it with them through the rest of their lives. What has been violated in contemporary eyes is the right to self-will. The technology that violates it, suasion, is no longer read as feminine and a possible route to empowerment; it is read as manipulation.

And it is here that we come on the crux of the argument for contemporary culture: *abuse* is defined as acts that are not just physical but manipulative in any way. For the nineteenth and early twentieth centuries, physical manipulation—coercion—was an old mode of discipline being challenged by nonphysical suasion. The only difference was whether bodies and force were involved. Consider in contrast the "Power and Control Wheel," a widely popular handout in domestic violence workshops across the United States at the beginning of the twenty-first century. The wheel originated with the Domestic Abuse Intervention Project, a program originally intended to standardize the practices of effective domestic violence programs. The project emphasizes self-empowerment for survivors and education for people at high risk of being in abusive relationships. Whereas nineteenth-century and Progressive Era culture focused on the presence or absence of physical violence, and women's culture proposed suasion as an alternative to that violence, early twenty-first-century culture insists that physical violence is only the last and most obvious symptom of an abusive relationship. Instead, any attempt to have power or control over someone else is defined as abusive. The Project's "Equality Wheel," in contrast, documents a healthy, nonabusive relationship not in terms of moral rather than physical manipulation but in terms of attempts at equality. Whereas the first wheel lists as abusive economic, verbal, and emotional manipulation as well as misuse of privilege and even "using children" to exert power over a partner, the "Equality Wheel" calls for "economic partnership," "negotiation and fairness," and other activities that abandon the battlefield of control. "Economic partnership," for example, contains an enjoinder to ensure that "both partners benefit from financial arrangements." Although models of healthy relationships a century ago relied on psychic manipulation to counteract physical coercion in keeping with an ideology that was not only subversive but key to first-wave feminism, American definitions of abuse have changed such that contemporary culture (claims that it) cannot abide any use of any kind of leverage in private relationships, especially between equals.

But as much the distinction between physical and nonphysical manipulation has been challenged, there remains an anachronistically gendered tone to discussions of abuse. I have argued that earlier culture defined moral suasion and other nonphysical modes of discipline as feminine and therefore that the debates that riddled the culture over which form of discipline was preferable carried with them inflections of gender. The same is true of contemporary discussions of power in personal relationships. For example, the Domestic Abuse Intervention Project's website, from which various wheels addressing power imbalance can be downloaded for free to be used in small groups and workshops, issues some very strange restrictions on republication of the wheels:

> Although some experiences of battered women may be similar to those of other groups, they aren't the same. Substituting gender-neutral language does not acknowledge the specific tactics used to control other groups of people, including men abused by women and people abused by their same sex-partner[s]. For these reasons, we *do not grant permission to substitute gender neutral language* on the Power and Control Wheel. (emphasis added)

Therefore, the wheel keeps abuse gendered. The section labeled "Using Male Privilege" warns the reader against "treating her like a servant." The section on "Using Isolation" focuses on "controlling what she does, who[m] she sees and talks to, what she reads, where she goes." To be fair, this language has been adapted by other users in clear violation of the copyright holder's wishes, but the fact that the project makes so explicit and details at such length its belief that women and men cannot experience abuse the same way resurrects the gendered divide that at first glance the wheels put to rest.[9] Although the wheels avoid questions of gendered power—the questions that informed the sexist debates about discipline one hundred years ago—they rely on gender divisions to discuss the effects of power. In other words, they remove gender distinctions from the production of abuse, but rather than eliminate that bias altogether, they simply relocate it to the consumption of abuse.

Although I have been making the point that there is a great divide between conceptions of power and abuse between 1900 and 2000, it is worth remembering that this divide was already taking shape at the end of the girls' novel genre. As early as 1903 and *Rebecca of Sunnybrook Farm*, the disciplining girls were using their discipline without cunning, in effect disavowing the manipulation they wielded so effectively. Although Rose in 1875 used her influence openly, and although girls up through Emily in 1923 continue to be able to discipline the people around them, the later girls do so without the conscious effort that lies at the heart of today's definition of manipulative behavior as abusive. In the wheels, for example, it is not actions that are judged as manipulative or healthy, but intentions. The financial dimension of a healthy relationship—as defined by the "Equality Wheel"—is not necessarily one in which both partners earn and spend in equal amounts but one in which bother partners *try* to share in amounts with which they are both comfortable. Therefore, a relationship is defined as abusive or healthy by consideration of what the partners intend to do. The early stirrings of this conception of healthy relationships manifest in *Emily*, who usually disciplines accidentally, and when she disciplines intentionally—by using the Murray look—she feels guilty about it. As such, this genre of novels constitutes a vital piece of the history of how Americans define healthy relationships. It begins steeped in the disciplinary practices of the sentimental novel and traces forward the changing notions of discipline until the origins of contemporary definitions of abuse can be seen at the end.

Notes

1. See, for example, Irene Gammel's introduction to *Making Avonlea* as well as various other articles in the collection, particularly Eleanor Hersey's article on the film version of *Anne*.

2. Lawrence Stone in particular explains the history of the family and its identity as defined by father or state. This is one of his central points, but its full implications only come to light in Jacques Donzelot's landmark *The Policing of Families*. Eventually, the pact between father and state would be betrayed by the state, which learned to use the child as a backdoor into family rule. Emphasizing the needs of the individual child as defined by his or her psychology—a history I trace throughout this book—provided an excuse for the state to supercede the pater familias and remove the father as proxy ruler of the family.

3. Carol Mattingly makes a similar point about temperance fiction: "Because temperance fiction became accepted as within the province of women's work, and because it could so readily be associated with many forms of injustices toward women, temperance offered women a popular cultural medium for discussing and exploring women's issues" (124).

4. Because Fauntleroy loves his mother and disciplines his adoptive father to behave as she wishes, he performs the same essential duties a girl at his point in the history of the genre might. In fact, Fauntleroy seems to be a boy mainly so that the line of inheritance to which the adoptive father is so dedicated can believably run through him. In other words, Fauntleroy is a boy mostly because being a boy better equips him to discipline the father in this one particular instance.

5. As Jabe Slocum says, Timothy manages events and people remarkably well, without "knowin' that he was managin' anything" (182).

6. *Rebecca* may seem a strange addition to this list, since one of her parents is still alive in the novel. In fact, although Rebecca's mother is deathly ill at the end of the book, she does live through to its end. However, *Rebecca* is consciously part of the tradition I am describing in these novels, and the distinction between Rebecca's social position and that of an orphan would not have been so stark to contemporaneous readers as it is to us today. Rebecca did meet the turn-of-the-century definition of "orphan" because she had lost her father, although she would not have been regarded

as a "full orphan," which was a term in common use to refer to a child who had lost both biological parents. For more on these definitions, see the work of Nurith Zmora and Joan Gittens. For more on the importance of social position to the definition of orphanhood, particularly compared with the importance of the death of both biological parents, see Susan Whitelaw Downs and Michael W. Sherraden's "The Orphan Asylum in the Nineteenth Century." Finally, whatever her strictest orphan status, Rebecca functions as an orphan in the novel: she is given up by her sole remaining biological parent, she lives on the charity of her adopters, and she is expected to fill an affective as well as a financial position in the adoptive household.

7. Mary Henley Rubio has recently questioned the common perception that *Anne* was written for young readers. She acknowledges that Montgomery initially accepted that her book would be perceived as written for girls, but she also points to Montgomery's eventual frustration with "being pigeonholed as a children's writer," and she documents how Montgomery asserted late in her career that she wrote *Anne* for adults (289). Although I am not yet convinced by Rubio's argument (it's not clear, for example, why the later Montgomery's word is more trustworthy than the early Montgomery's), her theory may add another way to connect Montgomery's oeuvre to sentimental novels written for adults, even if it loosens the place of *Anne* in the canon of children's literature.

8. See, for example, Nina Baym's *Woman's Fiction* and Alexander Cowie's *Rise of the American Novel*.

9. The third chapter of Karen Sánchez-Eppler's *Dependent States*, which focuses on the imagery of dead children in fiction and early photography, explores this subject more fully. Anne Higonnet's *Pictures of Innocence* also explicates the importance of the image of dead children in various forms of art.

10. E. Anthony Rotundo gives the history of manhood in America far more attention than I can here, so I only point to his work and his argument that during the late nineteenth century, bourgeois culture changed its criteria for manliness, deemphasizing moral character and stressing instead a manly physique and actions that bespoke physical power. These changes are an important part of the history of manliness on which I am building.

11. Further, figures who are central to the history of affective discipline that I recast repeatedly endorsed a deeply gendered conception of discipline. I point to many of these in later chapters, but for now, consider Lyman Cobb's celebration of the mid-nineteenth-century trend toward moral suasion, in which he says that those who have championed affective discipline have "elevated WOMAN to the true and dignified station, designed by her Creator. She it is, who, by her mild and persuasive tones and beneficent countenance, can and does, aided by Divine Revelation, 'win the young hearts of our children to duty'" (7–8). He later complains that the typical father is "generally in favor" of physical punishment, but the typical mother is "generally, (*to her great credit be it spoken*), *opposed* to it" (32). For Cobb, then, sentimental discipline was fundamentally gendered.

12. Again, this process is part of the history of masculinity that Rotundo recounts.

13. Strickland does go on to argue that Alcott herself, however, believed strongly

in women's suffrage. This makes her all the more interesting for my study since, as chapter 3 demonstrates, she still fictionalized instances of women relying not on masculine coercion but feminine suasion.

14. Nina Baym has made passing reference to a similar trend in midcentury Anglophone literature, speaking of how "a potentially individual woman matured into a type" (*Novels, Readers, and Reviewers* 100).

15. For the main arguments in this history, see Philippe Ariès's *Centuries of Childhood*, Linda Pollock's *A Lasting Relationship*, and Lloyd DeMause's *The History of Childhood*.

16. On the service to which the dying child is put in nineteenth-century fiction, see the third chapter of Karen Sánchez-Eppler's *Dependent States*.

CHAPTER 1: *THE WIDE, WIDE WORLD* AND THE RULES OF
SENTIMENTAL ENGAGEMENT

1. See Myra C. Glenn's *Campaigns against Corporal Punishment* for this example and many others, including chilling descriptions of the various weapons of corporal punishment.

2. In fact, this may be one of the ways in which the United States was "feminized" that Ann Douglas deplores. Such is certainly the implication of her disgust with less rigorous, anti-Calvinist shifts in American culture.

3. See Richard H. Brodhead's "Sparing the Rod" for how "literature was another venue in which the problems set by middle-class disciplinary theory were worked through, was even (as in *Uncle Tom's Cabin*) a chief medium through which that theory was vindicated and broadcast" (88).

4. Although the English title of Foucault's most famous work on the subject is *Discipline and Punish*, the importance of surveillance to a Foucauldian notion of discipline is better preserved in the French title, *Surveiller et punir*.

5. Claudia Nelson's "A Wealth of Fatherhood" is an exception. Her treatment of Captain Montgomery is telling: Nelson spends very little time analyzing Ellen's biological father, insightfully pointing out that his failures both within and outside the domestic space necessitate "father-substitutes" (167). She then goes on to study Warner's use of men who fill the biological father's place.

6. Jane Tompkins makes a similar point in her afterword to the novel. There, she even goes so far as to indicate that the novel can be read as subversive. For her, the novel endorses "the conviction that human events are, ultimately and inevitably, shaped by secret prayer," which "produces a view of society in which orphan girls like Ellen Montgomery, and writers like Susan Warner, can hope to change the world" (596).

7. In *Domestic Individualism*, Gillian Brown links this distaste for the frivolous with a sentimental disdain for the market; for Harriet Beecher Stowe in particular, Brown argues, the market is signified by a prevalence of the cosmetic over the useful, and the intrusion of the market into the home is the herald of disorder and inhumanity. It is odd, therefore, that other mainstays of the sentimental tradition have

no qualms about endorsing a femininity that is marked by adornment instead of pragmatism, so much so that they choose to fix the anticonsumer argument in an unlikable character, such as Fortune in the case of Warner's novel. Gale Temple's article on *Ruth Hall* makes a point similar to my own: although sentimental novelists seemed to distrust the mass market and the consumption that supported it, many of them went out of their way to mock characters who opposed consumption.

8. I use the masculine pronoun throughout my discussion of the Lockean educational model in order to help keep it separate from the orphans who populate the girls' novel as well as to reflect Locke and the early republic's investment of education and other forms of empowerment along gender lines.

CHAPTER 2: *THE HIDDEN HAND* AND MOMENTARY INDIVIDUALISM

1. Gillian Brown's *Domestic Individualism* contains one of the better-known analyses of how these two male authors criticized but borrowed from the feminine tradition of sentimental consumption.

2. "Yet, for the sake of my dear mother and Clara, I did violence only to my own natural manhood, and bore it all with the servility of a slave" (408).

3. One of Southworth's charms is how aware her narrator is of these breeches in verisimilitude. This particular scene is too serious for her to do more than have a character point out the problem, but earlier in the novel, when Capitola and Hurricane realize they neglected to ask a certain character's name—resulting in confusion that will enable a major plot point later—Southworth closes the chapter with a wink at the reader as Wool exclaims that they've just passed an awfully rough spot in the road (60).

CHAPTER 3. *EIGHT COUSINS* AND WHAT GIRLS ARE MADE FOR

1. See chapter two of Karen Sànchez-Eppler's *Dependent States*.

2. Rose's influence over Phebe fully bears fruit in the novel's sequel, *Rose in Bloom*, in which Phebe returns to America an accomplished singer. She leaves the family briefly to pursue a blossoming singing career, and she returns to it shortly thereafter to marry the eldest surviving cousin, thus ensuring her future security. Her social mobility, career prospects, and ability to meet her future husband on comparable social ground are all thanks to Rose's interest.

3. Bruce A. Ronda has suggested another disciplinary tradition with links to what I have been calling the Lockean tradition. Ronda states that Horace Bushnell's use of the term "organic" to describe the ideal nurturing family relationship descends from Locke (see Ronda 308), and Bushnell's own comments that the "only genuine teaching" is one in which a child loves his teacher and therefore follows his example (318) certainly describes the broad sense of Lockean discipline as well as the specific relationship between Alec and Rose.

4. The impending marriage is more than an idle possibility on the horizon of these novels, even though the first novels of these girls' series never end with a mar-

riage. In the sequel to *Eight Cousins*, Rose's marriage is a major issue, and the payoff of that marriage is carefully planned in *Eight Cousins*.

5. Alec's Lockean education of Rose is a success, as the reader discovers when Rose gives up her position in the leisure class (if only for a day) so her beloved servant can enjoy an Independence Day celebration in her stead.

6. Catherine Keohane's article on female charity in the eighteenth century covers the history of this issue well. In it, she points out that acting on behalf of the woman's imminent husband—even in cases when a woman had yet to be engaged to be married—a man could halt even good feminine spending without serious qualms.

7. Fern's novel is not a major part of the specific tradition I am considering—the formula in which an orphan girl enters a home that does not necessarily want her but is then transformed by her presence. However, *Ruth Hall* has become an unavoidable text in any discussion of individuality and sentiment. This is because the novel seems a perfect example to illustrate possessive individualism, the dominant theory of individualism in contemporary studies of sentiment. Therefore, scholars examining possessive individualism inevitably reference it, and other scholars—such as Temple and María C. Sánchez—proposing a different model by which to study individualism likewise find themselves obliged to reference it, if only to demonstrate that their competing models work well on the dominant model's ideal test case. Since I am interested in tracing the history of individualism out of sentimentalism, *Ruth Hall* looms deceptively large in my argument.

CHAPTER 4. *REBECCA OF SUNNYBROOK FARM* AND THE THREAT OF
AFFECTIVE DISCIPLINE

1. Wiggin is most precisely a second-wave U.S. kindergarten activist, and her ideology was deeply influenced by another reformer who played a role in the history of sentimental-style discipline, Elizabeth Palmer Peabody. Bruce A. Ronda's biography of Peabody is an excellent source for the links—and differences—between Wiggin and Peabody (see 312, 319–20, and 331–32 for especially eloquent anecdotes). Peabody is also an important forerunner to Wiggin in that she anticipates much of the ambiguous feeling in kindergarten theory about discipline and individualism. For instance, Ronda argues that Peabody rejected the individualism embraced by the transcendentalists with whom she spent a great deal of time (309), but he also documents how she championed the personal privacy of students, particularly in regard to their writing (8), a point that will become increasingly important throughout the history of the orphan girl novel.

2. In *Being a Boy Again*, Marcia Jacobson points to a similar concern over the threat to selfhood, particularly to masculine selfhood, in what she calls the "American boy book." Interestingly, Jacobson argues that these were only marginally books for boys, that they are best understood as books for men, among whom they had very high sales figures.

3. The child in these early kindergarten texts is always male, in part to distinguish the pupil from the teacher, who is always female.

4. One of the most interesting things about the ideology of the kindergarten is how similar it is to what Freud would articulate in subsequent decades. For Freud, the child always has a sexual nature, and there are natural desires and even natural machinery in place so that this nature will mature on its own. Adults, for Freud, therefore can best serve children by first refraining from imposing their own misconceptions of sexuality on children and second by learning to recognize when a child's sexual maturation has been derailed—usually by interference from the world of adult symbolics. It might be that the kindergarten movement was instrumental in laying the groundwork for Freud's argument about the desires of children.

5. Deidre Shauna Lynch makes a similar point about characterization and difference. See *The Economy of Character*, 248–49, for a witty example of her argument.

CHAPTER 5. *A LITTLE PRINCESS* AND THE ACCIDENTAL POWER OF STORIES

1. The fourth chapter of Karen Sánchez-Eppler's *Dependent States* points out the sentimental tradition of bringing up poverty in order to bemoan it, then throwing loose change at it until guilt over the disparity between the comfortable sentimental home and the inhumanity of poverty in capitalist America has disappeared. This is a frequent and valid complaint against the sentimental tradition, and *A Little Princess* is very much a novel about a rags-to-riches orphan restored to the upper class who was never really a member of any other class.

2. See Glenn Hendler's *Public Sentiment*.

CHAPTER 6. *ANNE OF GREEN GABLES* AND THE RETURN OF
AFFECTIVE DISCIPLINE

1. For example, it continues the genre's disapproval of public humiliation. When her first teacher in Avonlea, Mr. Phillips, punishes Anne, he does so by making her stand up before the class with these words written on the board: "Ann Shirley has a very bad temper. Ann Shirley must learn to control her temper." Phillips then reads the sentences aloud, "so that even the primer class, who couldn't read writing, should understand it" (168). Phillips is, by the end of the novel, replaced by a teacher Anne likes much more, a teacher who is also much more effective in her lessons and respectful in her discipline.

2. Make that an international phenomenon, as Erika Diane Rappaport has demonstrated in her extensive analysis of the public pleasures of shopping in London's West End.

3. Hunter makes this argument in her series of examples about children who saved and bought for themselves subscriptions to *St. Nicholas*, the most important venue for original juvenile fiction of the period (29–31). *St. Nicholas* is more than just a parallel example, for although *Anne* was not originally serialized there, many parallel books—including the original version of *A Little Princess*—were. The girls' novel genre was intimately and economically tied to the history of this particular magazine, and I return to its analysis in the conclusion to chapter 10. For more infor-

mation on this magazine and its role in the history of children's literature, see the excellent collection *St. Nicholas and Mary Mapes Dodge: The Legacy of a Children's Magazine Editor, 1873–1905*, edited by Susan R. Gannon, Suzanne Rahn, and Ruth Anne Thompson.

CHAPTER 7. *THE SECRET GARDEN* AND THE RAJAH'S MASTER

1. Kerber's book on republican motherhood is a powerful study of the origins of this mother, but we can still find her as late as Catharine Beecher's 1869 *The American Woman's Home*, coauthored to a debatable extent by her sister, the author of *Uncle Tom's Cabin*, arguably the most important sentimental novel. In Beecher and Stowe's book, there is attention given to the education of the child's spirit, but most of the advice they give has to do with physical care—for example, the entire chapter entitled "The Care of Infants" is devoted to the subject of taking care of children's bodies. For Beecher, as for the republican mother of Revolutionary America, the boy child must be cared for so that he can grow up to rule well. Although Beecher believes in expanding the sphere of women's influence, she consistently places faith in the moral use of power by those—explicitly men, as in her denunciation of suffrage—who already have it.

2. Gretchen Holbrook Gerzina's recent biography of Burnett calls into question Burnett's personal investment in Christian Science, an investment scholars have long taken for granted, but it is difficult to read scenes such as this one without thinking of Burnett's exposure to the ideas of Christian Science. Throughout *The Secret Garden*, Mary's ideas about healing are frequently set in opposition to those of medical opinion, and her successful disciplining of the boy has more to do with right feeling than it does medicine.

CHAPTER 8. *POLLYANNA* AND ANXIOUS INDIVIDUALISM

1. See, for example, a conversation between the housekeeper Nancy and Aunt Polly while they prepare for the child's arrival. Nancy, who is frightened of her harsh mistress throughout most of the novel, ventures to say that surely Polly would "want her—your sister's child," but Polly "haughtily" replies that she "can't see how I should particularly *want* to have the care of" the girl. Still, she says, "I hope I know my duty" (13). This word is, throughout the genre, a frequent marker for adults who must be disciplined into affection for their new charges, showing up in *The Wide, Wide World* as well as *Emily of New Moon*, the first and last books in the genre.

2. She even, as Pollyanna rejoices , calls her niece "dear" for the first time (171).

3. And in a sequel to *Emily of New Moon*, which is the last novel I consider, Emily suffers an accident that leaves her in much the same position as Pollyanna. Invalidism is also the target of affective discipline in *Heidi*, a European novel that in many ways fits into the orphan girl novel tradition between *Eight Cousins* and *Rebecca of Sunnybrook Farm*.

4. Pollyanna was often literally the central image of badges for real-life glad clubs,

such as the Pollyanna Society, whose lapel pins featured the words "Join the POLLY ANNA CLUB and BE GLAD."

5. Clay Lancaster's is the seminal article on this phenomenon.

CHAPTER 9. *EMILY OF NEW MOON* AND THE PRIVATE GIRL

1. Mary Henley Rubio's recent *Lucy Maud Montgomery: The Gift of Wings* notes an interesting distinction Montgomery herself made between definitions of sentiment. Rubio claims that Montgomery "loathed" sentimentality but saw sentiment— which Rubio defines as "the impulse that held societies together"—as an important literary goal dating at least back to Charlotte Brontë (301). Rubio notes Montgomery's pleasure over a review that declared *Emily* was marked by "sentiment that never gets over the line into sentimentality" (qtd. in Rubio 301). Rubio does not address Montgomery's place in a history of the genre of sentimentalism, but an "impulse that held societies together" might be a fair way to describe the affection that drives sentimental-style discipline.

2. For instance, he tells Emily that she has—in the spirit of a key scene in the European orphan girl novel *Heidi*—restored him to the Christian faith (324).

3. Jimmy represents a man whom the author herself stripped of his body and put to her own ends. Elizabeth Waterston, who edited Montgomery's selected journals, points to a 28 January 1912 entry not included in the volume, an entry in which she says Montgomery writes of "Cousin Jimmie Macneill, her grandfather's older brother." Macneill was, according to Montgomery, "a most eccentric individual—a curious compound of child and genius. He was a born poet. He composed hundreds of poems and would recite them to favored individuals" (Waterston xvii). This Jimmie is strikingly similar to Emily's cousin Jimmy, whose name does not have a consistent spelling in the novel. The fictional Jimmy is perhaps mentally impaired, though only slightly, following an accident as a child, and he recites his poetry—which he refuses to transcribe—only on certain nights, and only when his beloved Emily is in attendance.

4. "Perhaps she had been outgrowing it gradually, as childhood began to merge into girlhood—perhaps the bitter scene with Aunt Elizabeth had only shaken into dust something out of which the spirit had already departed. But, whatever the explanation, it was not possible to write such letters any more" (314).

5. Her apology, though, is a masterpiece of understatement: "I am sorry for anything I did to-day that was wrong," she says, "and I ask your pardon for it" (171).

6. Aunt Elizabeth uses her power in the same way when she refuses to let Emily have bangs, and the novel similarly marks Elizabeth's snide comment as poor form (87).

7. Margaret Steffler and Irene Gammel ("Eros") assume this thesis in their articles.

8. As I demonstrate, sentimentalism certainly worked against the kind of privacy *Emily* endorses, but the same cannot be said of the kindergarten movement, which, particularly in the strand of theorists who had direct influence on the late orphan girl novel, was never comfortable with the total access to children's hearts that sentimen-

talism assumed. Bruce A. Ronda has made this point, for example, about Elizabeth Palmer Peabody, whose ties with Kate Douglas Wiggin were extensive, noting how Peabody "dissented" from Bronson Alcott's insistence on reading his pupils' journals.

9. See, for example, Spacks's discussion of Laurence Sterne (*Privacy* 49).

10. The most obvious example is *Little Orphan Annie,* which hit newspapers one year after the publication of the first *Emily* novel and exploded in popularity through radio and film incarnations in the 1930s. But less well-known examples help illustrate a shift away from the nostalgic tone and settings of the orphan girl novels and toward more modern themes. Amy Bell Marlowe's *The Girl from Sunset Ranch; or, Alone in a Great City,* published in 1914, opens with the tragic orphaning of a girl in the rugged west, but it immediately transfers her to a city landscape marked by ethnic heterogeneity and public opinion shaped by mass media. Other Stratemeyer books, such as *The Moving Picture Girls; or, First Appearances in Photo Dramas* (by Laura Lee Hope, a pseudonym used for various Stratemeyer books), also published in 1914, featured girls negotiating new technology and revising cultural opinions attached to them. Harrison Bardwell's 1930 novel, *Roberta's Flying Courage,* follows with approval a girl who professionalizes herself and becomes an early and prominent female pilot, along the way overcoming assumptions about the proper place of young ladies.

CHAPTER 10. SPINNING SYMPATHY

1. See chapter 5 of Sánchez-Eppler's *Dependent States.*

2. Jerry Griswold has made exactly this point about the effect of Porter's novel at the turn of the century. He includes an example of "the Glad Kids, a group of prisoners in a penitentiary whose ages ranged from thirty-two to seventy-six." These prisoners modeled themselves after Pollyanna and happily acknowledged her influence on them.

3. See chapter 15, where the narrator describes this chain of events at length (190–91).

4. See David I. Macleod's *The Age of the Child,* 7–8.

5. This is Griswold's reading of *Pollyanna.* He dubs Pollyanna "a genius at 'reverse psychology'" (220) and thinks of characters such as Pollyanna as "audacious kids who refuse to be vanquished" (236).

CHAPTER 11. GIRLS' NOVELS AND THE END OF MOTHERING

1. See Parille's *Boys at Home* and Claire Chantell's "The Limits of the Mother at Home in *The Wide, Wide World* and *The Lamplighter.*"

2. The appearance of such a character representative of scientific motherhood in a book for girls also prepares the way for a later movement in girls' culture. Laureen Tedesco explores this in an article on the writing of *Scouting for Girls,* the Girl Scouts' handbook that was being composed in the late Progressive Era from about 1918 to 1922. Tedesco's point is that the handbook teaches Americanization and Pro-

gressive-style scientific self-improvement. Placed in the history I am theorizing, the handbook also provides a successor to Uncle Alec, a scientific authority that intercedes to teach girls how to mother well.

3. Carroll Smith-Rosenberg has demonstrated that a similar real-life pattern began to emerge in the midcentury. She points, for example, to letters written in the 1840s that record the habit boarding-school girls had developed of forging deep mentor relationships that often resulted in one girl calling another her "mother."

4. Gruner goes on to argue that in addition to these instances in which Sara explicitly replaces mothers, there are also instances in which she effectively replaces them in her roles as educator and storyteller.

5. Contrast this story with Cindy Weinstein's account of how midcentury courts differed from earlier incarnations in that they began privileging affective ties over consanguine ties. Weinstein also argues that the desires of the child—as figured in her affective privileging of one possible family over the other—gained *more* weight in influencing judicial decisions (see especially chapter two of Weinstein's text) in the midcentury.

6. Watson's comments stand in opposition to a great deal of midcentury thought, but his ideas are particularly striking in comparison with those of Lyman Cobb, who in 1847—shortly before the publication of *The Wide, Wide World*—laid the blame for poor discipline on fathers, whose punishment he characterizes as *"very severe."* Whereas Watson finds fault with mothers, Cobb locates it in fathers: mothers can hurt the children by being too lenient, but only, Cobb suggests, as they try to correct the cruelty of fathers (33). Elsewhere, Cobb praises mothers' discipline, saying that its "great secret . . . is the LOVE which she bears them" (104).

7. This is a point that Kimberley Reynolds makes in passing in her study of popular children's fiction at the turn of the century (94).

8. I am thinking here of course of Susan Warner's *The Wide, Wide World* (1850), but Chantell makes a similar point about *The Lamplighter*, Maria Cummins's 1854 orphan girl tale. Chantell argues that in both Cummins's and Warner's novels, the mother "must be translated from corporality into abstraction in order to achieve perfect influence over" their children, at which point the influence becomes "unassailable" (139).

9. Gillian Adams makes the point that the novel should be read in these two stages.

10. Burnett may have felt some personal pressure to refute this claim as she wrote *The Secret Garden*. At the time, she was widely known for the enormously, internationally successful *Little Lord Fauntleroy*, which touched off a craze of dressing boys in ringlets and lace. The backlash from this craze, which took *Fauntleroy* as the highest example of how women's writing threatened boys' masculinity, would follow Burnett for the rest of her career. By the time of *The Secret Garden*, the backlash was so widespread and so virulent that she can hardly have been unaware of it as she conceived the story of Colin, the hysterical boy. For more on the reception of *Fauntleroy*, see Anna Wilson's "Little Lord Fauntleroy: The Darling of Mothers and the Abomination of a Generation."

CONCLUSION. AFFECTION, MANIPULATION, PLEASURE, ABUSE

1. See my comments on this novel in the introduction, where I point out that *Fauntleroy* might as well be one of these girls' novels, except that it stars a (highly feminized) boy instead of an orphan girl.

2. And I can't resist mentioning that Brenda R. Weber has already listed me, although I appear incognito, in her article on devotees of Montgomery around the world (50).

3. Karen Sánchez-Eppler's *Touching Liberty* similarly deals with male bodies and the privileges attached to them: "All the 'men' who, Thomas Jefferson declared, 'are created equal' shed their gender and their race; in obtaining the right to freedom and equality they discard bodily specificity. The problem, as feminists and abolitionists surely suspected, was that women and blacks could never shed their bodies to become incorporeal 'men'" (3).

4. Although I am far from sharing Ann Douglas's disgust with sentimental fiction and the sentimentalization of U.S. culture, Sánchez-Eppler's claim strikes me as a point in her favor. The prefeminist (and Ann Douglas) sense that sentimental writers and women were out to emasculate men might be right, especially since intemperance and hypermasculinity were conflated. Thus, the Washingtonians created an all-male space but *imported* feminine discipline to conquer male behavior and reconnect themselves to the families they were (according to their own sentimental narratives) injuring.

5. Here I am paraphrasing and extending Sánchez-Eppler's argument about moral suasion ("Temperance" 6).

6. Instances of empowered boys, girls, and men advancing and retreating proliferate through these novels, but my favorite is one so obvious that it has attracted little commentary. In the climactic scene of *The Secret Garden*, the very scene in which Colin apparently supplants Mary as the protagonist of the disciplinary narrative, the narrator describes Colin as "a *laughable*, lovable, healthy" boy (231, emphasis added). The standard interpretation of this line is that Colin is laugh*ing*, but the text literally says that in the same moment he is to be loved and made healthy, Colin is to be *laughed at*. I do not want to make too much of what is only one word, and a word that was probably a mistake in the first place, but the mistake fits with the larger argument of these novels: boys should be lovable and healthy, but there is also something inferior about them. They should be respected and put in power, but the girls who give them that respect and power retain the right to giggle behind their fans. This point is similar to one that Barbara Ehrenreich has made about late-twentieth century texts. She demonstrates how the logic of New Right antifeminism is founded on the understanding that "*all* men are weak" (162). Evidently novels in the sentimental tradition are not the only texts to provide their readers with such pleasures.

7. Here I am drawing on a vast array of scholarship on the child. Philippe Ariès was instrumental in considering childhood itself as a cultural configuration, and although Linda Pollock disagrees with much of what Ariès says about affectionate bonds between parent and child, both agree that the nineteenth century was charac-

terized by a belief in love as the primary element in relationships between mothers and children. Ariès also provides lengthy sections on the history of children's rights. James R. Kincaid has argued in different venues that the nineteenth century saw an increase in the emphasis on children as "not-adult," as primarily nonsexual and nonlaboring. Lloyd DeMause and Lawrence Stone make similar comments about children and work. Finally, in her *Little Strangers*, Claudia Nelson has documented the increasing emotional investment in American children—significantly, orphans chief among them—that replaced the work value of children with sentimental value.

8. See Linda K. Kerber's *Women of the Republic* for the eighteenth-century origins of this relationship.

9. In fact, although I frequently worked with these kinds of handouts during sessions with survivors of and people at high risk for domestic violence, the only wheels I have ever seen that use such specifically sexist language are the Duluth Model wheels available at the project's website.

Bibliography

Abate, Michelle Ann. *Tomboys: A Literary and Cultural History.* Philadelphia: Temple UP, 2008.

Abel, Emily K. "Hospitalizing Maria Germani." *"Bad" Mothers: The Politics of Blame in Twentieth-Century America.* Ed. Molly Ladd-Taylor and Lauri Umansky. New York: New York UP, 1998. 58–66.

Ackerman, Alan. "The Right to Privacy: William Dean Howells and the Rise of Dramatic Realism." *American Literary Realism* 30.1 (1997): 1–19.

Adams, Gillian. "Secrets and Healing Magic in *The Secret Garden.*" *Triumphs of the Spirit in Children's Literature.* Ed. Francelia Butler and Richard Rotert. Hamden, Conn: Library Professional Publications, 1986. 42–54.

Alcott, Louisa May. *Eight Cousins.* 1875. Racine, Wisc.: Golden P, 1965.

———. *Little Women.* 1868–69. New York: Wanderer, 1982.

———. *Rose in Bloom.* 1876. Boston: Little, Brown, 1995.

Alger, Horatio. *Tattered Tom; or, The Story of a Street Arab.* Boston: Loring, 1871.

Ariès, Philippe. *Centuries of Childhood: A Social History of Family Life.* Trans. Robert Baldick. New York: Vintage, 1962.

Armstrong, Nancy. *Desire and Domestic Fiction: A Political History of the Novel.* New York: Oxford UP, 1987.

Avery, Gillian. *Behold the Child: American Children and Their Books, 1621–1922.* Baltimore, Md.: Johns Hopkins UP, 1994.

———. "Children's Books and Social History." *Research about Nineteenth-Century Children and Books.* Ed. Selma K. Richardson. Urbana: U of Illinois P, 1980. 23–40.

Bardwell, Harrison. *Roberta's Flying Courage.* Cleveland: World Syndicate Publishing, 1930.

Baxter, Kent. *The Modern Age: Turn-of-the-Century American Culture and the Invention of Adolescence.* Tuscaloosa: U of Alabama P, 2008.

Baym, Nina. *Novels, Readers, and Reviewers: Responses to Fiction in Antebellum America.* Ithaca: Cornell UP, 1984.

———. *Woman's Fiction: A Guide to Novels by and about Women in America, 1820–70.* 1978. Urbana: U of Illinois P, 1993.

———. "Women's Novels and Women's Minds: An Unsentimental View of Nineteenth-Century American Women's Fiction." *Novel: A Forum on Fiction* 31.3 (1998): 335–50.

Beecher, Catharine E., and Harriet Beecher Stowe. *The American Woman's Home; or, Principles of Domestic Science: Being a Guide to the Formation and Maintenance of Economical, Healthful, Beautiful and Christian Homes.* 1869. Watkins Glen, N.Y.: Library of Victorian Culture American Life Foundation, 1979.

Berlant, Lauren. "Poor Eliza." Davidson and Hatcher 292–323.

Boeckmann, Cathy. *A Question of Character: Scientific Racism and the Genres of American Fiction, 1892–1912.* Tuscaloosa: U of Alabama P, 2000.

Brodhead, Richard H. "Sparing the Rod: Discipline and Fiction in Antebellum America." *Representations* 21 (Winter 1988): 67–96.

Brown, Gillian. *The Consent of the Governed: The Lockean Legacy in Early American Culture.* Cambridge, Mass.: Harvard UP, 2001.

———. *Domestic Individualism: Imagining Self in Nineteenth-Century America.* Berkeley: U of California P, 1990.

Buchan, William. *Advice to Mothers, on the Subject of Their Own Health; and on the Means of Promoting the Health, Strength, and Beauty, of their Offspring.* Philadelphia: John Bioren, 1804.

Burnett, Frances Hodgson. *Little Lord Fauntleroy.* New York: Charles Scribner's Sons, 1886.

———. *A Little Princess.* 1905. Philadelphia: Lippincott, 1963.

———. *The Secret Garden.* 1911. New York: Henry Holt, 1987.

Bushnell, Horace. *Christian Nurture.* 1847. New York: Charles Scribner's Sons, 1916.

Cadogan, Mary, and Patricia Craig. *You're a Brick, Angela! A New Look at Girls' Fiction from 1839 to 1975.* London: Gollancz, 1976.

Carley, Rachel. *The Visual Dictionary of American Domestic Architecture.* New York: Henry Holt, 1994.

Chantell, Claire. "The Limits of the Mother at Home in *The Wide, Wide World* and *The Lamplighter.*" *Studies in American Fiction* 30.2 (2002): 131–53.

Chapman, Mary, and Glenn Hendler, ed. Introduction. Chapman and Hendler 1–16.

———. *Sentimental Men: Masculinity and the Politics of Affect in American Culture.* Berkeley: U of California P, 1999.

Chavasse, P. H. *The Physical Training of Children.* Philadelphia: New-World Publishing, 1871.

Cobb, Lyman. *The Evil Tendencies of Corporal Punishment as a Means of Moral Discipline in Families and Schools, Examined and Discussed.* New York: Mark H. Newman, 1847.

Coolidge, Susan. *What Katy Did.* 1873. New York: Garland, 1976.

Cowie, Alexander. *The Rise of the American Novel.* New York: American Book Company, 1951.

Davidson, Cathy N. *Revolution and the Word: The Rise of the Novel in America.* New York: Oxford UP, 1986.

Davidson, Cathy N., and Jessamyn Hatcher, eds. *No More Separate Spheres! A Next Wave American Studies Reader.* Durham, N.C.: Duke UP, 2002.

DeMause, Lloyd, ed. *The History of Childhood*. New York: Psychohistory P, 1974.

DiQuinzio, Patrice. *The Impossibility of Motherhood: Feminism, Individualism, and the Problem of Mothering*. New York: Routledge, 1999.

Dobson, Joanne. "The Hidden Hand: Subversion of Cultural Ideology in Three Mid-Nineteenth Century American Women's Novels." *American Quarterly* 38.2 (1986): 223–42.

——. Introduction. *The Hidden Hand or, Capitola the Madcap*. By E.D.E.N. Southworth. 1859. New Brunswick, N.J.: Rutgers UP, 1998. xi–xlv.

Domestic Abuse Intervention Project. "Wheel Gallery." www.theduluthmodel.org/wheelgallery.php. Accessed 2 March 2010.

Donzelot, Jacques. *The Policing of Families*. Trans. Robert Hurley. New York: Pantheon, 1979.

Douglas, Ann. *The Feminization of American Culture*. 1977. New York: Anchor, 1988.

Downs, Susan Whitelaw, and Michael W. Sherraden. "The Orphan Asylum in the Nineteenth Century." *Social Service Review* 57.2 (1983): 272–90.

Ehrenreich, Barbara. *The Hearts of Men: American Dreams and the Flight from Commitment*. Garden City, N.Y.: Anchor, 1983.

Foucault, Michel. *Discipline and Punish: The Birth of the Prison*. 1975. Trans. Alan Sheridan. New York: Vintage, 1979.

Gammel, Irene, ed. "The Eros of Childhood and Early Adolescence in Girl Series: L. M. Montgomery's Emily Trilogy." Hudson and Cooper 97–118.

——. "Making Avonlea: An Introduction." Gammel, *Making Avonlea* 3–13.

——. *Making Avonlea: L. M. Montgomery and Popular Culture*. Toronto: U of Toronto P, 2002.

——. "Safe Pleasures for Girls: L. M. Montgomery's Erotic Landscapes." Gammel, *Making Avonlea* 114–27.

Gannon, Susan R., Suzanne Rahn, and Ruth Anne Thompson, eds. *St. Nicholas and Mary Mapes Dodge: The Legacy of a Children's Magazine Editor, 1873–1905*. New York: MacFarland, 2004.

Gatens, Moira. "Privacy and the Body: The Publicity of Affect." Rössler 113–32.

Gerzina, Gretchen Holbrook. *Frances Hodgson Burnett: The Unexpected Life of the Author of "The Secret Garden."* New Brunswick, N.J.: Rutgers UP, 2004.

Gillen, Mollie. *Lucy Maud Montgomery*. Markham, Ontario: Fitzhenry and Whiteside, 1999.

Gittens, Joan. "Friendless Foundlings and Homeless Half-Orphans." *Chicago History* 24.1 (1995): 40–72.

Glassman, Peter. Afterword. Spyri 381–33.

Glenn, Myra C. *Campaigns against Corporal Punishment: Prisoners, Sailors, Women, and Children in Antebellum America*. Albany: State U of New York P, 1984.

Griswold, Jerry. *Audacious Kids: Coming of Age in America's Classic Children's Books*. New York: Oxford UP, 1992.

Grossberg, Michael. *Governing the Hearth: Law and the Family in Nineteenth-Century America*. Chapel Hill: U of North Carolina P, 1985.

Gruner, Elisabeth Rose. "Cinderella, Marie Antoinette, and Sara: Roles and Role Models in *A Little Princess.*" *The Lion and the Unicorn* 22.2 (1998): 168–87.

Hendler, Glenn. "Bloated Bodies and Sober Sentiments: Masculinity in 1840s Temperance Narratives." Chapman and Hendler 125–48.

———. *Public Sentiments: Structures of Feeling in Nineteenth-Century American Literature.* Chapel Hill: U of North Carolina P, 2001.

Hersey, Eleanor. "'It's All Mine': The Modern Woman as Writer in Sullivan's *Anne of Green Gables* Films." Gammel, *Making Avonlea* 131–44.

Higonnet, Anne. *Pictures of Innocence: The History and Crisis of Ideal Childhood.* London: Thames and Hudson, 1998.

Hope, Laura Lee. *The Moving Picture Girls; or, First Appearances in Photo Dramas.* New York: Grosset and Dunlap, 1914.

Hudock, Amy E. "Challenging the Definition of Heroism in E.D.E.N. Southworth's *The Hidden Hand.*" *American Transcendental Quarterly* 9.1 (1995): 5–20.

Hudson, Aïda, and Susan-Ann Cooper, eds. *Windows and Words: A Look at Canadian Children's Literature in English.* Ottawa: U of Ottawa P, 2003.

Hunter, Jane H. *How Young Ladies Became Girls: The Victorian Origins of American Girlhood.* New Haven, Conn.: Yale UP, 2002.

Inness, Sherrie A. "'Anti-Barbies': The American Girls Collection and Political Ideologies." Inness, *Delinquents and Debutantes* 164–83.

———, ed. *Delinquents and Debutantes: Twentieth-Century American Girls' Cultures.* New York: New York UP, 1998.

———. Introduction. Inness, *Delinquents and Debutantes* 1–15.

Jacobson, Marcia Ann. *Being a Boy Again: Autobiography and the American Boy Book.* Tuscaloosa: U of Alabama P, 1994.

Johnson, Deidre A. "Community and Character: A Comparison of Josephine Lawrence's Linda Lane Series and Classic Orphan Fiction." *Nancy Drew and Company: Culture, Gender, and Girls' Series.* Ed. Sherrie A. Inness. Bowling Green, Ohio: Bowling Green State U Popular P, 1997. 59–73.

Jones, Paul Christian. "'This Dainty Woman's Hand . . . Red with Blood': E.D.E.N. Southworth's *The Hidden Hand* as Abolitionist Narrative." *American Transcendental Quarterly* 15.1 (2001): 59–80.

Justice-Malloy, Rhona. "Little Girls Bound: Costume and Coming of Age in the 'Sears Catalog': 1906–1927." Inness, *Delinquents and Debutantes* 109–33.

Kenealy, Arabella. "The Talent of Motherhood." *National Review* 16 (1890): 446–559.

Keohane, Catherine. "'Spare from Your Luxuries': Women, Charity, and Spending in the Eighteenth Century." *Studies in Eighteenth-Century Culture* 31 (2002): 41–59.

Kerber, Linda K. *No Constitutional Right to Be Ladies: Women and the Obligations of Citizenship.* New York: Hill and Wang, 1998.

———. *Women of the Republic: Intellect and Ideology in Revolutionary America.* Chapel Hill: U of North Carolina P, 1980.

Keyser, Elizabeth Lennox. "'The Whole of the Story': Frances Hodgson Burnett's *A Little Princess. Triumphs of the Spirit in Children's Literature.* Ed. Francelia

Butler and Richard Rotert. Hamden, Conn.: Library Professional Publications, 1986. 230–43.

Kidd, Kenneth B. *Making American Boys: Boyology and the Feral Tale*. Minneapolis: U of Minnesota P, 2004.

Kincaid, James R. *Child-Loving: The Erotic Child and Victorian Culture*. New York: Routledge, 1992.

———. *Erotic Innocence: The Culture of Child Molesting*. Durham, N.C.: Duke UP, 1998.

Kostof, Spiro. *A History of Architecture: Settings and Rituals*. New York: Oxford UP, 1985.

Ladd-Taylor, Molly. *Mother-Work: Women, Child Welfare, and the State, 1890–1930*. Urbana: U of Illinois P, 1994.

Ladd-Taylor, Molly, and Lauri Umansky. Introduction. *"Bad" Mothers: The Politics of Blame in Twentieth-Century America*. New York: New York UP, 1998. 1–28.

Lancaster, Clay. "The American Bungalow." 1958. *Common Places: Readings in American Vernacular Culture*. Ed. Dell Upton and John Michael Vlach. Athens: U of Georgia P, 1986. 79–106.

Landry, H. Jordan. "Of Tricks, Tropes, and Trollops: Revisions to the Seduction Novel in E.D.E.N. Southworth's *The Hidden Hand*." *Journal of the Midwest Modern Language Association* 38.2 (2005): 31–44.

Lemons, J. Stanley. *The Woman Citizen: Social Feminism in the 1920s*. Charlottesville: University Press of Virginia, 1990.

Lewis, Jan. "Mother's Love: The Construction of an Emotion in Nineteenth-Century America." *Social History and Issues in Human Consciousness: Some Interdisciplinary Connections*. Ed. Andrew E. Barnes and Peter N. Stearns. New York: New York UP, 1989. 209–29.

Lindey, Sara. "Overhearing Children's Stories: Children's Rights in Fanny Fern's Newspaper Writing." *Children's Literature Association Quarterly* 34.2 (2009): 138–56.

Lynch, Deidre Shauna. *The Economy of Character: Novels, Market Culture, and the Business of Inner Meaning*. Chicago: U of Chicago P, 1998.

Macleod, David I. *The Age of the Child: Children in America, 1890–1920*. New York: Twayne, 1998.

Mann, Horace. "Ninth Report, for 1845." *Life and Works of Horace Mann*. Vol. 4. Boston: Lee and Shepard, 1891.

Mann, Mary Tyler, and Elizabeth P. Peabody. *Moral Culture of Infancy and Kindergarten Guide*. Boston: Burnham, 1863.

Marlowe, Amy Bell. *The Girl from Sunset Ranch; or, Alone in a Great City*. New York: Grosset and Dunlap, 1914.

Mattingly, Carol. *Well-Tempered Women: Nineteenth-Century Temperance Rhetoric*. Carbondale: Southern Illinois UP, 1998.

McLean, Deckle. *Privacy and Its Invasion*. Westport, Conn.: Praeger, 1995.

Merish, Lori. *Sentimental Materialism: Gender, Commodity Culture, and Nineteenth-Century American Literature*. Durham, N.C.: Duke UP, 2000.

Michel, Sonya. "The Limits of Maternalism: Policies toward American Wage-Earning Mothers during the Progressive Era." *Mothers of a New World: Maternalist Politics and the Origins of Welfare States.* Ed. Seth Koven and Sonya Michel. New York: Routledge, 1993. 277–320.

Mills, Alice. "Pollyanna and the Not So Glad Game." *Children's Literature* 27 (1999): 87–104.

Mitchell, Sally. *The New Girl: Girls' Culture in England, 1880–1915.* New York: Columbia UP, 1995.

Montgomery, L. M. *The Annotated Anne of Green Gables.* 1908. Ed. Wendy E. Barry, Margaret Anne Doody, and Mary E. Doody Jones. New York: Oxford UP, 1997.

———. *Emily of New Moon.* 1923. New York: Bantam, 1993.

———. *The Selected Journals of L. M. Montgomery.* Vol. 1. Ed. Mary Henley Rubio and Elizabeth Waterston. Oxford: Oxford UP, 1985.

Mott, Frank Luther. *Golden Multitudes: The Story of Best Sellers in the United States.* New York: Macmillan, 1947.

Murray, Gail Schmunk. *American Children's Literature and the Construction of Childhood.* New York: Twayne, 1998.

Nelson, Claudia. *Boys Will Be Girls: The Feminine Ethic and British Children's Fiction, 1857–1917.* New Brunswick, N.J.: Rutgers UP, 1991.

———. *Little Strangers: Portrayals of Adoption and Foster Care in America, 1850–1929.* Bloomington: Indiana UP, 2003.

———. "A Wealth of Fatherhood: Paternity in American Adoption Narratives." *Gender and Fatherhood in the Nineteenth Century.* Ed. Trev Lynn Broughton and Helen Rogers. New York: Palgrave Macmillan, 2007. 165–77.

Newfield, Chris. *The Emerson Effect: Individualism and Submission in America.* Chicago: U of Chicago P, 1996.

O'Keefe, Deborah. *Good Girl Messages: How Young Women Were Misled by Their Favorite Books.* New York: Continuum, 2000.

Parille, Ken. *Boys at Home: Discipline, Masculinity, and "The Boy Problem" in Nineteenth-Century American Literature.* Knoxville: U of Tennessee P, 2009.

———. "'The Medicine of Sympathy': Mothers, Sons, and Affective Pedagogy in Antebellum America." *Tulsa Studies in Women's Literature* 25.1 (2006): 93–115.

Patell, Cyrus R. K. *Negative Liberties: Morrison, Pynchon, and the Problem of Liberal Ideology.* Durham, N.C.: Duke UP, 2001.

Paul, Lissa. "Enigma Variations: What Feminist Theory Knows about Children's Literature." *Signal* 54 (1987): 186–202.

Pawley, Christine. *Reading on the Middle Border: The Culture of Print in Late-Nineteenth-Century Osage, Iowa.* Amherst: U of Massachusetts P, 2001.

Pearson, Karl. *The Ethic of Freethought.* 2nd ed. London: Adam and Charles Black, 1901.

Petronio, Sandra. *Boundaries of Privacy: Dialectics of Disclosure.* Albany: State U of New York P, 2002.

Phillips, Jerry. "The Mem Sahib, the Worthy, the Rajah and His Minions: Some Reflections on the Class Politics of *The Secret Garden.*" *The Lion and the Unicorn* 17.2 (1993): 168–94.

Pollock, Linda. *A Lasting Relationship: Parents and Children over Three Centuries.* Hanover: UP of New England, 1987.

Porter, Eleanor H. *Just David.* New York: Grosset and Dunlap, 1916.

———. *Pollyanna.* 1913. New York: Dell Yearling Classic, 1990.

Rahn, Suzanne. "*St. Nicholas* and Its Friends: The Magazine-Child Relationship." Gannon, *Making Avonlea* 93–110.

Rappaport, Erika Diane. *Shopping for Pleasure: Women in the Making of London's West End.* Princeton, N.J.: Princeton UP, 2000.

Renza, Louis A. *Edgar Allan Poe, Wallace Stevens, and the Poetics of American Privacy.* Baton Rouge: Louisiana State UP, 2002.

Reynolds, Kimberley. *Girls Only? Gender and Popular Children's Fiction in Britain, 1800–1910.* Philadelphia: Temple UP, 1990.

Romero, Lora. *Home Fronts: Domesticity and Its Critics in the Antebellum United States.* Durham, N.C.: Duke UP, 1997.

Ronda, Bruce A. *Elizabeth Palmer Peabody: A Reformer on Her Own Terms.* Cambridge, Mass.: Harvard UP, 1999.

Rössler, Beate. "Privacies: An Introduction." In Rössler, *Privacies* 1–18.

———, ed. *Privacies: Philosophical Evaluations.* Stanford: Stanford UP, 2004.

Rotundo, E. Anthony. *American Manhood: Transformations in Masculinity from the Revolution to the Modern Era.* New York: HarperCollins, 1993.

Rubio, Mary Henley. *Lucy Maud Montgomery: The Gift of Wings.* Toronto: Doubleday Canada, 2008.

Ryan, Mary P. *The Empire of the Mother: American Writing about Domesticity, 1830–1860.* New York: Haworth, 1982.

Sánchez, María C. "Re-Possessing Individualism in Fanny Fern's *Ruth Hall.*" *Arizona Quarterly* 56.4 (2000): 25–56.

Sánchez-Eppler, Karen. *Dependent States: The Child's Part in Nineteenth-Century American Culture.* Chicago: U of Chicago P, 2005.

———. "Temperance in the Bed of a Child: Incest and Social Order in Nineteenth-Century America." *American Quarterly* 47.1 (1995): 1–33.

———. "Then When We Clutch Hardest: On the Death of a Child and the Replication of an Image." Chapman and Hendler 64–85.

———. *Touching Liberty: Abolition, Feminism, and the Politics of the Body.* Berkeley: U of California P, 1993.

Sandage, Scott A. "The Gaze of Success: Failed Men and the Sentimental Marketplace, 1873–1893." Chapman and Hendler 181–201.

Schrum, Kelly. *Some Wore Bobby Sox: The Emergence of Teenage Girls' Culture, 1920–1945.* New York: Palgrave Macmillan, 2004.

Smith-Rosenberg, Carroll. *Disorderly Conduct: Visions of Gender in Victorian America.* New York: Knopf, 1985.

Southworth, E.D.E.N. *The Hidden Hand; or, Capitola the Madcap.* 1859. New Brunswick, N.J.: Rutgers UP, 1998.

Spacks, Patricia Meyer. *Privacy: Concealing the Eighteenth-Century Self.* Chicago: U of Chicago P, 2003.

——. "The Privacy of the Novel." *Novel: A Forum on Fiction* 31.3 (1998): 304–16.

Spilka, Mark. *Hemingway's Quarrel with Androgyny.* Lincoln: U of Nebraska P, 1990.

Spyri, Johanna. *Heidi.* 1880. New York: William Morrow, 1996.

Steffler, Margaret. "Brian O'Connal and Emily Byrd Starr: The Inheritors of Wordsworth's 'Gentle Breeze.'" Hudson and Cooper 87–96.

Stone, Lawrence. *The Family, Sex and Marriage in England, 1500–1800.* New York: Harper and Row, 1977.

Stoneley, Peter. *Consumerism and American Girls' Literature, 1860–1940.* Cambridge: Cambridge UP, 2003.

Stowe, Harriet Beecher. *Uncle Tom's Cabin; or, Life among the Lowly.* 1851. New York: Norton, 1994.

Strickland, Charles. *Victorian Domesticity: Families in the Life and Art of Louisa May Alcott.* Tuscaloosa: U of Alabama P, 1985.

Tedesco, Laureen. "Progressive Era Girl Scouts and the Immigrant: *Scouting for Girls* (1920) as a Handbook for American Girlhood." *Children's Literature Association Quarterly* 31.4 (2006): 346–68.

Temple, Gale. "A Purchase on Goodness: Fanny Fern, *Ruth Hall*, and Fraught Individualism." *Studies in American Fiction* 31.2 (2003): 131–63.

Theriot, Nancy M. *Mothers and Daughters in Nineteenth-Century America: The Biosocial Construction of Femininity.* 2nd ed. Lexington: UP of Kentucky, 1996.

Thom, Douglas A. *Everyday Problems of the Everyday Child.* New York: Appleton, 1927.

Tompkins, Jane. Afterword. *The Wide, Wide World.* By Susan Warner. New York: Feminist P, 1987. 584–608.

Vallone, Lynne. *Disciplines of Virtue: Girls' Culture in the Eighteenth and Nineteenth Centuries.* New Haven: Yale UP, 1995.

Van Horn, Catherine. "Turning Child Readers into Consumers: Children's Magazines and Advertising, 1900–1920." *Defining Print Culture for Youth: The Cultural Work of Children's Literature.* Ed. Anne Lundin and Wayne A. Wiegand. Westport, Conn.: Libraries Unlimited, 2003. 121–38.

Walter, Henriette R. *Girl Life in America: A Study of Backgrounds.* New York: National Committee for the Study of Juvenile Reading, 1927.

Warner, Susan. *The Wide, Wide World.* 1850. New York: Feminist P, 1987.

Warren, Eliza. *How I Managed My Children from Infancy to Marriage.* Boston: Loring, 1866.

Waterston, Elizabeth. Introduction. Montgomery, *The Selected Journals of L. M. Montgomery.* xiii–xxiv.

Watson, John B. *Psychological Care of Infant and Child.* New York: Norton, 1928.

Weber, Brenda R. "Confessions of a Kindred Spirit with an Academic Bent." Gammel, *Making Avonlea* 43–57.

Weinstein, Cindy. *Family, Kinship, and Sympathy in Nineteenth-Century American Literature.* Cambridge: Cambridge UP, 2004.

Wexler, Laura. *Tender Violence: Domestic Visions in an Age of U.S. Imperialism.* Chapel Hill: U of North Carolina P, 2000.

Wiener, Martin. *English Culture and the Decline of the Industrial Spirit, 1850–1980.* Cambridge: Cambridge UP, 1981.

Wiggin, Kate Douglas. *Children's Rights.* Boston: Houghton, Mifflin, 1892.

———. *Rebecca of Sunnybrook Farm.* 1903. New York: William Morrow, 1994.

———. *The Relation of the Kindergarten to Social Reform.* San Francisco: California Froebel Society, n.d.

———. *The Relation of the Kindergarten to the Public School.* San Francisco: C. A. Murdock, 1891.

———. *Timothy's Quest.* Boston: Houghton, Mifflin, 1898.

Wiggin, Kate Douglas, and Nora Archibald Smith. *Froebel's Gifts.* Boston: Houghton, Mifflin, 1896.

Wilson, Anna. "Little Lord Fauntleroy: The Darling of Mothers and the Abomination of a Generation." *American Literary History* 8.2 (1996): 232–58.

Woolf, Virginia. *Orlando: A Biography.* New York: Harcourt, 1928.

Wright, Gwendolyn. *Building the Dream: A Social History of Housing in America.* New York: Pantheon, 1981.

Zboray, Ronald J. *A Fictive People: Antebellum Economic Development and the American Reading Public.* New York: Oxford UP, 1993.

Zmora, Nurith. *Orphanages Reconsidered: Child Care Institutions in Progressive Era Baltimore.* Philadelphia: Temple UP, 1994.

Index